MW00440806

Torn by War

Miss. Mary Adelia Byers.
Batesville
Arkansas

Portrait (probably from an
ambrotype), 1863, and signature of
Mary Adelia Byers

TORN BY WAR

The Civil War Journal of Mary Adelia Byers

Transcribed and edited by Samuel R. Phillips

INTRODUCTION BY GEORGE E. LANKFORD

UNIVERSITY OF OKLAHOMA PRESS : NORMAN

Library of Congress Cataloging-in-Publication Data

Byers, Mary Adelia, 1847–1918.
Torn by war: the Civil War journal of Mary Adelia Byers / transcribed and edited
by Samuel R. Phillips.
   p.   cm.
Includes bibliographical references and index.
ISBN 978-0-8061-4395-8 (pbk. : alk. paper)
1. Byers, Mary Adelia, 1847–1918.
2. Batesville (Ark.)—History—19th century—Sources.
3. Arkansas—History—Civil War, 1861–1865—Sources.
I. Phillips, Samuel R., 1935–
II. Title.
F419.B38B94 2013
976.7'26—dc23
                                   2013006314

The paper in this book meets the guidelines for permanence and durability of
the Committee on Production Guidelines for Book Longevity of the Council on
Library Resources, Inc. ∞

In memory of Mary's daughter
Clare Neill Phillips
and her granddaughter
Clare Phillips Dowell
with love and thanks for encouragement

Contents

Illustrations

Maps

Figures

*Unless otherwise noted, all illustrations are
from the collection of Samuel R. Phillips.*

Preface and Acknowledgments

On May 3, 1862, Maj. Gen. Samuel R. Curtis and his United States Army of the Southwest occupied Batesville, Arkansas, bringing the Civil War home to the town's residents for the first time since secession in 1861. Mary Adela Byers, a girl of fifteen, saw the occupation as a turning point in her life and began her journal as Curtis was preparing to leave the northern Arkansas town and advance on Little Rock.

Mary was my great-grandmother. Her journal passed to my grandmother and guardian, Clare Neill Phillips, and then to my father, Neill Phillips. In 1973 my father wrote to his cousin, genealogist Marion Stark Craig, that Mary "kept an absorbing diary as a youthful female prodigy during 'The War' that I am now trying to annotate."

My father described the origins of the three Byers brothers—William, Tom, and John—lawyers and sons of Dr. John Byers of Pennsylvania Scotch-Irish stock. Within a few years of arriving in Batesville, however, Tom, John, and William's wife all died young. Tom was unmarried and childless, but John ("Pa") left his widow, Esther ("Ma"), and four children, including Mary. William stopped work on his country place, Catalpa Hall, resuming only after his second marriage, to a rich widow Emma Wilson: "Uncle William carried on magnificently, took care of John's widow and children, and just lasted out the Civil War when his whole world collapsed around him in tragedy. All during the time, Uncle William's wife, the sophisticated Mrs. Emma, with her beautiful clothes and her opera box in New Orleans, and our g.g. grandma Mrs. John, a dedicated little midwestern Methodist who was horrified by cards, theater, or dancing, carried on a polite feud mitigated by mutual respect. It's in Grandma Neill's diary."[1]

---

1. Neill Phillips to Marion S. Craig, Sept. 1, 1973.

In a contrasting version of family history, Mary's son Ernest Neill wrote to his niece, Clare Phillips Dowell (to whom this book is dedicated):

> My great-grand-dad was a doctor, and . . . his sons obtained fair educations in the small Ohio town where they grew up, but the family had no money and the sons worked during their childhood and youth, and to some extent were self-educated. All three were chair makers until they had studied law sufficiently to obtain a license to practice.
>
> Our grandfather [John Hancock Byers] died young with t.b. [tuberculosis] but was considered by the Batesville bar (and the B. bar at that time was even more outstanding as to ability than that of Little Rock, I am told) as an unusually bright young lawyer and of the highest character. I got this from the late Judge U. M. Rose, who lived here at that time, having begun his legal career here.
>
> Grandfather's brother, William, later judge of our court, was not so bright but was of the highest character, and until he broke, with financial trouble following the Civil War, too hard-boiled a second wife, and too much "licker," he stood at the top in many respects.[2]

My father's melodramatic description and my uncle's more reflective one whetted my appetite to complete the transcription of the diary and make it available to my family, then as the project grew, to a wider audience, hence this book. The many pages that my father had written (still by hand but at least in a script familiar to me) were immensely helpful as were his comments, for he remembered his grandmother and knew many other participants. For instance, I have retained his remark on Mary's dislike of music (mentioned regarding her entry of November 18, 1862).

---

2. Ernest Neill to Clare Phillips Dowell, Sept. 16, 1943. Ernest himself was a lawyer, and Judge Rose had founded the Rose Law Firm in Little Rock (the firm received unwelcome notoriety during the Clinton presidency, 1993–2001) and the American Bar Association. Rose is one of the two Arkansans featured in the Hall of Statuary in Washington, D.C.

Mary wrote her journal in a former ledger of accounts dating from 1841; sample pages appear herein. She also used its narrow pages to practice her penmanship and to write her name along with those of the young men who appear in the journal. I found her style literate and her choice of topics often mature beyond her years. In fact, if she were typical of fifteen-year-old girls of the time, one can only marvel at the high intellectual standards and regret their passing.

Now to the practical problem of making the transcription. So that my eyes need not leave their place on the journal page, the obvious method was to dictate. A secretary and tape recorder helped me transcribe a few pages in 1987, but the project was laborious and eventually interrupted. Twenty years later a computer and voice-recognition software provided at least the illusion of technological progress, but they were not trouble-free; my speech, halting while deciphering Mary's writing and relying on her nineteenth-century vocabulary, often fooled the software. Many of the "recognized" words were wrong (although, of course, spelled perfectly). I have conformed spellings of proper names, inserted paragraph breaks, and added punctuation and, in brackets [ ], connectives, identifiers, and missing words. I have italicized names of steamboats; other italics are Mary's.

Mary's handwriting was well-disciplined and would have been easy to read had she had a decent pen. In the first half of the journal, her long, vertical strokes (as in a lower-case "p") simply disappear, leaving only blobs of ink at stroke reversal. (Oh, for time travel—I certainly would have taken her a box of Japanese roller-ball pens.) I checked the completed product by reading aloud from the journal while my wife, Mitzi, followed along with the typescript. Yet errors likely remain. For instance, in the entry dated August 3rd, 1863, appears the word "bobonet." Originally I transcribed this as a nonsense word, "bobonkt," but a seamstress friend pointed to the more likely "bobbinet." Sure enough, a closer look at the "k" revealed it to be an "e" plus a tiny ink drop in just the wrong place.

Recalling my grandmother's recounting of how Mary's journal had luckily escaped the 1926 fire that ravaged Batesville's neighbor, Newport, I had the document professionally copied with an oversize flatbed scanner (the page size is an inconvenient six-by-fifteen inches), with the resulting discs stored safely. A collateral benefit was that in checking the transcription, instead of risking further damage to the fragile original, I could use the scan with increased magnification and contrast, which eased reading and place-keeping.

I am grateful for encouragement and writing advice from Mitzi and for assistance with research and illustrations from Swannee Bennett, Ray Hanley, and Don Heuer. Thanks also to Jo Blatti, Marilynn Chlebak, and Brian Langston of the Independence County Historical Society and to Elizabeth Jacoway, Don Ross, and my cousin Robert A. "Lit" Craig.

Nancy Britton and George Lankford, whom I met through the Independence County Historical Society, have been extremely helpful in sharing their vast knowledge of nineteenth-century Batesville, which must seem at times more real to them than the present day. Much historical research and a great deal of the annotations for this book were provided by Nancy, who brought to bear her experience as the decades-long editor of the historical journal *Independence County Chronicle* and as author of books on church and county history. Her help and George's contribution of the introduction add greatly to the value of Mary's writings for scholars.

My editors at the University of Oklahoma Press—Charles E. Rankin and Alice Stanton—and production manager Emmy Ezzell guided me through the publication process. Bill Nelson added his cartographic skills, and copy editor Kevin Brock's knowledge of Civil War Arkansas and concern for detail improved the book in many ways.

During e-mail collaboration with my daughter Amanda while editing maps, I wondered how Mary would have liked having her most personal thoughts and observations, carefully hidden from her devoted sister and mother, revealed a century and a half later and, worse, discussed via what she would have regarded as an overgrown telegraph.

Dramatis Personae

In approximate order of appearance, with their ages at the start of the journal.

Family

The author	Mary Adelia "Mollie" Byers, fifteen.
Sarah (Sister)	Sarah "Sallie" Byers, seventeen, her sister.
Ella	Ella Aurelia Byers, thirteen, her sister.
Willie	William Wilson Byers, eleven, her brother.
Ma	Esther Ann Wilson Byers, thirty-nine, her widowed mother.
Pa	John Hancock Byers, her father, died 1855, when Mary was eight.
Uncle William	William Byers, fifty-two, her uncle (John's older brother) and family benefactor.
Aunt Emma	Emily Burton Wilson Byers, about forty, second wife to William.
Cousin Preston	William Preston Byers, twenty-six, child of William by his first wife, Lucy A. Manning. Soldier, CSA.
Cousin Ann	Ann Grow Byers, twenty-three, Preston's sister.
Cousin Rilla	Aurelia Adelia Byers Smith, twenty-four, Preston's sister.
Cousin Henry	Henry C. Smith, thirty, Rilla's husband. Merchant and occasional soldier, CSA.
Byers	Robert Byers Smith, five, son of Cousins Rilla and Henry.

Not exactly Byers family, but important relations:

Burton sisters   The influential daughters of Dr. Philip P. Burton:
Emily Burton Wilson Byers (Aunt Emma)
Nancy Burton Burr
Mary Burton Weaver
Rosalie Burton Hynson Archer

Mary's Social Group

Burr, Emma   Daughter, sixteen, of E. T. and Nancy Burton
               Burr. Mr. Burr was a wealthy merchant, born in
               Massachusetts. Mrs. Burr was a sister of Uncle
               William's wife, Emily Burton Wilson Byers. The
               Burrs lived at their home on White River, Engleside.

Case, Mary   Daughter, fourteen, of George and Sarah Ridgway
               Case.

Harpham, Anna Daughter, sixteen, of Reuben and Martha Harpham,
               tailor and seamstress, from Pennsylvania. They and
               several other families with Unionist sympathies
               remained in Batesville unmolested.

Maxfield, Lutie   Lucretia Noland Maxfield, sixteen, daughter of shoe
               manufacturer and merchant Uriah Maxfield and his
               wife Leah. Also called "Lute." Kept wartime journal.

Maxfield, Vene   Elvena Maxfield, nineteen, Lutie's sister. Also called
               "Vena." Kept journal.

Maxfield, Will   William Elijah Maxfield, Lutie's brother and Mary's
               sometime beau. Second lieutenant, CSA.

Maxfield, Theodore Lutie's brother. Soldier, CSA.

McGuire, Will   Farmer, nineteen, head of the household of his
               deceased father. Also kept a journal before, and briefly
               after, he was wounded in Confederate service.

Perrin, Sarah   Schoolteacher, twenty, much admired by the younger
               girls.

Perrin, Frank   Sarah's brother. Soldier, CSA.

Perrin, Jim   Sarah's brother. Soldier, CSA.

Smith, Puss	Cynthiana Desloges Smith, sixteen, daughter of wealthy planter Robert Smith and his second wife, Susan McIlvain Smith. Also called "Annie."
Smith, John	Puss's brother, eighteen. Sometime beau of Mary and soldier, CSA.
Wilson, George	Son, twenty-two, of Aunt Emma by her first husband. Soldier, CSA.
Wilson, Nannie	Nannie Manning Wilson, twenty, George's sister. With her cousins, Emily Weaver and Emma Burr, formed a trio of Confederate belles in wartime Batesville.
Wycough, Mary	Daughter, sixteen, of carpenter and merchant Samuel Butler Wycough and Malinda H. Bandy Wycough.

Genealogy

John Hancock Byers (Pa)
Esther Ann Wilson (Ma)

} Sarah Byers (Sister)
Mary Adelia Byers (Mollie)
Ella Aurelia Byers
William Wilson Byers (Willie)

William Byers
(Uncle William)
(2) Emily Burton Wilson
(Aunt Emma)

} Four young children

Frank Rhea Wilson
Emily S. Burton

} George Burton Wilson
Nancy Manning Wilson (Nannie)

William Byers
(Uncle William)
(1) Lucy Adelia Manning

} William Preston Byers (Cousin Preston)
Ann Grow Byers (Cousin Ann)
Aurelia Adelia Byers }* (Cousin Rilla)

Col. Robert Smith, Jr.
(1) Finnetta Stuart

} Henry C. Smith   }* (Cousin Henry)

Col. Robert Smith, Jr.
(2) Susan McIlvain

} John Smith
Cynthiana Desloges Smith
(Puss or Annie)

*Rilla and Henry's son, Robert Byers Smith (Byers)

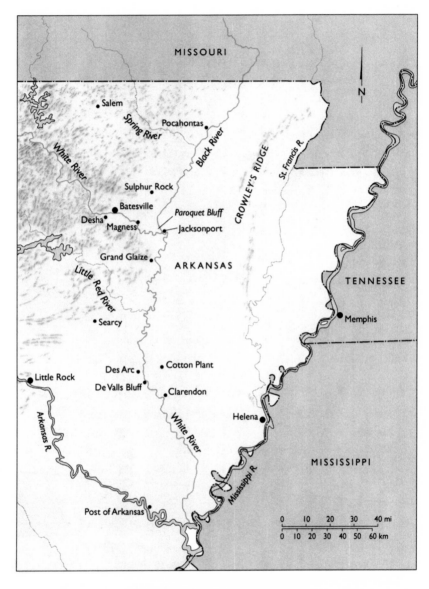

Northeast Arkansas and vicinity.

Based on *Shaded relief map from Center for Advanced Spatial Technologies, University of Arkansas.* Used by permission.

Depending upon which way the men, horses, wagons, and guns were heading, the White and Black Rivers were either highways or barriers. The White was navigable year round to Batesville and in flush water into Missouri. Jacksonport, of course, profited by its location at the confluence of the White and Black.

In later years the U.S. Army Corps of Engineers has built dams, creating the lakes shown and nearly stopping the flooding of the White River at the former sites of (Cousin) Henry Smith's farm near Grand Glaize and (Uncle) William Byers's plantation, Double Trouble, near Des Arc. Batesville may owe its site in the Ozark foothills above the alluvial plain to its founders' fear of this annual inundation.

Independence County, 1855.

Fragment of Arkansas map published by J. H. Colton & Co., New York, and reprinted by
Hearthstone Legacy Publications, www.hearthstonelegacy.com. Used by permission.

Batesville

This town was the seat of Independence County, a significant port on the White River, and a center for farming. Situated in the Ozark foothills, it had a healthier climate than Double Trouble. See Appendix 1.

Grand Glaize

This village was a prosperous White River port at the time, below Jacksonport and near the present hamlet of Possum Grape. It was the site of Henry Smith's farm.

In later years the north and west boundaries of the county changed.

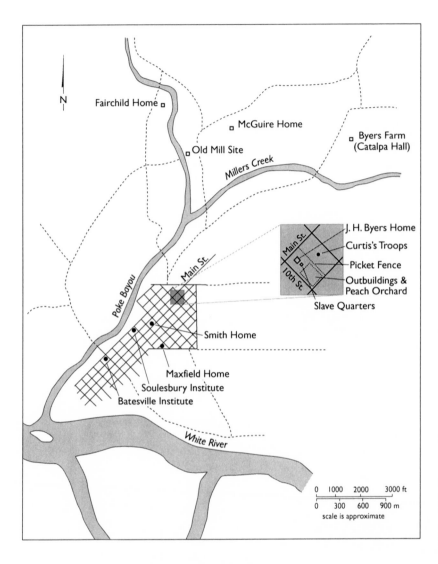

Batesville and vicinity, 1863.

Batesville Institute

The Batesville Institute "for the promotion of the Fine Arts, Mechanism, Science, Education, Commerce and Agriculture, and the Diffusion of Knowledge" was completed in 1858 as one of the grandest buildings in Arkansas, but it was destroyed by fire a few months later. Almost immediately the citizens rebuilt it. In 1864 it served as headquarters for the Federal quartermaster, surviving the war. John H. Byers (Mary's father) and Henry A. Neill (her future father-in-law) were among the founders.

Catalpa Hall

The home of Uncle William and Aunt Emma, located two miles north of Batesville. See Appendix 2.

Mary's home (modern site: 1014 Main Street)

In 1847 Uncle William bought a whole block in the School Addition for $99.50. The following year he sold half to Mary's father, who built the house shortly thereafter. (Britton, "Methodists, Slavery, and Secession in Independence County.") A century later Mary's son Ernest recalled that the "house was small, maybe four rooms including kitchen, a small front porch and maybe a small storeroom attached to the kitchen. The dwelling of the slave woman, 'Leanna,' was a short distance from the house and was but one room. The kitchen may have been detached during slavery." (E. Neill to Neill Phillips, 1962.) The remaining half block was occupied by Federal troops in May 1862.

Introduction

George E. Lankford

When the three Byers brothers arrived in Batesville in 1837, they were joining their family story to a far bigger national narrative, one about seeking the dream that lay to the west. The young men were born in western Pennsylvania, sons of a doctor, but their family had moved to Ohio, where the three had grown up and "read law."[1] Like so many others, they were bringing with them money for investment, an entrepreneurial spirit, and a hope for prosperity in a land of bright promise—the new state of Arkansas.

The details of their arrival in Batesville are not known, but it is likely that they came by steamboat, for in the six years since the *Waverly* had arrived at the wharf at the foot of Main Street, it had become the primary mode of transportation for those who could afford it. Batesville was located at the first major shoal in the White River as travelers headed upstream from the Mississippi Valley toward the springs that were the sources of the ancient river draining the southern Ozarks. Although only 200 feet higher than the nearby Mississippi floodplain, Batesville offered a noticeably healthier climate.

The town sat close to the mouth of Poke Bayou as it poured into the White, and beneath the soil's surface were remains of prehistoric Indian houses, early French hunting camps, and early American trading houses serving the fur trade. The modern town, though—the one seen by the Byers brothers as they stepped off the boat—had been founded in 1821

---

1. Most of the information about the history of the Byers family was taken from the research of Dr. Marion S. Craig, a descendant. See Craig, *My Byers-Bonar-Shannon and Allied Families.*

as the seat of Independence County in the new Territory of Arkansas.[2]

Before the stumps were cleared from the streets, a two-story brick courthouse had been built in the public square just two blocks up from the wharf, a sight that must have been reassuring to the professional gaze of the three lawyers. Houses and storefront buildings were springing up on both sides of Main Street, and within a year the first church building (Methodist) would be erected. William Byers, the oldest of the brothers, immediately began settling in. He rented a house, bought land, and began construction of a house on Main for his wife, Lucy Adelia, and his brothers, John and Thomas. He also founded Batesville's first newspaper, the *Batesville News*, in 1838 and hung up his lawyer's shingle. William set out to be a man of influence in the new town, and his rapid purchases of land and slaves bear witness to his success. The 1840 census lists for their household William and Lucy, Thomas, John, and five slaves.

It was a good time for people who had money for investment, for the dream bubbles of speculation that brought so many newcomers westward were turning into the Panic of 1837. But it was an unfortunate time for Arkansas to have become a state, with all the financial burdens that came with the new status. The backing from Washington, D.C., was never completely given, and the brand new State Bank of Arkansas, one branch of which was located in Batesville, ended up in receivership. Property of all kinds was available at low prices, and William became a successful investor.

His brothers had different plans, though. After four years in Batesville as a lawyer, Thomas moved to the town of Columbia in Chicot County in the southeast corner of the state, where he became a slave trader. William, however, sold Thomas some land in Independence County, probably as a way of anchoring him to his brothers in addition to giving him an investment for security. But John returned to Ohio, where he married Esther Ann Wilson and set up a law practice. In 1845 his first child, Sarah, was born, followed in 1847 by Mary, who later

---

2. Lankford, "Town-Making in the Southeastern Ozarks."

Judge William Byers (Uncle William), 1810–81.
Courtesy Independence County Historical Society.

became the author of this journal. Just months later, John, Esther, and their two babies moved to Batesville for good, probably because tragedy had struck William's family.

Already wealthy by the middle of the decade, William had started building a large country house a few miles northeast of town. He wanted to get into farming in a serious way (that was how fortunes were being built in the 1840s), and he also needed more space for his household. He and Lucy had two children, Preston and Aurelia, and he had brought to Batesville Lucy's family from Ohio: Aurelia, Wharton, Vesta, and William Manning. In 1846 Catalpa Hall was finished enough to permit the Byers family to move in. Lucy, however, did not benefit. Already having lost a baby to illness while visiting in Ohio, she herself succumbed to disease in the new house. In his grief William erected a large monument to her and the baby in the town cemetery, where it still stands.

The next year John and his family arrived in Batesville. They probably moved into Catalpa Hall while they constructed a permanent home. John bought half of Block 40 on Main Street in the School Addition from William and built a four-room house with a detached kitchen and a small cabin for their servant, Leanna. This was Mary's home through the Civil War, when she was keeping her journal. In 1849 John was appointed prosecuting attorney for the Third Judicial District. This included Marion and Searcy Counties, which were the locale for the "Tutt-Everett feud," which kept law-enforcement officials busy, including John, who was forced to be away from home for extended periods. Even so, his daughter Ella Aurelia was born in 1849, and William, their last child, arrived in 1850.

That year also marked the beginning of a new chapter in William Byers's life, for he married again. The new mistress of Catalpa Hall was Emily Burton Wilson Byers. She was the daughter of Dr. P. P. Burton, who had moved to Batesville in 1840 with two sons and a daughter from Holly Springs, Mississippi. When one of the sons was killed, the family became the center of a notorious murder case involving a number of local people.[3] The uproar lasted for most of the 1840s, but Emma was not directly involved, for she had married the son of the editor of the Whig newspaper in Holly Springs, coming to Batesville only for visits to her sisters. On one of her visits after she was widowed, she met William Byers. After they married in 1850, she moved to Catalpa Hall, bringing her children George and Nancy Wilson.

Catalpa Hall became the center of a successful plantation, judging by the fact that William frequently bought slaves of all kinds from people across north Arkansas, spending $8,260 during the decade for thirteen slaves.[4] From his initial three in 1850, Byers in 1860 was the owner of

---

3. See Lankford, *Surprised by Death*.
4. Independence County Deed Records, Batesville.

thirty-two slaves, all living in six slave houses at Catalpa Hall and his plantation, Double Trouble, near Des Arc on the lower White. That is a clear indication of the seriousness of his turning to agriculture as a path to wealth. It also is an explanation of his concern to move his slaves when the Union army approached, as recounted in Mary's journal.

As William increased his fortune during that last decade before the Civil War, tragedy struck his two brothers. In 1855 John Byers, having contracted tuberculosis some years before and exhausted by his job as prosecutor, died of the disease in Batesville. He was buried in the Public Graveyard (now Pioneer Cemetery). William served as his brother's attorney to settle the estate. The debts were paid, leaving little in the hands of the widow, but William saw to it that she was able to keep Leanna and her daughter since his sister-in-law was "entitled to her dower in said slaves."[5] It is likely that he also bought the house and property, thus enabling John's family to continue living there without fear of creditors. Mary makes it plain in her journal that they were dependent on "Uncle William's" generosity, frequently expressing gratitude.

That was in 1855. The following year Thomas, by now proprietor of Howe's Cotton Harvester in Chicot County, went into financial collapse. He became ill of an unknown malady and went to Batesville for help from William. He lingered until 1858, when he died and was buried in Pioneer Cemetery next to John. Thomas left only $100 in his estate, which did not cover his bills. His remains accompanied John's when they were moved to Oaklawn Cemetery after it opened in 1872, probably by the initiative of William.

Mary's Social Group

Mary Byers gives the reader only a few years out of her long life, and those are not really years at all. They are the selected memories of things that happened to her on scattered days, and they are mostly single incidents or bits of information, many of them accompanied by her own

---

5. See John Byers's estate inventory, reproduced herein.

A true and full Inventory of the Personal Estate of John H. Byers Deceased late of Independance County

One Bay Horse	75.00
" Clay Bank Horse	110.00
" Brown Horse	65.00
" Horse Waggon & Harness	65.00
" Cow	12.00
" Wheelbarrow	5.00
" Negro Woman & Child	1100.00
	1432.00
Moneys on hand	403.48

State of Arkansas } S.S.
County of Independancy

I Esther A Byers Administratrix of the Estate of John H. Byers Deceased do Solemnly Swear that the foregoing is a full inventory and description of all the moneys goods chattles books papers and Evidences of debt and of all debts due or becoming due to said John H. Byers as far as I have been able to ascertain them
So help me God Esther A Byers

Sworn to and Subscribed before me this 16th day of Aprl 1856

George Case JP

Estate inventory of John H. Byers, 1856.
Craig, *My Byers-Bonar-Shannon and Allied Families.*

John H. Byers's Estate, 1856

A true and full Inventory of the personal estate of John H. Byers, deceased, late of Independence County

One	Bay Horse	75.00
"	Clay Bank Horse	110.00
"	Brown Horse	65.00
"	Horse Waggon & Harness	65.00
"	Cow	12.00
"	Wheelbarrow	5.00
"	Negro Woman & Child	1100.00
		$1432.00
	Money on hand	403.43

State of Arkansas } S.S.
County of Independence }

I, Esther A. Byers, Administratrix of the Estate of John H. Byers, deceased, do solemnly swear that the foregoing is a full inventory and description of all the moneys, goods, chattles, books, papers, and evidences of debt and of all debts due or becoming due to said John H. Byers as far as I have been able to ascertain them.

So help me God [signed] Esther A. Byers
Sworn to and subscribed before me this 16th day of April 1856
    George Case, J. P.

———

Editor's Note: On the 1860 census schedule, Esther is listed with real estate valued at $2,000 and $2,500 of personal property, both above average for Batesville. From Craig, *My Byers-Bonar-Shannon and Allied Families,* 54, 61. Nevertheless, William's financial support was vital in getting her and her children through the war.

wry judgment. It is even more difficult to interpret her self-understanding in these pages because she never gives the reader a good idea of why she is writing this journal. For whom is she writing? Who is her imagined audience? That is important because everyone writes for the understanding of a particular mind, altering what is said to bring about the desired response of the person to whom she is "speaking."

By getting acquainted with the people with whom she spent time, though, the reader becomes aware of Mary's social network. First comes family. Her widowed mother; her older sister, Sarah; her younger brother and sister—they are her constant concerns in her writings. She makes the reader aware of the presence of the slaves, Leanna and her daughters. Mary muses on her lack of affection for them in comparison to her mother's feelings, but she makes it clear that she learns to respect the labor they provide as she assumes their duties. Purnell is an infrequent part of her chronicle, and the reader is left to figure out that he is most likely the man in Leanna's family. He was probably the closest thing to a husband allowed in the race-based slave system since marriage was not legally permitted to slaves on the principle that they were property and therefore could not enter into legal contracts, including wedlock.

Mary's contempt for and dislike of Henry Smith reveals the complexity of her relationships with Uncle William's family, the Catalpa Hall group. While she shows her affection for some—Uncle William, Aunt Emma, the children—her resentment of the imposition of Henry, his wife (William's daughter Aurelia), and child (young Byers Smith) on the household is a dominant theme. Although Henry favors the Confederacy, his lackluster support of the war effort places him very close in Mary's mind to the Union officers who board in the house. They are all barely tolerated antagonists and irritants in her home life.

The joy in Mary's adolescent world appears to come from her friendships with her female peers. The reader becomes familiar with them since they are the group with whom Mary makes daily and overnight visits to other homes and goes on recreational trips to local places of interest. Her friends are particularly delighted in gathering with their "beaux"—Confederate soldiers who enjoy competing for the attention of the young women. Other Batesville girls are mentioned in the journal but rarely named. It is clear that there were many more people in Mary's age group than were part of her circle of friends. It is one of the tasks of the reader to figure out which comments about them are reflections of the town's class structure and which are about them as individuals. From Batesville's founding, there had been distinctions of social classes, for the migrations that built Independence County included a wide spectrum of geographic origins, education, religious beliefs, and wealth. By the 1840 election, it was already clear that the nearby Whig gentry tended to run the town, although the county as a whole voted Democratic. That old political division can occasionally be sensed behind the words of the journal.

Besides their peers, the girls included in their social circle an older group of married friends as well as elderly women, many of them widows, on whom they frequently called. The young ladies also uncomplainingly performed other visits that were part of their duties as responsible members of the community. Chief among those was "setting up" at night with the gravely ill and dying. Even a cursory reading of Mary's journal reveals that early death, whether of children or young adults, was frequent. By the end of the war, many of the young women had become hardened visitors and nurses at the bedsides of the wounded and sick soldiers in the military hospitals in Batesville.

The two major institutions beyond the family that figured in Mary's life were the churches and the schools. Most of her set of friends could be found at services of one or both of the two churches with buildings in town. The Methodist church was built in 1838 and served as the town's only place of worship for a decade until the Presbyterians built a church on Main Street in 1848.[6] Modern readers may find it unusual that most of the young women were not considered "members" of a church until after they had made a solemn commitment, even if they had been baptized as a child. That may be the reason why Mary and her friends attended services fairly frequently and across denominational lines, especially during the war, when services were not certain.

---

6. Britton, "Methodists, Slavery, and Secession in Independence County"; Lankford, "Presbyterians, Slavery, and Secession in Independence County."

Mary and Sarah's tuition bill, 1855.
Craig, *My Byers-Bonar-Shannon and Allied Families.*

Tuition Bill for Mary and Sarah, 1855

Miss Mary A. Byers
    To H. J. Newell Jr.
For Tuition in Common
Branches Session

"	closing May 30, 1855	$8.00
"	Writing & Materials.	.50
"	Incidental expenses	.50
	Amount	$9.00

Miss Sarah Byers
    To H. J. Newell, Jr.
For Tuition Session closing

	May 30th, 1855	$8.00
"	Writing & Materials	.50
"	Incidental Expenses	.50
	Amount	$9.00
	Whole Amount	$18.00

—

Editor's Note: Newell taught at the Soulesbury Institute.
Craig, *My Byers-Bonar-Shannon and Allied Families,* 57.

Batesville had done fairly well in maintaining access to education. In a day when there was no public education, subscription schools were the norm, but these depended on the presence in town of someone competent to teach and willing to earn only a meager living doing so. As early as 1833, before any church building existed, the Methodists and Presbyterians joined in sponsoring a weekly "Sabbath school" under Aaron Lyon that focused more on secular education than religious.[7] From that time on, Batesville nearly always had at least one subscription school ("academy") in operation—sometimes for females, sometimes for males, often for both, with various grades and subjects. From the Batesville Academy to the Soulesbury Institute, schooling was available if a family could pay. Even with the straitened circumstances of Mary's life after her father's death, she and her siblings went to school, probably though the generosity of her uncle.[8] Indeed, the existence of her journal is the demonstration of an educated person, and it fits into a group of diaries kept by the young of Batesville during those years.[9]

Batesville was fortunate in having such literary young adults who kept these historical records. Elvena Maxfield wrote hers for 1861 and 1862, then quit (or destroyed the later pages), only to return to her writing more than a year later. In the meantime her younger sister Lucretia (Loutie), began keeping a journal, almost as if by agreement. Will McGuire kept his infrequently, but he had responsibility for his fatherless family, went to war several times, and was badly wounded at one point.[10] As might be expected, the styles and interests of the writers vary. Will, as a soldier, gives the most trustworthy military comments, whereas the Maxfield girls are much more useful in describing the affairs of civilians, primarily those in town. Mary is the youngest of the diarists

---

7. Lyon, "History of Batesville Sabbath School."

8. See the family's school bill, reproduced herein.

9. This was not a new thing. For the previous generation, see an 1844 "friendship book" of messages that displays astonishing literary knowledge and skill by young Batesvillians. Agnew, "Speaking of Things."

10. See, for example, E. Maxfield, "Elvena Maxfield Journals"; L. Maxfield, "Lucretia Noland Maxfield Journal"; and McGuire, "W. L. McGuire Journals."

and begins late. Even so, her viewpoint seems surprisingly mature at times, especially as her understanding of human behavior in times of extraordinary political and military stress grows. It may be more than luck that she is the only one of the diarists who gives the readers an insight on slaves confronted with choices of freedom and survival at the same time that they are trying to maintain a normal posture in a white family facing its own choices of poverty and doing without the laborers on which they had always depended. Mary's journal is not redundant. It is an addition to the understanding of Batesville's Civil War.

Mary's Civil War

If the reader relies solely upon Mary's journal (or even all four diaries) to understand the Civil War as it occurred locally or in Arkansas, it will lead to confusion. Mary herself does not appear to understand what was happening. One reason was the lack of accurate information. From the viewpoint of a comparison of the diaries from the area, augmented by letters and diaries written by visitors during the war, it seems clear that Batesville lived on rumor. Except for brief periods of time when the Union army maintained a telegraph line, there was no rapid communication into the region. All the diaries reflect that reality, by commission (incorrect assertions of victories and defeats) and by omission (Mary never mentions Shiloh or Gettysburg, even later when the information must have reached the area). As the months go by, the reader can watch the growth of Mary's skepticism about the value of the "news" in town.

Another reason for the limitations of Mary's journal as a key to understanding the war is that she, like the other diarists, was young. It is unlikely that she concerned herself with issues of military strategy and tactics. It is probable that most of the people of Independence County had early realized the marginal position of Arkansas on the western edge of the Confederacy and had drawn a wrong conclusion from that fact: that there would be little actual military activity in the region. As it turned out, Batesville had little to offer as a target for either side, but it was an important place to serve as a bivouac, a launching spot on a navigable river for military units heading either south or north. During the war, the town was occupied three times by Union units and more than three times by Confederate forces. Farmsteads and small towns in the area were burned to the ground, but Batesville remained intact. Its role was to be a headquarters.[11]

What was going on around Batesville and Independence County from 1862 through 1864 was nonetheless of great interest and some importance.[12] After the Confederacy's loss at the Battle of Pea Ridge in 1862, its leaders decided that Arkansas was more expendable than the states to the east and ordered Maj. Gen. Earl Van Dorn and his army to Mississippi. One consequence was that Arkansas suddenly found itself without an effective defense, most of its soldiers now east of the Mississippi River just as General Curtis and the Army of the Southwest maneuvered toward Little Rock from the north. Arkansas governor Henry Rector threatened to secede from the Confederacy if it did not return troops to the state, then realized he could not wait. He called upon Maj. Gen. Thomas Hindman of Helena to devise a defense and a new army as quickly as possible.

Hindman's solution was to introduce into the Trans-Mississippi war a new element, permission for locals to form "independent" units of ten or more men, trained or untrained, whose task was to harass the Union forces by any means possible. His intention was to create guerrilla units that would keep the Federals off balance and cautious while costing little money or energy from the regular forces as they were restructured. He achieved that, but the "independent" units evolved into many small, mobile companies that could not be distinguished from outlaws. To complicate the situation in north-central Arkansas even more, the

------

11. The best military account of Independence County's Civil War is Mobley, *Making Sense of the Civil War in Batesville-Jacksonport and Northeast Arkansas.*

12. For further research on the war in this region, see Lankford, "Chronicle of Independence County's Civil War." This unpublished volume contains first-person narratives from these and other diaries as well as letters from many Union and Confederate visitors to Batesville, organized in chronological sequence through the war years.

sizable minority of citizens who were pro-Union were forced to create defensive militia units to protect their homes, companies that were also "independent." One of the immediate results was an ongoing argument among Union and Confederate military leaders over issues of identification of legitimate units and proper treatment of prisoners.

It is doubtful that people in Batesville were aware of this unprecedented military confusion. In fact, historical awareness of the importance of this development has only been recognized and discussed in the last few decades.[13] While Brig. Gen. John S. Marmaduke and Col. Joseph O. Shelby organized forces in the Batesville area in 1863 for a diversionary assault on Union troops to the north in Missouri, Mary and her friends were enjoying its romantic side as a pleasant spring and summer with young soldiers. The war in occupied Batesville seemed very civil, and so life appeared in Mary's journal, but the civilians just a few miles from the occupied zone were terrorized as paramilitary groups of questionable allegiance roamed through the area.

The Confederate military strikes north failed, and when Union forces again occupied Batesville in the winter of 1864, their mission was to capture or exterminate the remaining independent units and bring peace to the region. When Col. Robert Livingston's command withdrew in June, though, they were immediately replaced by General Shelby's men, who had the same mission: destroy these units claiming Confederate allegiance but in reality outlaws and bring peace to the area. During these months of activity by the official army units of both sides, hundreds of "brigands" of the "uncivil war" in the Ozarks, as it has been called, were captured and executed. Of these things Mary and her friends knew little. Her conversations with the Union officers who boarded with them and those with her Confederate admirers all avoided these topics, with the result that the journal's war entries focus on the news of deaths of friends and her excited reactions to rumored victories.

---

13. On Unionism, see Johnston, "Peace Society in Fulton County"; and DeBlack, "Remarkably Strong Union Sentiment." On guerrilla warfare, see Sutherland, *Savage Conflict*; and Mackey, *Uncivil War.*

Mary expressed her disgust at the men of Batesville and Independence County for taking the "loyalty oath" and becoming citizens of the United States again. But these men were already envisioning the approaching end of the worst war in American history and trying to figure out how the new order would be established and recovery achieved.

The Journal of Mary Adelia Byers

1862

I am commencing to keep a journal for several reasons. It is very improving both in penmanship and in learning any one to commit his thoughts to paper with accuracy. I should have commenced when the war began or at least when the Federal army entered Batesville.[1] Poor Batesville! You have suffered much at the hands of this army, but not so much as you will suffer if it remains here longer. Report says that they leave in the morning and as Gens. Steele's[2] and Osterhaus's[3] divisions left yester[day] and today, I believe it is true. Some say that we will fare worse with the Southern army in the country than with the other, but we are prepared for anything now short of hanging.

---

1. Maj. Gen. Samuel R. Curtis's Army of the Southwest had occupied Batesville beginning May 3.

2. Maj. Gen. Frederick Steele, USA.

3. Brig. Gen. Peter J. Osterhaus, USA. Osterhaus was one of many Germans who had immigrated to St. Louis. At the outbreak of war, he joined the Twelfth Missouri Volunteers, a mostly German regiment, rising to commanding officer of the Second Brigade. Batesville residents felt fear when the German troops arrived. Emily Weaver Reed recalled: "when happening to glance toward the window, I saw what literally paralyzed me with fright, and instant death loomed before me, for there at the window were crowded a lot of hideous, grinning 'feds,' jabbering in Dutch and pointing toward me. . . . [I]n they poured, back door and front door, crowding and jabbering some orders in Dutch, which, of course, none of us understood." "Batesville: Personal Recollections of 1863," 24–25. Another resident recorded: "One morning I was standing in front of my store and a German Cavalry troop galloped through the main street with their knives in their mouths and pistols in each hand. . . . At the end of the street they halted and slowly returned. When they saw our sign over the store 'Hirsch & Adler,' they cried out 'Juden Secesh!' (Secessionist Jews!) and some 50 of them dismounted, entered the store and packed up everything in it, also a few new wagons that we had in the yard, and carried same to their quarters. . . . The Germans were particularly unfavorable to me because I was a Jew." Hirsch, "Memoir."

JUNE 24TH

This day has been an eventful one. Gen. Curtis with his men have left town. They have gone to Jacksonport and expect to proceed from there to Des Arc,[4] then to Little Rock. I hope they may be repulsed before they reach there. They expect to meet other obstacles than swamps before they reach there. Lieut. Crabtree says there would be but little glory in taking a town as they took this. He came today to say, "Good-bye," but I was away. He left his "kind regards." Lieut. Curry left word that "the swamps had dried up." I had laughed no little at their idea of swamps between here and L. R., a thing never before heard of.[5]

Parilee Tucker is dead. Is it to be wondered that we should hate them when they cause the death of the beautiful and good? Bill is very near distracted; her death was so sudden and unexpected. We have troops camped around us again. The 3rd Illinois Cavalry and a battery [are] said to be stationed for the summer but they cannot get water, and I think they will be compelled to leave.

Sarah went to Mrs. Fairchild's[6] today for the first time. I know she will have a pleasant time. Miss Isabel did not leave yesterday and [I] doubt whether she gets off at all.[7]

---

4. Jacksonport was a strategic port at the confluence of the Black and White Rivers with an estimated population in 1860 of 1,000 people. Des Arc was an early settlement in eastern Arkansas named after the nearby Bayou des Arc. It had around 400 residents in 1860.

5. Mary at age fifteen seems a bit young to be keeping company with officers, especially Federals.

6. Clarissa "Tennse" Fairchild (b. 1817) and her husband, Hubert F. Fairchild (b. 1818), lived at Sun Fish, their plantation north of Batesville. Mr. Fairchild served as a justice on the Arkansas Supreme Court until resigning in 1863.

7. Crossing the porous and constantly shifting battle lines must not have been difficult. As the armies alternately occupied Batesville, Mary often mentions people auctioning their property and "leaving" as refugees for a place of safety: for the Unionists, Ohio, and for the Confederates, as far away as Texas. The Federals later instituted a system of oaths and passes for temporary crossings.

John Smith[8] had quite an adventure the other night; came very near spending it in the guard-house. I guess he will be more particular in future how he blacks himself and appears before a Gen. Of.[9]

JUNE 25TH

There has not much of note transpired today. I spent both yesterday and today at Cousin Rilla's.[10] Cousin Henry has taken quite a fancy to Sarah and I and wants us to come down often; he is much pleasanter then he used to be.

Anna Harpham was thrown from her horse on Monday while riding with one of these Officers. She is not dangerously hurt. No news from the army; don't know anything of their movements except that they have nearly all gone to Jacksonport.

JUNE 26TH

I have the headache this evening. Was at Mrs. Perrin's this morning.[11] They are great talkers. Lieut. Crabtree talked very differently [there] to what he did here. I have been reviewing my conduct toward him since Mrs. Perrin told me about him, and I have been angry with myself for treating him as I did, and if he ever returns here I will treat him differently. He shall know that I am indeed Southern in principle. He will think from my conversation on Sunday that there is an inclination the other way. I have learned that the adage, "The longer we live, the more we learn," is true, for I am a great deal wiser then I was 8 weeks ago, but whether I will be any better for it I don't know. "For though the

---

8. The eighteen-year-old son of Col. Robert Smith, Jr., and Susan McIlvain Smith, John was brother of "Puss" Smith and half-brother of "Cousin Henry" Smith. He was a sometime Confederate soldier and beau of Mary.

9. See entry for June 29th for further details of this event.

10. Cousin Aurelia "Rilla" Adelia Byers Smith and her husband, Henry C. Smith, lived at Catalpa Hall, her father's estate, two miles north of Batesville. See Appendix 2.

11. Nancy (Mrs. David) Perrin, stepmother (?) of Sarah, Frank, and Jim.

spirit is strong, the flesh is weak." They have been out today throwing up embankments or, as they say, "Digging holes for the Secesh to fall in." I don't think those breastworks will ever protect Uncle Sam's soldiers from Rebel troops; this is the name I glory in now.

JUNE 27TH

Wonder upon wonder. Mr. Lyon and Miss Hutchins[12] are married—married last night at Dr. Allen's.[13] Most people think it the best thing that has happened, but I don't. I think Miss Hutchins much too good, smart, and everything else for such an old doty thing as Mr. Lyon. Old Mrs. Bates is dead.[14] Cousin Ann and Nannie were in town today. They are very much troubled out there,[15] especially since Steele's guards left. They were very attentive; the others are very careless. The farce is now being acted, and nothing but the absence of scenery and footlights prevents it from being equal to any ever played in the Drury Lane Theater. Gen. Curtis makes a splendid stage manager, the only objection being that he does not shift scenes with sufficient rapidity. They are now barricading the Court House, and what is the use? For those walls are not proof against a Minié ball. They want to ruin the town as much as they can without applying the torch and to get the report circulated through the country that the town is strongly fortified and that it will be held at all hazard. O, for someone to communicate it to our noble army! They could take the town within twenty-four hours and that without a

---

12. Aaron W. Lyon was a prominent Presbyterian, land speculator, merchant, and public servant. A widower in his early sixties at the time of his wedding, he and young Caroline Hutchins went on to have three children. Lyon helped establish Arkansas College, now Lyon College (renamed after the family of Frank Lyon, a modern benefactor).

13. John F. Allen, physician and prominent Presbyterian.

14. Mary Bates, sixty-two, married to innkeeper and Irish immigrant, Robert Bates. Batesville was named after James Woodson Bates (1788–1846), lawyer and territorial delegate to Congress; he was not related to Mary and Robert.

15. Catalpa Hall.

fight, for this army would ske-daddle, to use an expression very much in vogue with them at present but not admired by me.

JUNE 28TH

I am prone to judge people too harshly. I must quit it for I wrong others as well as myself. But I am always boasting of my perception and I find out to my chagrin that I am very often sadly mistaken.

Word came yesterday that none of the forces had crossed Black River, but I think they have, for another [wagon] train of sick left the hospital this morning.[16]

Later. The attack has commenced. As to whether it will become general, we cannot tell. Mr. Kennard[17] thinks it will. He says they never would come within three-fourths of a mile and then retire if an attack were not in contemplation, for it would put them on their guard. One piece of artillery has been ordered to the Court-House; the other two pieces are awaiting orders. All is now quiet. One of the men of Davis' Battery say[s] that three were taken prisoners. One man was killed. Uncle William wants us to go to his house, but I don't want to go. If we go out we won't have anything to come [back] to. The street is now filled with soldiers. We don't have to go to Uncle William's this evening. Col. Washburn could not be found. Mr. Wilkins[18] has come home;

---

16. Ill health was often a greater problem than battle wounds for soldiers during the Civil War. For example, by the time Company A, First Battalion, Arkansas Union Infantry was mustered out in St. Louis at the end of 1862, its members had been constantly in ill health due to poor food, medical care, and sanitation, thus they had seen no combat. About 150 of the original 380 men in the unit had died of disease. *Boone and Gibbs.*

17. Michael Shelby Kennard was the twenty-nine-year-old son of Rev. George W. and Eliza Kennard. He was formerly a law partner of Judge U. M. Rose, editor of the *Independent Balance,* delegate to the Secession Convention in March 1861, and until Fort Sumter, a strong supporter of the Union. After the war he became a well-known educator. Mary refers to both men as "Mr. Kennard," usually distinguishing the reverend as "old Mr. Kennard."

18. Possibly Edward L. Wilkins, a thirty-six-year-old brickmason from Pennsylvania residing in Batesville with his wife, Mary.

he says our boys are at Tupelo [Mississippi], below Corinth.[19] Philmore says Richmond has fallen but with a heavy loss on the Federal side.[20] No victory to boast of.

JUNE 29TH

Everything quiet. The Southern troops had come to guard some men who had come home to see their families. When they were ready to go back [they] thought they would have some fun and scare the Yankees, fired on them, shot one man all to pieces, and took five prisoners when they retreated. There were fifty Southern men.

Evening. John Smith and Mrs. Kennard have been here this evening. John was very pleasant and amused us no little in telling of his adventure the other night. He dressed up as a negro woman intending to go to a negro wedding, when Col. Washburn ordered him to the guard house. But Dolph Wycough[21] interfered, and he was released.

JUNE 30TH

All the troops are leaving here. [They] received orders last night at ten o'clock to march to Sulphur Rock and wait further orders. They were up at half-past two and now, eight o'clock, they are all gone except one company that is staying as a rear guard. There was a fight of five hours on Saturday at Salem. We have not heard how it terminated. It is thought that there is to be a fight either at Jacksonport or Des Arc soon and that is what they [will do] with these troops here as they have not sufficient force.

---

19. A consequence of the transfer of the trained troops of Maj. Gen. Earl Van Dorn's Army of the West from Arkansas to the region east of the Mississippi River, deemed more important by authorities in Richmond.

20. This, of course, was only one of the recurrent rumors.

21. Marion Adolphus "Dolph" Wycough, son of carpenter and merchant Samuel Butler Wycough and his wife, Malinda, and brother of Mary Wycough.

Mrs. Cox[22] was arrested on Saturday and released on promising that she would go home. I would like to see Lieut. Curry now to tell him something of their good treatment of prisoners. I wouldn't care if the "Secesh" caught him and put him in the chain gang.

There is not a Fed in town now except seven at the hospital that were too sick to be removed. The Confederates are expected hourly. There has been heavy skirmishing in Jackson County for two days, and yesterday quite a general engagement.

Meeting in camp, Gens. Steele and Carr[23] told Gens. Curtis and Osterhaus that if those negroes[24] were not driven out of camp they would break their swords, disband their troops, and go home, that their men were on less than half rations and that there were five and six hundred negroes lying around camp, eating up the provisions and doing no duty and that they would stand it no longer. Gen. Curtis therefore issued a proclamation for all persons having negroes in camp to come and they might have them.

Mrs. Poe was arrested yesterday on the charge that the guard who was at her mother's had been taken prisoner, and she was to be held until his return, but, the guard coming in, she was released.

Later. I can just hear the sound of a distant drum. I hope it may be the last time that the sound of a Federal drum will greet mine ears. The army is now cut off from all supplies here. There are trees felled across White River so that boats cannot travel. They are obliged to cut their way through to Des Arc. They stayed in Batesville eight weeks and two days.

---

22. Laura Erwin Cox, wife of lawyer Thomas Cox, who was then away with the Confederate army. According to local tradition, the Cox home on Main Street was used as headquarters by both armies in turn. After her husband's death, she married Dr. D. C. Ewing.

23. Brig. Gen. Eugene A. Carr, USA.

24. Runaway slaves.

JULY 3RD

Just two months today since the Northern army entered Batesville and if [it] were not for the destruction of property, we would not know they had been here. The night of the 1st the wind blew the United States flag down, and yesterday evening Col. Sweet with 150 Texas Rangers[25] reared the Confederate. The people were pleased, but fear almost outbalanced pleasure, for, if the Federal troops ever return, woe unto us, for they have sworn that the town shall be laid in ashes.

Martha Womac is dead,[26] another victim of the war; her husband is in the Southern army. There are more lies told in this war than would take to sink the Great Eastern. It was all a lie about Steele's and Curtis's quarrel and the proclamation. Last night they had a bigger one than ever has been told, that Curtis had sent Hindman[27] word, "if he would just let him get out of Arkansas, he never would trouble him any more." I don't know what the world is coming to. I think the devil will have to send Beauregard[28] the letter the old woman told about, viz., please not to kill any more Yankees, for we hadn't house-room for them.

JULY 4TH

It is dry and warm, and I have been sick for three days. This is the anniversary of the Declaration of Independence. If the Federal army had stayed here until now there would have been a grand celebration; as it is there was some speaking and a flag raised. The flag was made by the

---

25. Col. George W. Sweet and the Fifteenth Texas Cavalry.

26. Probably related to Thomas Wamac, a forty-eight-year-old carpenter in the 1860 census and partner with S. B. Wycough in a general store. Also, "Womack."

27. Maj. Gen. Thomas C. Hindman, CSA, new commander of the Trans-Mississippi Department.

28. Gen. P. G. T. Beauregard, CSA.

ladies, at Mrs. Neely's.[29] Capt. Gibbs[30] came home yesterday but did not get off his horse. Came again today, got some clothes for himself and Purnell,[31] made a short speech to the good people of Batesville and then returned to head-quarters, where that is they won't tell, but it is supposed to be about Searcy. He met Mr. Kennard; the first thing he said was [that if Dick's wife had left with the Northern army,] Purnell said he'd follow her to the end of the world [and] bring her back.

John Smith sent me a large basket of plums today, but I had taken blue snake[32] and could not eat any.

There is to be a ball tonight at the Batesville Institute. If Sarah was at home she would be nearly crazy to go.[33]

JULY 6TH

What a long warm day this has been, and the day is not gone yet. The sun seems [to be] trying how hot he can shine, and everything combines to draw the minutes out to their utmost tension. Mr. Kennard has just returned from over White River. He brought two pair shoes that I [had] bought, some that were taken from the sutlers. Cousin Preston has come home. I have not seen him. He will probably come here tomorrow; if he does not I will know the reason.

---

29. Margaret Desha Denton Neely, the wealthy widow of lawyer William F. Denton and then of Judge Beaufort H. Neely, lived in a large house on Main Street. She was a forceful and outspoken supporter of the Confederacy and an exhorter (lay speaker) for the Methodist church.

30. Capt. William E. Gibbs commanded Company K, 1st Arkansas Mounted Rifles, the first company of Confederates organized in Independence County in 1861. He was reported missing in action at the Battle of Wilson's Creek (Oak Hills), but he later returned to Batesville. His sister, Margaret, was married to Judge Rose.

31. Dick Purnell, Leanna's "husband" and Captain Gibbs's servant.

32. This may have been a local name for blue mass, a mercury-based nostrum for everything from constipation to syphilis. Just after his inauguration, Abraham Lincoln is supposed to have stopped taking it (for depression)—it made him "cross."

33. The journal does not indicate the whereabouts of Sarah, the gay, worldly sister. Mary, the prim bluestocking, apparently did not consider going to the Confederate officers' ball herself.

I have been down at Mrs. Cowle's this evening.[34] People talk about love in marriage; that is a match of convenience, and if they ain't a *happy* couple I never saw one. He was smoking and she reading a novel and each quarreling with the other for not stopping. Tobacco smoke was disagreeable to her, but Mr. Cowle did not care, said he meant to keep on until Agnes quit reading novels. Mrs. Cowle said she would not quit novels 'til he'd quit smoking. So they have it, each one is prepared for a siege and a protracted one. All ye lovers of matrimony or ye who contemplate it, come see and take warning.

JULY 15TH

I have neglected you, my journal, for several days, but I have been on such a pleasant visit to Mrs. Fairchild's and only returned yesterday and am contemplating one equally as pleasant tomorrow out at Mrs. McGuire's.[35] Will (I suppose he has arrived at the dignity of "Mr. McGuire" now) came this evening accompanied by Jim Perrin (what a detestable puppy he is) to invite Sister and I out to an "Apple bee." He will come by for us tomorrow in a wagon, or as Jim Perrin interposed, something better if it could be obtained. I expect he will think it will devolve upon him to do the honors of the occasion. I am glad Frank is not here or goodbye to all pleasure for me; he would bother me so. It is a sin for any one to dislike a family as cordially as I do that one and yet keep up a familiarity which is increasing instead of diminishing, but I really like Miss Sarah. I expect a pleasant time indeed. My. . . . [entry incomplete]

---

34. Rev. John Cowle was a preacher and presiding elder of the Methodist Episcopal Church, South. Born in England, he, his wife Agnes, and four small children lived just down the street from Mary. He presided over the Batesville, Jacksonport, and Harrisburg Districts. A strong proponent of slavery, Cowle once gave a three-hour oration to a large crowd, charging that the M. E. (sometimes called "Northern") church was an organization of abolitionists.

35. Catherine Lewis McGuire, widow of wealthy planter Elam S. McGuire and mother of Will McGuire (a friend of Mary's), lived near Catalpa Hall.

JULY 17TH

I have been asleep and feel very drowsy, but I will compel myself to write, for if I neglect writing as I have done for two weeks I will soon give it up entirely. The visit yesterday was quite as pleasant as anticipated. There were nineteen persons from town out. Will Maxfield was there, and of all the *airs* that I ever saw man put on he beats, Jesse Searcy[36] not excepted. W. tried to make the table move but did not succeed.[37] Afterward had Will Maxfield as Prof. of Phrenology to examine our heads. Thinks I would make a splendid horse-jockey, can keep a secret with two to help me, and that the bump of perseverance was not very strongly developed. Mote Folsome[38] is very sick; the Dr. thinks he will die.

JULY 20TH

This is Sunday, but it does not seem so to me. I went to church last night also again today. This evening I went up to Mrs. Fairchild's with John Smith. I don't understand him; last night he came to Cousin Rilla's with me from church. This evening coming home as we passed the telegraph he asked if I wouldn't send him some dispatches when they got to Little Rock. I said, "Of course," when the telegraph is established. He then asked if I would not answer his letters when he wrote to me. I said that I would, but my letters wouldn't be interesting, for I couldn't write good letters. He said that was what the girls always said. We then spoke of drinking and playing cards. I asked him neither to touch liquor or cards until he returned. He replied that he would not for one reason, because

36. A forty-year-old lawyer, veteran of the Mexican War, and nephew and heir of the prominent Richard Searcy.

37. Table tipping and other forms of spiritualism became popular in America in the middle of the nineteenth century. President Lincoln was said to have participated in séances during the war. Fair, "Spiritualism & the Civil War."

38. Believed to be Martin Folsom, fourteen-year-old son of physician and landowner Isaac Folsom and his wife, Lucy. Other records note that the boy died the following day. See, for example, E. Maxfield, "Elvena Maxfield Journals."

it was my advice; that he would tell me when he came back (and he expected to get a furlough in about a month), and I should see how good he was at keeping promises. When I came home I told Ma; she does not want me to correspond with any gentleman.

I went to Aunt Emma's today to help Nannie make a dress to wear to the party tonight. Cousin Annie wanted Sarah to go too, but Ma did not want her to go. She did not tell her positively that she should not go, told her she might do as she pleased, but if she went it would be against her expressed wishes. Sarah wanted very much to go but was afraid to after that, and the thought of Ma's displeasure would have prevented all pleasure. It is the anniversary of the battle of Manassas, and the Texas soldiers leave tomorrow, and I thought Ma might have let her go. I tried to persuade her to, but all arguments were of no avail. Probably it is for the best, but I can't see the wisdom in it now for I had set my heart upon her attendance. For myself I had no desire to go, but a few more refusals and Cousins Ann and Nannie will ask us no more. Sister had a hearty cry and composed herself to disappointment, and now she is sitting by my side darning stockings, quite different employment to what she and I both anticipated for her two hours ago, but the cup of happiness was dashed to the ground just as she raised it to her lips. I will try to think it for the best. Sarah does wrong by crying; she weakens her own cause; it only angers Ma, who thinks it rebellion against her authority. I think she and I have gone to our last party (and first, too). Ma will never consent to our going to another. I told Mrs. Kennard to tell John about the letter writing.

The Texas soldiers left today. Mr. Kennard was very much affected at parting with his family. John came over to say, "Goodbye," and tell a parting lie. He is the most notorious liar in the county. Mrs. Maxwell came up this evening. She wants either Sarah or me to assist her in teaching, as she expects to go in the Institute. I won't go into that old

Esther Ann Wilson Byers (Ma), 1823–91.
Courtesy Independence County Historical Society.

Methodist concern that never did anything but rise, make a show for
five months, then fall and be nearly buried in the ruins.[39] Mrs. Maxwell
will not hold out any better, and when I make my debut as a teacher
I want it to be under more favorable auspices. I wish I had accepted
Mrs. Fowler's offer and gone to school to her. I intend going to see her

---

39. Mary probably means Soulesbury Institute (College). It is now apparent to
her that she must think about earning a living for herself and her family, since they
were living on Uncle William's bounty, and as the war continued, he grew poorer.

tomorrow. I am making a pink gingham sacque and can't get it to fit. I am in a bad humor and have slightly angered Ma by hinting that she too was mad. I would that I could take a peep into futurity and see how I shall pass the next six months.

JULY 24TH

I have today called on Mrs. Lyon, the second bridal call I ever made. The first I made was on Mary Montgomery, and Sunday when I went riding she was in the cabbage patch with a little white-headed young one in her arms. Her husband is in the Army. I could not help contrasting her condition with mine. She troubled about her husband and the child to care for and I happy and careless of the future. But her future may be much brighter than mine, for as yet my sky has been o'ercast with few clouds.

Willie is sick today. I wish we had his daguerreotype, not that I consider him dangerous, yet since Mote Folsome died I am uneasy. He (Mote) was as strong and healthy as any one.

JULY 25TH

This has been a very pleasant day. Mary Case, Lutie, Sister, and I went to Mrs. Slater's to see Mrs. Fowler. A rain coming, we were sent home in the carriage. People say Mrs. Slater is a tartar, but in conversation she is one of the most pleasant women I ever met.

Rutherford's[40] Co. is in town again. Nothing reliable from the seat of war, many conflicting rumors. Curtis still at Helena. Lieut. Crabtree's three months are almost out, and the Confederacy is still in existence.

JULY 28TH

I am decidedly blue or as the French would say I am affected with *ennui*. (There, I have written it, but I know not how to pronounce it.) Harriet Wilkinson died last evening. She had a congestive chill Saturday night.

40. Capt. (later Col.) George W. Rutherford, CSA.

She has been sick for some time but not confined to her bed. It is now raining; they will have a wet evening to bury her. Mrs. Maxwell wants me to help her teach but I don't want to.

It is now reported that Curtis's army has been reinforced and is advancing on Little Rock, and Steele upon Batesville, but I think it is only camp rumor. It is supposed that from Curtis's march from Pea Ridge to Helena he lost by sickness, death, and desertion between three and four thousand men. They will remember the march through Arkansas unto the last day of their lives.

Later. I have just returned from Harriet Wilkinson's funeral. Coming down I walked with Mr. Guillam.[41] We had a long discussion about religion. His religion seems to me like it lay near the surface, his conversation like he was afraid to talk about serious matters for fear young people would avoid him as being too sober and afraid to give full vent to his spirits and enjoy himself with all the hilarity of youth for fear his conduct would not be in accordance with his profession. His conversation does not make me feel as if I should like to be a participant in that religion in which he professes to find so much enjoyment as Mr. Dannelly[42] does. When Mr. Dannelly talks to me I feel as if I should like very much to be a possessor of religion.

JULY 31ST

The last day of July. I spent the morning sewing. This evening Puss Smith sent for Sister and I. Sarah wouldn't go until a second summons. We tried to make the table move but did not succeed.

41. Rev. William H. Gillam, Methodist Episcopal Church, South. During the war, Gillam "went north," remaining in Arkansas but transferring into the M. E., or "Northern," Church. In 1864 he was active in restoring the M. E. congregations in Batesville, both black and white. See Britton, *First Hundred Years;* and "Methodists, Slavery, and Secession in Independence County."

42. George A, Dannelly, traveling elder of the Methodist Episcopal Church, South. His daughter Jennie was about Mary's age.

AUGUST 4TH

This has been as warm a day as I ever spent. Mrs. Wycough and Mrs. Cowle spent the day here today. I have not laughed as much for long time. [Each] seemed to exert herself, and each vied with the other in saying amusing things. Mrs. Cowle as usual came off victor. There is to be a party tonight at the Batesville Institute, a compliment to the soldiers. There can't one company of soldiers pass through here but there is a party given them. We have a picnic Wednesday. It is a kind of female affair, none of the other sex permitted except three boys.

There is an amusing thing in a L. R. paper received today. At Hilton Head the Federalists have sent male and female missionaries to instruct the negroes, and now the northern papers are loud in their denunciations of these ladies that instead of teaching they are seen riding and walking with officers and with blue coat sleeves around their waists listening to airy nothings which fall from the lips of said officers and are received by these Christian damsels like the dews of summer are by the parched earth in August.

AUGUST 8TH

Mary McGuire[43] [died] on the 5th; she was sick but four days. Emma Robison, Minerva, and Rena Lowe[44] are in town today. They want Sarah and I to go home with them. I would like very much to go but I want my tooth plugged [filled], want to finish my white dress, help make Purnell's breeches, and to go and see White Brickey present a flag, and one or two other things to be done. There has been a Mrs. Rogers here whose husband is sick at the hospital.

---

43. The nineteen-year-old daughter of Elam S. McGuire. Her younger sister Delia was also to die during the war.

44. Minerva and Rena Lowe were daughters of D. H. Lowe. With Mary and Emma, they were friends of Mary's and Sarah's from rural White River Township.

AUGUST 15TH

I came home today from Mrs. Womac's. I never had as dull a visit in my life; I suppose it was home-sick[ness]. They all told me so; if it was, it was the first attack I ever had. I would have given worlds had they been at my disposal just to have [been] at home. I think it will be the last time I go to Mrs. Womac's. At Mrs. Lowe's it was not much better. There [were] so many there, too, but they are not the kind of people that I fancy. Mr. Garthwaite[45] came today. He wants us all to go to school to him that we may take French, music, and anything that they teach, free of charge.

AUGUST 17TH

I fear that I am not a good historian of facts, for many things have occurred that should have been recorded. Old Mrs. Ruddell is here. She has no more sense than she ever did. She is telling about what she said and done when the Federals were here—the first thing to be told when two persons meet who have not seen one another since they left. I went to Sunday School this morning but did not stay to church, came home in time to receive the old woman. People say that Curtis is crossing at Clarendon, intending to advance on Little Rock. If it was not that Little Rock was the capital of Arkansas and that they are gaining a foothold in the state, I would rejoice to hear of their arrival. The aristocrats over there say that the people of Batesville should have repulsed the army. This is Judge Bevens,[46] who, after he had run from here to escape from them, cries disgrace to Batesville, that it will never be respected again because the people submitted to be tamely run over.

AUGUST 21ST

I went to a picnic yesterday. It was one of the most pleasant days I ever passed. Jim Perrin was there; as usual he was my *besetting sin*. All of the

---

45. Rev. W. S. Garthwaite, a Presbyterian and a school principal.
46. Probably Judge William Casper Bevens, Third Judicial District.

girls and boys hate him, but he is invited on every excursion. Mr. Dennis, the Texas soldier that waits on the wounded Lieut. at Mr. Case's,[47] was there. He is a specimen of the uneducated backwoodsman: says *seed, this here, that thar,* etc. All of the girls except Puss Smith tried to cut Jim Perrin up on every occasion and make him appear as ridiculous as possible. Frank Campbell lost none of his gallantry during his campaign. He is going in the army again in about a month. Fifty-six Federal prisoners crossed Ramsey's ferry yesterday.[48] They are on parole of honor until regularly exchanged. Today I have been ironing.

SEPTEMBER 6TH

It is raining. Commenced studying French Sept. 12th and geometry on the 16th. Which will I complete the first?

OCTOBER 2ND

I have not written in my journal for more than a month. Much has transpired that should have been recorded. Mr. Dannelly and Jennie were in town from Saturday until Tuesday. We, that is Sarah, Mary Wycough, and I, made an engagement to go to Mr. Guillam's this evening, but Ma says that as I have never been in the habit of visiting at Mrs. Guillam's I had better not stay there to supper and we have nothing fit to invite him to sit down to if he should come home with me, leaving me no alternative but to stay at home and break my word. Oh, poverty, you are indeed a curse, and I have tasted of it as deeply as most of my age, but as Ma says I may have some days before my life closes that will make me reflect on these that I am now passing as bright and beautiful. But even this does not make me more cheerful or resigned to my lot.

---

47. George Case, father of Mary's friends Mary Case and Eliza Jane Case Lewis.
48. The modern bridge that spans the White River at Batesville stands on the site of Ramsey's Ferry.

OCTOBER 26TH

There has been a great change in the weather. Friday was a warm, bright day; in the evening the wind commenced blowing and it looked very much like rain, but yesterday morning when I rose it was snowing. It continued until 3 o'clock when the snow was about three inches deep; then the sun shone and the snow began to melt. By this time tomorrow there will be but very little on the ground. Whoever saw snow before there had been frost to kill bean and tomato vines?

Thursday, Eliza Lewis's[49] baby died. She has been sick since June. Dr. Hendren[50] vaccinated her and she has not been well since. Eliza has lost two children. Her two little girls, Fannie and Ava, sleep side [by side] in the church-yard.[51] Her husband is in Kentucky with Kirby Smith.[52] She has not heard from him since August; then he had no clothes but those he wore and but one dollar that said he must spend that day.

Ann Legget[t][53] died on Wednesday with typhus fever. "They say" that she was engaged to Chaplain Williams, but he denied it last spring when I teased him about her. If it was so he will not feel her death much for there is the girl in Mississippi with whom he was enamoured last spring, so I don't think he will be inconsolable.

It is rumored that the Feds are coming, and it would not surprise me in the least if they were in here next week. Very well I know they could come if they tried for there are no troops at Pocahontas except McBride's conscripts, who are only half armed [and] that would run at the first fire. The hospitals are broken up at last, though a good many of the men are still about town. There cannot possibly be as many fools in

49. Eliza Jane Case Lewis.

50. Dr. William Hendren and his wife, Ann, a teacher, lived next door to the Lewises.

51. Mary herself would lose three of her ten children in infancy; her daughter Clare, three of her five.

52. W. J. Lewis, a watchmaker who enlisted at the start of the war and would be killed at Atlanta in 1864. At this time his unit was serving with Maj. Gen. Edmund Kirby Smith's Confederate army during the Perryville Campaign.

53. The eighteen-year-old daughter of Jeremiah and Elizabeth Leggett.

the whole Confederate army, in one regiment I mean, as there was in this one of Col. Shaler.[54] For aside from the officers of the regiment they were the most foolish, ignorant set of men I ever saw or heard tell of. Avy was as smart a one as there was among them, and his song-ballads (as he termed them) and love letter that he wrote for and to Sarah were such as any twelve-year-old boy with half sense ought to have written. Sarah did not answer the letter, and, the next time Mr. Avy came over, only passed through the room once; Mr. Avy took the hint that his attentions were not very agreeable and left. My time has been occupied to day in writing what has transpired in the last week, and I will try now to keep the journal regularly.

OCTOBER 27TH

This morning I heard of the death of Nellie Mix, one of our scholars and a very pretty little girl, her mother's only daughter. The school did not close for her funeral as it should have done; Mr. Garthwaite is very neglectful of such things.

I think I will make my fortune crocheting nets for the hair. I have already made three and have two more in house and the promise of three more.

This evening I was sitting on the porch alone when a gentleman rode by, bowing very familiarly and with a "Good evening, Miss Mary," he passed on. I bowed but could not imagine who it could be, studied about it until Ma came in from walking and asked her, but she had not seen him. After supper, Ma and I went down to Cousin Rilla's, mentioned about it, and Sarah had met the same man and was equally puzzled. We sent over to Mr. Womac's, as he had been there, found out it was Ad Robinson.[55] He had been taken prisoner by the enemy, paroled, and allowed to come home.

---

54. Probably Col. James R. Shaler, an unpopular Missourian commanding the 27th Arkansas Infantry, organized in July 1862 from volunteers and conscripts at Yellville, Arkansas. Gerdes, "27th Arkansas Infantry."

55. Probably A. W. Robinson, twenty-three, living with his in-laws, the John Womacs.

NOVEMBER IST

I hardly know what to put down first, for, as the old saying is, my wits are wool-gathering, though I tell Mamma that I am as calm and unconcerned as I should be, if there were not so many conflicting rumors about the Federal army. They now say that there are four thousand Northern troops camped around Judge Cain['s], about 4 miles this side of Pocahontas, and they are believed to be only the advance of a very large army. A man arrived in town today just from Ironton [Mo.]; he reports that there is a great deal of baggage and army stores arriving on every train. Sam Hirsch[56] was in Memphis a few weeks ago. While he was there Gen. Osterhaus's division went up the river to Cape Girardeau. The two Baxters[57] were along with it and sent word to their wives that they would be home in a few days, that the army would be here, and as Miss Abbie[58] says, "make things happen." The prisoners taken in a skirmish near Cotton Plant told the same, also said that Steele's command was coming, too. Everything goes to confirm these reports so I suppose we may look for the Feds any day. Mr. Womac bought wagons [and] teams, packed up, sold out, and left yesterday. They were not sure that they would go until in the morning and were off at four in the evening. Mr. Womac does things with a rush. Emma Wycough has moved her

---

56. Aaron Hirsch's brother.

57. Brothers Elisha and Taylor Baxter. They had arrived from North Carolina in 1852, and although they had owned slaves, both held strong Unionist sympathies. In 1869 Elisha would buy Catalpa Hall and in 1872 be elected governor of Arkansas. Taylor later moved to Kansas.

58. Abby Eastman, sister-in-law of Vermont-native and Unionist Calvin C. Bliss, later elected lieutenant governor of Arkansas. Despite her Yankee politics, "Miss Abba" was popular with Mary's friends. Yet by the following year (1863), conditions in Independence County were becoming dangerous for Union men. Bliss was away when his wife decided it was no longer safe for the family to live in Batesville. She, her two children, her sister Abby, and several other families started north across enemy lines on June 20. Via Rolla and St. Louis, the Bliss family finally arrived in Bradford, Maine, where the sisters' parents lived. Boone and Gibbs, "Calvin Comins Bliss."

things to her father's and intends going to her Papa's. Col. Coleman[59] has left town, and nearly every man is going to leave.[60] There is a dreadful cry raised that the Federals will force every negro to leave, put the torch to everything, and will be no respecter of persons, but I can hardly believe it. I cannot think that they would destroy a house that a family was living in and that they will deprive us of our honors, for there was an army of twenty thousand through here last spring, and if there was one woman ruined unwillingly, I have never heard it.

Old Mr. Kennard[61] has lost all the sense he ever had. He went away today, took Ellen and Jule, left Mrs. Kennard, Lida, and those three little children alone, with winter coming on and no provision for it. He is the greatest coward I ever knew. He is too old to conscript and did not take the oath last spring, and there could not have been the least danger in him remaining. The men don't seem to have any sense anyhow. They act like a parcel of sheep: whatever and wherever one goes they all have to go.

NOVEMBER 3RD

We have had quite an exciting day of it. Sarah and [I] stayed at home from school to help to make two shirts and a pair of pants for Purnell, who came last Thursday evening. I have a sore place on my thimble finger and have sewed all day with my thimble on next to the little finger. Miss Sarah Hawkins spent the greater part of the morning here. She came to get Ma to dye a bonnet for her sister, Mrs. Daugherty. This evening there was a good deal of commotion in the kitchen. Uncle William thought Leanna[62] and her children had better go south with him as the

---

59. Col. W. O. Coleman, CSA. His 4th Missouri Cavalry and 46th Arkansas Mounted Infantry operated "independently" as a quasi-guerrilla unit.

60. The military-aged men were leaving for fear of Federal conscription.

61. Rev. George W. Kennard, Baptist. Ellen and Jule were his house slaves. "Mrs. Kennard" here is his daughter-in-law, Mrs. M. Shelby Kennard, and Lida was her slave.

62. Leanna Purnell, Ma's slave.

Federals were forcing all negroes,[63] both male and female. Leanna was very unwilling to leave, and Purnell used all his eloquence and brought forward all the arguments he could think of, and finally Ma promised not to send them.

NOVEMBER 5TH

This morning Mrs. Kennard, Lida, Sarah, Ella, and I went down to Dr. Carrigan's[64] drug store to bring up some things which she wished to secure should the enemy come in. Mrs. Kennard told us that, if there was anything which we wanted, to take it. I got two small stands of beef marrow, some bottles of extract to flavor with, an inkstand, a puff for powder, a box of rouge (this last I have no use for) and a bottle of sarsaparilla.[65]

Uncle William started yesterday with all his negroes except old Aunt Barbary and Lou. Cousin Rilla sent all of hers except Cynthia. Nannie says that there was a very affecting time at their house when the negroes started. They had not intended to take Emmeline, as she is *enceinte*, but she said, "Wherever Master goes, thar I'se gwine," so they took her.[66] While I was writing the last sentence, Cousin Preston came to get some powder that was in Cousin Rilla's bureau here. He is going over to camps tonight; that is eight miles. They have in [Uncle William's] train ten wagons [and] sixty-seven negroes, besides lead horses and cattle.

Little Fraze Kennard[67] is quite sick. Ma is uneasy, thinks he is threatened with winter fever. Mrs. Cowle talks of moving down on Crowley's

---

63. Residents feared that any occupying Federals would force the slaves to leave their masters.

64. Dr. John M. Carrigan, forty years old in 1860, a physician and druggist who came to Batesville in the late 1850s and died in 1862.

65. This seems a curious collection to withstand a siege.

66. Uncle William was heading for his plantation near Des Arc, well behind the Confederate lines. He took with him the bulk of his slaves, which represented a large part of his wealth, and left Aunt Emma in charge at Catalpa Hall with a skeleton staff. The Hirsch and Adler interests, listed as "negro traders" in the 1860 census, were said to have moved their "merchandise" to Texas, then on into Mexico.

67. The two-year-old son of M. Shelby Kennard.

Ridge. She too is *enceinte* (this is all the use I have ever put my French to).

NOVEMBER 7TH

George Wilson[68] has been heard from. He was a straggler as was supposed. Being worn out with the two days' battle, on the third day he went off the road a few miles, got in some house, and was not able to return to camps for several days, and had not come in when the report was made out but had before the courier started. The Arkansas troops are to be re-mounted, and when the agent came for George's horse, Aunt Emma wanted him some clothes made, and Sarah and I stayed at home yesterday and today to make a pair of drawers apiece. Mr. Garthwaite has accepted the chaplaincy of a regiment in Shaver's[69] Brigade. Mrs. Lyon and Mrs. Garthwaite teach in the school. John Miller came today and got his little girl's pantalettes and paid me $2 1/2, gold piece, the first I ever had of my own, and I earned it, too.[70] Fraze is a little better this evening. I sat up with Mrs. Bliss last Friday night. Dr. Allen came also; she thought she was going to die, although she had had but one chill.

NOVEMBER 8TH

This morning [I] came up from Mrs. Cowle's before breakfast. After breakfast I ripped up an old dark calico dress and made a new one of it. I have but two calico and one worsted dress for this winter. I never had so few dresses, and there are no hopes of me getting any more. At nine I went over to Mr. Ford's[71] to get a piece of beef, but he had none. Mrs. Ford[72] was out at Mrs. Hykes's. Late this evening she came in, bringing

---

68. Aunt Emma's son.

69. Col. Robert G. Shaver, CSA.

70. The "little girl" was probably the daughter of John's son, William Reed Miller, future governor of Arkansas (1877–81).

71. Moses Ford, a blacksmith and prominent Unionist. He may not have wanted to sell beef to a secessionist family.

72. Harriet Ford.

Mrs. Hykes with her. The Union people did not find the affinity for each other until the Northern army left them amidst Seceshionists.

Soon after I came home, Cousin Annie came in to spend the day. They are in a pickle out there. The Messrs. Ansell have come to take their negroes to Texas, and they will be left with Aunt Barbary, who is so crippled with rheumatism that she has to be raised up in the bed, and Lou and Jim and he [sic] has to start to Little Rock with George's clothes, and nobody but old McGregor will be left to cut the wood. Nannie has taken the culinary department and Cousin Annie that of housemaid. Nan is Betsey and Annie, Bridget.

Mr. Cowle came home this evening. Now they will know whether they will move. I teased Mrs. Cowle this evening by telling her (she was here and got up to go home when Mr. Cowle came) that it was the first time that I had ever known her to be glad or even pleased when he came and that the millennium must be coming.

Dr. Allen pronounce[d] Fraze's fever typhus with a touch of diphtheria, but it is my opinion that he knows nothing about either and is needlessly alarmed, although the child is very sick.

NOVEMBER 9TH, SUNDAY NIGHT

This does not seem much like Sunday. Mrs. Cowle spent the day here again today. Mr. Cowle came from Conference yesterday, thinks that they will leave next Thursday. Mr. Hickison[73] is Presiding Elder on this district. The circuit and station are thrown together, and Mr. Foster[74] is to minister. I went down to Mrs. Wycough's this evening. Henry has just come from Little Rock, where he had gone with Mr. Wycough

---

73. Rev. J. M. P. Hickerson preached in the Methodist Episcopal Church, South, then apparently changed to the M. E., North, then to the Methodist Protestant churches in the years following the war. He was eventually expelled from the ministry for "being married to a woman who has a living husband," the husband having disappeared during the war but apparently reappearing. Hickerson eventually moved to California.

74. Rev. William Foster.

(who is elected to the Lower House) and to take Shirley. I must start to school tomorrow. I have been but one and a half days this last week. If it was not for my French I would quit entirely. Sarah and I told Mrs. Cowle that we would be down next year to Conference and try to catch a Parson, as I had never had an offer and was anxious to receive one.

NOVEMBER 10TH

I had to assist some in teaching today. Mrs. Lyon is getting very cross and ugly; I think from present appearances there will be a young Lyon or Lyoness some day. Mrs. Wycough came up this evening and Mrs. Cowle was here again. Her married life has been very unhappy, and if she had more compassion for others we would feel more for her. I shall be very sorry when she moves away for good, as the children say. Sarah went to stay with Mary Wycough tonight, and I shall have to stay with Mrs. Kennard. When Fraze gets well, and he is much better now, I shall very politely decline staying. I have stayed from home so much that I hardly [know] when I am at home, home is as strange as other places. Old Mr. Kennard has fallen desperately in love with a dashing young widow over the river and has to go over now every Saturday. The niggers and the———& time. [*sic*]

NOVEMBER 13TH

Cousin Rilla and Byers spent two days with us this week. Nannie is still cook; she holds out better than was expected. Mr. Trawick[75] was in town yesterday. He came here [and] wished to know how "Sallie and Mollie" were, said he had charge of the school in Searcy and next spring, if the country was not overrun with Federals, he would have a very full school and would be obliged to employ an assistant and that he did not know

---

75. Yet another Methodist Episcopal Church, South, preacher, Rev. Sidney R. Trawick was probably brought to Batesville to teach at the Soulesbury Institute.

Journal pages for November 10–18, 1862

Fragment of the journal entry for November 13, 1862.
Mary begins a new handwriting style.

of anybody whom he would rather have than Sallie or Mollie. [He] hoped Ma would raise the subject to us (we were at school) and we might ponder it. Perhaps he would be over again, if not there could be communications by mail, etc. I told Sarah the people were determined to make schoolma'ams of one or the other of us. Mrs. Lyon has made one of me: I have two arithmetic classes under my particular charge. When Mr. Trawick was leaving, he discovered Cousin Rilla's piano. "Why, Sister Byers, you have a piano. You did not use to have that," and Ma, truthful in everything, replied that it was Mrs. Smith's. I told her that she should have told him that we had got it recently, to punish him for his impertinence. Yesterday he told Mrs. Wycough to tell Sarah and I to come down to Mr. Case's to see him for he had not time to come up again. Self-conceit is a very good thing in him, especially for he is the only one who has a good opinion of him (Mr. Trawick, I mean) except Betty, and she thinks Mr. Trawick the best handsomest, the best educated man living. Ma gave him a branch of Archie (my geranium). Betty, he said, had told him to be sure and bring her a piece of geranium. I believe I am through with the Trawick subject.

Mrs. Cowle comes up tomorrow to spend the day, the last time for a long while, I expect. Johnny[76] went today in the wagons that came for the furniture. She is sick now and will not be able to leave before Saturday. We have Mrs. Em Wycough's[77] clock now, and it makes time fly more rapidly to know how and when it goes. Col. Smith's shirts are not done yet nor likely to be this week. Jennie Dannelly will be in tomorrow to spend two days before they leave for Searcy. I asked Mr. Dannelly to bring her in on Tuesday, but he said she had her clothes to wash and

---

76. John Cowles, age nine.
77. Emma Bevens Wycough, twenty-four, wife of Dolph Wycough.

iron. I tried to get Crouch[78] to take mine and Sarah's ambrotype for her, but he would not. Helen Miniken brought me a net to crochet, which will be the ninth I have crocheted in the last four weeks.

NOVEMBER 14TH

Ma bought Mr. Cowle's wood saw and buck, and she and I have made an agreement that, as I will not sweep, I am to get up and saw wood half an hour every matin (French) before breakfast. This evening I got to school an hour and a quarter too late. Mrs. Lyon said we were to write compositions this evening and as she had not scolded on account of the lateness of the hour, I introduced a little delicate flattery in mine which was not at all displeasing to the lady. Jennie did not come in today; perhaps she will tomorrow. Sarah is taking music lessons from Cousin Rilla, and now she is looking over the music, seeking for something to sing.

NOVEMBER 18TH

It has rained incessantly since Saturday night. Saturday evening, Mr. and Mrs. Dannelly and Jennie came in. We went to Sam Hirsch's auction and got ribbon and bought lining for our hats. Mary Wycough and Jennie stayed here all night. After supper, Ma trimmed Jennie's hat. We did not go to bed until eleven. About one, Sarah's tooth began to ache

---

78. William A. Crouch, thirty, an artist, jeweler, silversmith, and proprietor of Crouch's Daguerreian Gallery. After invention in France and England by Daguerre and Fox Talbot, the precursors of photography spread more rapidly in America than in Europe. Beginning about 1855, the popular form was the ambrotype, from the Greek *ambrotos* (immortal). Using a collodion-coated glass plate, it avoided the metallic sheen and much of the cost of the daguerreotype. The negative image is usually made to look positive by displaying it on a black background. By the end of the war, the ambrotype was being superseded by the more durable tintype. Daguerreian Society, http://daguerre.org.

and did not cease until this evening, when Dr. McClure[79] extracted it. Ella is keeping up such a banging on that old piano that I'd defy Jeff Davis's secretary to write. Mr. Dannelly has been playing and teaching Sarah and Ella to play, and my ears demand a rest,[80] so I'm going over to stay with Mrs. Kennard tonight. I know that both she and Sarah will say that I go over merely to hear from John, for as we came up (she went [with] Sarah to have her tooth pulled, and I met them as I came from school), she told me a great pack of nonsense that John had said about me in a letter that she received a few days ago.

NOVEMBER 19TH

This morning I sat down to darn stockings, determined to darn one pair before I went to school if it took me until ten clock. Twenty minutes of nine, the bell rang. By a quarter after, the stockings were finished, and I began to get ready for school. All of my dresses were torn in some way, and I put on one that Cousin Ann had given Ella and started. Had got as far as Mrs. Weaver's,[81] and it began to rain, and looking down I saw three holes in my dress, upon which I turned around and came home with the determination not to go anymore until I could do so with a whole dress on. By noon, I had two mended.

NOVEMBER 28TH

Today. . . . [entry incomplete]

---

79. Dr. Moses McClure may have been the first professionally trained dentist in Batesville, arriving from Illinois in 1858. He became involved in many other enterprises too: newspaper publishing, timbering, and running a hotel, a sawmill, and a flour mill.

80. According to family history, Mary had no ear and really disliked music, though her sisters loved it.

81. Mary Burton Weaver, sister of Aunt Emma. Mr. Weaver was away most of the time serving in the Union army, while several of the couple's sons were in Confederate service.

DECEMBER 7TH, SUNDAY

A profitless day it has been to me. All day long have I sat before the fire and read Blackwood's Magazine.[82] Sarah begged that I should go to church with her today, but I see enough of Mr. Garthwaite during weekdays with an extra dose on Sundays.

Last night I rolled Sarah's hair up, and today it was curled very prettily. That was what made her so anxious to go to church.

Tomorrow is Monday, and if I was a catholic I should dread confessional day no worse than I do tomorrow, for I must go to school. I would give anything to be permitted to stop, but, going in the way we do, that is impossible. French was all that I took much interest in, and now I have lost a good deal of that, and since Mr. Garthwaite came from the Army he is more despicable than ever and I feel toward him like a prisoner might feel towards the judge who condemned him to the dark, dreary, and monotonous life of an imprisoned convict.

DECEMBER 21ST

Old Journal, I have most shamefully neglected you during the last three weeks. Only three days until Christmas! What a short, eventful year this has been. It has been full of changes, yet upon the whole a very happy one. It has been nearly a year since I have had a real mad fit or rather a fit of anger and hate. It was three days before New Year's. I had been at Uncle William's for several days and came home to get Ma to let Sarah and I attend a party on New Year's Eve. Sarah had been corresponding with Mark Wycough[83] ever since he had been in the Army, for nearly seven months. But, she had not liked the tone of his last letters and

---

82. This journal offered satire, reviews, and fiction; published in Edinburgh from 1817 to 1980.

83. Marcus Aurelius Reinhart "Mark" Wycough, younger brother of Dolph, was a Confederate soldier and would be captured during Price's Missouri Raid (1864) and held prisoner until the end of the war. He was later elected deputy sheriff, tax collector, and county clerk.

resolved that the next letter she wrote to him she would request that the correspondence be dropped, yet do this in so delicate a manner that his feelings or his pride be not touched.

Before Christmas, however, and before she had written again, Dolph Wycough went up to camps (they were then in winter-quarters in Clarksville), and while there, he was instructed by Mark to purchase a ring and send it to Sarah as a Christmas present from him. That day before Christmas, I think it was, Dolph sent it. (It was a beautiful plain gold ring. Mary [Wycough] wears it now.) Sarah did not wish to accept it and took it to Em—Dolph was not at home—gave it to her [and] told her that she did not wish to accept presents from young gentlemen. Em told her that she did not blame her, and Sarah left a letter to be sent to Mark and came away. In this letter, she apologized for not accepting the ring and told him that it was the advice of her mother and she (Sarah) thought it best also that the correspondence be dropped.

In a few days the answer came. He first said that they had lived for years side by side, that he could see no impropriety in accepting a ring of friendship, that so he had offered it, that they were children together and that should not break the friendship that had continued so long and a good deal in the same strain. Then it took another turn. He [had] thought that her mother had a friendly feeling for him, that she wished him well and that which had confirmed this feeling was the manner in which she had parted with him the morning he left, but she was a hypocrite like the rest of her vile race, and when he was no longer here to do errands for the family, go to the post office, etc., (N.B. he had gone to the P.O. for Aunt Jennie when she was here but never for Ma) but a poor soldier in the service of his country, she cast him off. That he never wished to do another favor for, or receive one from, one of the name, he was perfectly independent, and wound up by saying that he supposed "our little whiskey-jug Cousin Preston" had prejudiced "her dear mother" against him, made her think that he had designs against her darling child that hereafter he meant to show the world that he was a man, worthy of the name and some more that I have forgotten. In a P.S. he said that he supposed our high-strung family would now be above associating with his, and signs himself, "your enemy until death."

On reading this letter, I became very angry but said [little] except asked Sarah what she thought of it. She replied that when she read it, she was so angry that she cried. This was all that was needed, that raised my blood to the boiling point. I do not know what all I said; among others I know that I said that I would not shed a tear if I saw him in the flames of h—ll. I defied Mark Wycough to bring a tear to my eye. Ma made me stop and I have had but one real angry fit since; that was with a Fed. Him I boldly ordered out of the house and when he would not go I sat down vexed beyond endurance. Presently he left, then I wished him in a warmer region than Dixie. Those were the only mad spell[s] I have had within a year. I used to have them at least every month.

1863

Time rolls on and brings many changes. We have been ushered into a new year. How little we know today what will happen tomorrow! To begin at the beginning, three weeks ago Gen. Marmaduke with his division of the Confederate army came here. They had come from a raid in Missouri. They 'pressed all wagons, horses, and mules that they could find. The citizens of Arkansas have never liked Missouri troops since the battle of Oak Hill[s].[1] In north Arkansas especially they are held in the greatest aversion. It is now twice that they have been posted to protect our border, and it is now twice that they have fallen back.[2]

FEBRUARY 6TH

I left off last night rather abruptly. Yes, the Missourians fell back, and on Tuesday [the] 3rd we heard that the Feds were coming but placed no confidence in the report for we hear so many false ones.

During the last two weeks the girls have been meeting at each others' houses and spending the evening in pleasant converse. Tuesday was

---

1. The Confederate name for the Battle of Wilson's Creek, near Springfield, Missouri, August 10, 1861. It was the second major battle of the war and the first in which men from Batesville fought. "Battle Summaries: Wilson's Creek, Mo.," Civil War Sites Advisory Commission, www.nps.gov/hps/abpp/battles/mo004.htm.

2. Brig. Gen. John S. Marmaduke, CSA, and his Fourth Division reached the White River across from Batesville on January 18, 1863, half-frozen and exhausted by their raid on Springfield and Hartville (Marmaduke's "First Missouri Expedition"). U.S. War Department, *War of the Rebellion,* ser. 1, 34:194–98 (hereafter cited as *OR;* all citations are from series 1 unless otherwise stated). There would be two more diversionary thrusts attempted from Batesville: Marmaduke's "Second Missouri Expedition" in the late spring of 1863 and Maj. Gen. Sterling Price's Missouri raid in the fall of 1864.

the night appointed to go to Mrs. Smith's, accordingly we went. But John Smith had come home a week ago, and on Tuesday Mrs. Kennard gave John a dinner, and Sarah and I were invited over. Puss and Delia McGuire came up and with them brought a Capt. Kay, a gentleman who was staying at Mrs. Smith's in company with Gen. Jeff Thompson's nephew.[3] We spent a very pleasant day.

There was a party at the [courthouse], and Capts. Kay and Thompson remained only a short time after we arrived at nine. John and K. returned. We had such a very pleasant evening. At half-past eleven we came home. John had gone with me the evening before to Mrs. Wycough's, and he had made an engagement with me that I was to stay at home on Wednesday night in order that he might come up.

Wednesday morning, Mrs. Lewis came up to teach me to spin. At one we saw a party of Marmaduke's scouts coming in, in a hard gallop. We knew that the enemy must be after them, and Mrs. Lewis, Sarah, and I ran down to Mrs. Weaver's gate. The scouts told us that the Feds fired on them, killing one (the Feds say two) and wounding one. We then ran on as far as Mrs. Smith's. There the wounded man had been thrown from his horse and hurt much worse. The Yankees were two miles behind. Sarah and I came home in a state of high excitement. John Smith was down the street when the news came, came up home and got his coat and arms, and Col. Smith was trying his best to get him out of town. John was either very cool or tight, I could not tell which. He put on his clothes very deliberately, turned, and shook hands with me and was off. Half an hour after, I was in Mrs. Kennard's getting some yarn to knit some gloves which for John had asked me to do it three days ago, and looking out the window, there stood the gentleman. He had gone home, got his gun, and said that the Feds were six miles off. At three Abe Weaver[4] came up and said that there was not a Fed this side of Hookrum.[5] At this, we rested easy.

---

3. Brig. Gen. M. Jeff Thompson, the "Swamp Fox of the Confederacy," was the former mayor of St. Joseph, Missouri. Commissioned in the Missouri State Guard, he became the leader of what Union forces always considered guerrilla activity.

4. A Confederate soldier, son of Mary Burton Weaver.

5. Probably near Evening Shade, twenty-two miles north of Batesville.

About an hour after, Ma came in saying, "Well, Cousin Henry escaped only by the skin of his teeth. The Feds are at your Aunt Emma's." It was snowing very hard. We brought down some of the corn from the stable and put it in the smoke house. We then concluded that they (the Feds) would not be in until morning. Ma started to the bedroom, but as she opened the door she jumped back, crying, "Good God, here they are now!" I ran to the door and took a peep. There stood at least 200 cavalry. No one can tell all that we done and said during the next hour. Sarah went to the door, shook her fist at them, ran to the kitchen, and brought all the children[6] in the house.

Presently I opened the door. They were marching down the street. They went to the tavern, kicked down the doors, scared the women, making them scream like wildcats, and done I can't tell how much more devilment.

We heard some steps upon the porch and a quick knocking at the door. Ma opened it; there stood four men. I trembled. I was certain one was a negro, but I was mistaken. They wished to bring a man in who had been thrown from his horse and to get supper for twelve men. Of course they had to come in, and such a night as we had of it. The wounded man was a Lieut., by name Gilpin, the Capt. named Spencer. At eleven, Capt. Spencer told Ma that we would have to make ourselves as comfortable as possible in the other room, for they would be obliged to spend the night here. There were about 14 stayed here. The Lieut. slept in the bed and got lice on the blanket. The next morning we had to get breakfast for 14, but they furnished their own rations. After breakfast they heard that Marmaduke had been reinforced and was meditating an attack on them. Then they *got*. This room looked like horses had been stabled in it. This evening Marmaduke sent word for all to be ready to leave, for he intended to shell the town if the Federals came in again. Now I am sleepy and another night must sleep in my clothes, making three nights.[7]

---

6. Probably the children of the slave Leanna, who were in the detached building that housed the kitchen.

7. Capt. G. C. Rose led the "dash" of Brig. Gen. John W. Davidson's Union cavalry, driving Marmaduke's forces out of Batesville. To escape, some Confederate troops had to swim the frigid river. *OR*, 34:227.

FEBRUARY 7TH

Ma waked Sarah and I up this morning, telling us that the pickets were standing out in the street. "Feds or Southerners?" asked Sarah. "They are our men." I was standing in the front door when Capt. Sinclair rode up to the gate and spoke to me. There were nine Southrons this side of the river. He was here to supper this evening. About 9 ½ o'clock I was sitting in the other room crocheting as busily as possible on John's gloves when Sarah called to me that here was John. He had crossed over, called [a] minute a[t] home, and came up here on his way out to Aunt Emma's. Before he got back, his parents became uneasy for fear the Federalists would come up and catch him. Mrs. Smith got on an old horse that the Feds had left there when they stole her good one and rode out there. She went one road, John came another, and presently John rode up to the gate [and] came in. I believe he was tight. Col. Smith seeing him come in here sent Frank up here, but he did not come any farther than Mrs. Kennard's. Then he sent Jim. Jim had a dram a head and came here and would not leave until he got John off. I have not heard whether they got him over the river or not. The Feds broke down the doors of Dr. Carrigan's drug store, and the people have been carrying off everything.

Mrs. Fowler died Monday, February 2nd. Her death will be felt in Batesville. She was the best female teacher that ever taught in our schools, a native of Ohio. She has been here but two years. Fannie Rice[8] has another baby, a little boy. Three children, and father drinks like a fish, and the mother acts as though she weren't three removes from an idiot, though I believe silly people have children faster than intellectual ones.

It is now Saturday night, and I shall wash and undress and go to bed right, hoping that the Feds won't be here by morning. The general opinion is that there is a large body not very far off, waiting for the snow to

---

8. Probably Frances Denton Rice, twenty-two, daughter of the indomitable Mrs. Neely by her first husband, lawyer William French Denton. Fannie married Methodist reverend John Rice, who, serving as a Confederate chaplain, would be shot in a skirmish on Saffold's farm in March 1864. One child died, and Mrs. Neely kept the two survivors during the rest of the war.

go off the ground, when they will advance. Gen. Price has succeeded Holmes,[9] and Kirby Smith's division of the Army has crossed the Mississippi. All the Arkansas boys will be home then.

FEBRUARY 8TH

All's quiet this morning. Mr. Lacefield was at the gate this morning before breakfast to inquire the cause of firing which was heard down street yesterday evening and occasioned great disturbance. Two of the officers of Marmaduke's staff came over, got more liquor than was good for them, came up here, and fired their revolvers merely to frighten the people. Mrs. Bliss went down street an hour ago to carry some news to the "Federal Sisterhood," I suppose. The prisoners from the Post of Arkansas were taken to St. Louis.[10]

Twelve o'clock. The news has just come in that there are no Federalists this side of Hartville [Mo.] except those that were in here. They came down on a scout and robbing expedition.

Evening. I went to take dinner at Mrs. Kennard's. While there I received a note from John. This evening he came up. While here the conversation turned to Ford. It seems that Ford was at home three weeks ago [and] was sick. Dr. Hendren went to see him twice; the third time he called, the bird had flown. He began to suspect that all was not right but said nothing about it until the Federalists came and left, then he ups and tells it. Most people think nothing of this but it is my humble opinion that Dr. H. is not as true Southron as he might be. This evening we heard that Ford had come home again. John, after leaving here, went around there, inquired for him, receiving an answer that he

---

9. Lt. Gen. Theophilus Holmes, CSA.

10. On January 11, 1863, Maj. Gen. William T. Sherman and his Army of the Mississippi captured the Confederate garrison of Fort Hindman at the territorial outpost of Arkansas Post on the Arkansas River. The 4,800 Rebel troops, outnumbered six to one, constituted the largest surrender of forces in the Trans-Mississippi before the final capitulation in 1865. Mark A. Christ, "Battle of Arkansas Post," Encyclopedia of Arkansas History & Culture (article last updated Dec. 31, 2010), www.encyclopediaofarkansas.net/encyclopedia/entry-detail.aspx?entryID=525.

was not there, dismounted, searched the house, except one closet which was locked, demanded the keys of it. Upon not receiving [them], swore that he would burst the door down. When they were delivered, Ford was not there, and John was compelled to leave without accomplishing anything. Now if the enemy do return they will visit punishment on Col. Smith for this rash act of John's, for Mrs. Ford is strong Union.[11]

This evening [a flag of truce sent out by Marmaduke yesterday morning was returned]. It occasioned us a great fright, for we, not knowing of its going out, supposed that they were the enemy coming back.

Mrs. Maxwell got me to promise to assist her in teaching in one or two classes if she had more scholars than she could attend to. People are determined to make a school-ma'am of me whether I will or no.

FEBRUARY 9TH

Nannie came in town this morning. I fear her wedding will have to be deferred. L. L.[12] told her that when he returned next, if she still wished it, he would wait until the war is over, and now he cannot come on account of the Federals.

There was a great commotion in town this morning. The Federal flag of truce that came in yesterday morning went out today. They were very anxious to cross the river, but *that* Gen. Marmaduke wouldn't permit. One of our soldiers stole a revolver from one of the escort. He was intoxicated and raised a great noise about it but finally the Southrons succeeded in getting him out of town. This was a rash act, and our officers will punish the soldiers severely for this breaking the rules of honor, that is, if they find it out, which I hope they will not. I'm going home with Nannie if the horse will carry double.

All Northern papers that we can get speak very discouragingly of the war, and the very men who Lincoln had arrested at the beginning of the war are being elected to the Legislature. This augurs favorably to our cause.

---

11. John would have had no authority for this home invasion.
12. L. L. Moore, a prosperous merchant in Jacksonport.

FEBRUARY 10TH

Nannie had a beau yesterday evening,[13] and I did not go home with her. She was coming today, but the rain has prevented her. Loafink[14] came back this morning. He went off with the Federals. The citizens have arrested him. Mrs. Weaver goes before the court as witness or pleader in his behalf, notwithstanding Abe reported on him, she (Mrs. Weaver) being fully convinced of his innocence.

Pate Tucker[15] came this morning. At the battle of Murfreesboro, Will Womac, Frank Denton,[16] and Jeff Stone were slightly wounded, and two of that company were killed; I have not learned their names.[17]

By a St. Louis paper, Mr. Kennard is imprisoned for a violation of his oath.

FEBRUARY 16TH

Sixteen today! Sixteen years since this earth was blessed, or cursed as the case may be, with my presence. This age is called the happy one, and "Sweet Sixteens" are supposed to be the heyday of youth. What will this year bring forth for me? Pleasure or unhappiness? I speak here as though happiness consisted in pleasure alone, but I have lived long

---

13. This despite Nannie's engagement to L. L. Moore—Mary would have used Moore's name here if he had been the "beau."

14. Probably one of the Weavers' slaves.

15. Thomas Peyton "Pate" Tucker, a twenty-nine-year-old farmer, became a trusted courier and scout for Confederate troops. After normal mail was disrupted, he carried letters, messages, and money back and forth from the boys in camps to their families back home—the "Tucker Express."

16. Franklin Denton, twenty, son of Mrs. Neely, enlisted in Company H, Eighth Arkansas Infantry and would be wounded several times. He went on to found the *Batesville Guard* newspaper, still operating in 2013.

17. Over three days, from December 30, 1862, through New Year's Day, 1863, the Battle of Stones River in Tennessee inflicted over 30 percent casualties on both sides but boosted Federal morale. "Battle Summary: Stones River, TN," Civil War Sites Advisory Commission, www.nps.gov/hps/abpp/battles/tn010.htm. Womac and Stone served in Captain Gibbs's company. Stone would be killed at Chickamauga, Georgia, in September.

enough to learn that all that is styled pleasure is not happiness. Yet I have not tasted of that which the Christian calls true happiness.

The night that we were at Mrs. Smith's I invited the girls to come up here to-night, but it has rained since noon and they have not come. Sarah was sitting by the window wishing that, if the girls did not come, some good-looking soldier would, and looking up she beheld Sinclair. He was here a week ago and called this evening to get his supper, I have no doubt, but we had only two meals to-day so he missed it.

Cousins Henry, Rilla, and Byers stayed two days with us last week. Cousin Henry auctions the remainder of his goods this week.[18]

FEBRUARY 17TH

It has rained all evening. There has not been two weeks of sunshine this year. L. L. Moore came up this evening. Nannie and he were to marry this time when he came, but he came in town to stay tonight, and I regard this as a very good sign that she has jilted him. Poor Nannie! If she does not take L. L., I don't know who she will marry unless she bewitches Cousin Preston[19] again, for she has behaved in such a manner that I fear her good name is lost in Batesville forever. Wash Watkins[20] is the only man she ever cared anything about, and she only consented to marry Moore to keep people from saying that Wash flirted her, and now that she finds that her mother is very anxious for the match she refuses. But as she is quite notionate, probably Mr. Moore can prevail upon her to become his "loving spouse."

She rejected him four years ago, and in the meantime he has courted Cousin Annie three times, and just before he engaged himself to Nannie wanted to know of her if there was no hope for him if he waited, and receiving the reply that there would be none, immediately courted

---

18. Henry had decided to close his store because of the war.

19. William Preston Byers. He apparently had a crush on his stepsister Nannie Wilson, as did many of the other young men.

20. Probably William L. Watkins, twenty-three. Originally from Missouri, he had been "reading law" in Batesville.

Nannie. This looks strange. Cousin Henry will stop [by] tomorrow; and then I will know if I am to have a new Cousin-in-law.

Mrs. Southworth[21] has written of many bold, wild, and beautiful girls, but if she knew all the incidents of Nannie Wilson's life, she could weave it into a romance more thrilling than any of hers that I have ever read. If I should ever attempt to write a novel, it should be "Catalpa Hall" and all the characters be drawn from life. But as I shall never attempt this, Nannie's life will never be committed to posterity.

FEBRUARY 25TH

Rain, rain, rain. Yesterday was a beautiful day. Cousin Henry commenced auctioning his goods on last Thursday and has not sold all yet. I have been every day except Saturday; then it rained. Nearly everybody goes; the girls go for the fun of it. Yesterday I enjoyed talking to Charlie Goodwin.[22] He is *dead* in love with Cousin Annie. Last night we went down to the auction for the negroes; it was as good as a monkey show.

As I came up I stopped at Mrs. Crouch's and sat up all night. Both Lionne and Willie are sick, and the lady herself is [far] from well.[23] This day has been a blue day in earnest, but I suppose from all reports that the frequent rains are the cause of the Federals remaining away. The latest report is that the army or a portion of it is at Forsythe in Missouri, building boats to bring corn down, and that when the weather becomes settled so that the infantry and artillery can travel, we shall be favored with a more prolonged [visit] than the last.

Nannie's wedding is put off until the war is over. I have been romping with Cousin Henry and bruised my shin. I expect to have my peace to make with Mr. Dannelly for dancing, from what Mr. Hickison told me

---

21. Mrs. E. D. E. N. Southworth (1819–99), perhaps the most widely read American novelist of the era.

22. Charlie, twenty-three, and Fannie Goodwin (mentioned later in this entry), twenty, were children of A.G. Goodwin, a merchant and druggist. Goodwin's other children were named Eugene and Lizzie.

23. Elizabeth Alice Light Crouch (1837–1905). Her husband, William A. Crouch, was away in the Confederate army. See at Nov. 13th, 1862, note 78.

last week. My French progresses but slowly since I left school. The Sunday School will be organized next Sunday. I wish to be in Mrs. Hickison's class, and I expect that Fannie Goodwin will not be pleased, for I have been in her class for two years and she is very sensitive and will not understand my motives for leaving.

FEBRUARY 26TH

Mary Wycough is staying all night here tonight. I have been reading parts of my journal to her and Sarah. Cousins Henry and Rilla went home today. He is not going to auction any more.

The soldiers in town are in the habit of serenading the girls; they have not come here yet. I got acquainted with a gentleman named Trone at Mrs. Case's. He said that he was going to bring them here but he mistook the place and they went to Mrs. Weaver's. Cousin Ann laughed at me and told Cousin Preston that I could not find an officer nor a single man and had to take a blacksmith with six children. Miss Kate McCutchen offered $100 reward for the first Missourian who was not an officer nor a single man who would marry her for three years or the war.[24]

Saturday Sarah will be eighteen. Ma got me a barege dress at Cousin Henry's, but it is as ugly as sin. There is a blister on my tongue and a pimple on my nose.

FEBRUARY 27TH

This morning I thought I would do a good day's work, but after Mary and Sarah left, Ma and I thought we would make some jelly of this jelletin. We made it very nice except that it was not sufficiently spiced. Then as I was getting out my work, Cousin Ann came in; afterwards I went to Mrs. McClure's with her, came home at 1 ½, and heard Cousin Henry blaze away at the Missourians and especially those with whom

---

24. After experimentation with three-month terms at the beginning of the war, "three years or the war" was becoming the normal term of enlistment in both armies.

Cousins Ann and Nannie have been going. After dinner[25] he told me to come down to the store and get a pair of white kid slippers that I had won as a bet last summer. Cousin Ann came up; she had been at Mrs. Aikin's since leaving Mrs. McClure's and we went down together. Capt. Eastman had taken a horse out for her and brought her in. And as he is a stranger here and one of whom the general opinion is that he is skulking around the country merely to keep out of the army, although he professes to be raising a flying artillery company for Price, Cousin Henry took it upon himself to reprove her for allowing him to associate with her. He told her that if he ever saw them together he would knock him down, and she replying in no very pleasant manner he got in a passion and told her to go to the d—l! Poor Cousin Ann; she has a sore time between Aunt Emma and Cousins Rilla, Henry, and Nannie.

As I came up street, I stopped a few minutes at Mrs. Perrin's, received a few compliments on my good looks, pretty dress, collar, etc., came home, and so ends the day, having performed nothing except two calls and to gather the skirt of a dress. Sarah sits up at Mrs. Crouch's tonight, and as Cousin Henry auctions for the negroes tonight he will stay here. I have not heard Ella's or Willie's lessons this week; I must begin again on Monday.

The latest report of the enemy is that they are the other side of Pocahontas a few miles, destination unknown. I think we will have peace before next fall. Since the blockades at Charleston and Galveston, hope has been high in my bosom. Either some kind of negotiations are being made or an attack is meditated on several points at once, for we all know that a calm precedes a storm, and now there has not been any fighting for some months.

MARCH 1ST

The first day of Spring, a bright beautiful day. This morning the Sunday School recommenced with twenty-seven scholars. I did not go

---

25. Unless speaking specifically of a formal evening occasion, by "dinner" Mary means the midday meal.

to church but came home and tried to read one of Alexandre Dumas' novels, "The Queen Margaret." This evening Sarah and I were at Mrs. Case's a few minutes.

I don't know what we are living for, or why we live, we do no one any good, our lives are aimless. Every year we get poorer and there is no way to retrieve our fortunes. So it has been since Pa's death, and so it will continue to be until the end of time or our lives. We are entirely dependent on Uncle William. I suppose I might make a little by teaching school, but in this community the teacher is in a manner looked down upon and I am proud, though no one would suspect it by my bearing. I am not proud of fine clothes, my beauty, if I could lay claim to any, but of myself, of Mary Byers, of my position in society. I don't know that the opinion or the friendship of those who would think less of me for earning my own support is worth having or that I would lose much by losing it.

I have commenced teaching Ella and Willie lessons, but I get out of patience so soon, especially with Willie. I am really afraid the child never will know anything. He is no fool; he has plenty of sense, but none of it runs in the right direction. Go to explain anything, his head is as thick as a board. I don't believe boys are naturally as smart as girls, for I can make Ella understand twice as easily as Willie, although I got fretted with her one morning and called her a fool. It was about her grammar. I can't make her comprehend the rules; she learns it by rote and when it comes to the application is as ignorant as though she had never seen a grammar. It is nearly the same with Willie in regard to arithmetic but not quite so bad. I don't know whether it is their fault or that of their former teachers. They were very careless. Patience, patience.

MARCH 10TH

Yesterday I came home from Aunt Emma's, where I had been a week. This morning before I was dressed, Mrs. Maxwell came over to see about getting me to teach for her, but I had rather not. I don't know whether I did right, but Ma told me to do as I pleased.

Eight years on last Sunday since Pa died. What a long, long time, yet it passed quickly. I am assured that Ma will never marry again. This used

John Hancock Byers (Pa), 1814–55.
Courtesy Independence County Historical Society.

to trouble me a good deal. I could not bear the idea of a stepfather, but Ma has never shown by word or action that she was inclined that way. The good of her children is all she desires.

There is a review of Marmaduke's command on Thursday. A great many ladies are going over [across the river]. Sarah as usual is desirous to go.

This morning I got angry at the spinning wheel and said, "Confound the thing." It is nearly ten, and I am sleepy, so Good Night.

MARCH 11TH

This morning, after hearing Ella's and Willie's lessons, Sarah and I dressed and called on Mrs. Aikin and Mrs. Mix. They were all talking about the review, and I got in the notion of going. At dinner we spoke of it. Cousin Henry did not object and offered one of us his horse. Mr. Trone (a gentleman, married, and six children, who boards at Mr. Case's) brings me one. Mrs. Kennard made us a nice jelly cake. Cousin

Annie is going with Cousin Henry down on the Arkansas River to Uncle William.[26]

MARCH 15TH, SUNDAY MORNING

This is a bright, beautiful day. Such a day it seems to me that children of God would thank and praise him with a heart swelling with gratitude. There is a kind of holy and religious feeling pervades our being. I am going to Sunday School, but I shall not stay to church.

MARCH 17TH

Within the last week we have had a great deal of company. Thursday we went to the review, and Friday night Mr. Trone and Bob Case[27] came up. Saturday Mrs. Maxwell brought a Capt. Pollok over. Soon after, Mr. Trone came again and Dr. Fulkison with him. Sunday Mr. Holland came up to see Cousin Ann. Then we went down to Mrs. Cox's to see Mr. Bulkley. Col. Gordon came up to go home with her and a Lieut. Bledsoe with me. Yesterday Dr. Wallace came to get Sarah and I to go to Mrs. Mix's to a party. Soon after, Capt. Pollok came for the same purpose. Fannie Rice had just died and we were going to her funeral. This morning Mr. Trone was here and again tonight.[28]

MARCH 20TH

John came home on Tuesday. He was here that evening and again last evening with Col. Slayback. There was a party at Mrs. Mix's. Sarah and I were at Mrs. Lyon's yesterday. John and Mr. Holland came in; they insisted on our going to the party, but we declined. Mrs. Maxwell went.

This morning I had to do an errand for Mamma at Bryant's and

---

26. Yet Des Arc, the location of Uncle William's plantation Double Trouble, is on the White River far above the Arkansas. Possibly Mary refers to another plantation.

27. Bob Case was the son of George Case and brother of Mary's friend Mary Case.

28. The officers named in this entry were probably members of General Marmaduke's staff.

afterwards went to Harris to see about my shoes. As I came up, Puss called me and I went over. Col. Slayback commenced teasing me about John, wanting to know if I came to see he or John. He stayed for half an hour, and we kept a continual war of words. Puss and I took a long ride in John's buggy. I saw Capt. Head. Tomorrow I go to Mrs. Fairchild's with John.

MARCH 22ND

Mrs. Fairchild was not at home so we did not stop. When we came back we rode down to the ferry. There was a Captain buried with military honors yesterday; 150 guns were fired. Mr. Trone came up yesterday evening, stayed to supper and until nine. He brought me an acrostic on my name that he had got someone in camps, he would not tell who, to write for him. There is to [be] a review of the division next week or this week. This is Sunday. The officers are very anxious for the ladies to come over, promise that the other shall be a tame affair compared with this. Col. Gordon told the ladies that they must come and take dinner with him, but Col. Shelby[29] say[s] not so but with him. I wish to go. If Cousin Annie goes and if I can get Cousin Henry's grey pony, I am going. Mr. Trone said last night that he was afraid to take over there anymore for he had heard nothing scarcely in camps but my name and Puss Smith's. They tease him about me because he went with me over and was so attentive. I had only to speak and he was at my service or.... [entry incomplete]

APRIL 9TH

Disappointed today.... [entry incomplete]

MAY IST

[Out of sequence, on a partial page within the entry for June 14.]
It is evening. I am on the porch, and from the hospital opposite come

---

29. Col. (later Brig. Gen.) Joseph Orville "Jo" Shelby, CSA.

the groans of a dying man. Many things have occurred since last I wrote in my journal. Marmaduke's division ha[s] moved north and by this time is halfway to the Missouri River.[30] Mrs. Maxwell's school were going to have a . . . [entry incomplete]

JUNE 10TH

I have not written for three months, and in those three months much has transpired that I ought to have written. Mary Wycough spent the day here, Ma helping her to trim a hat. This afternoon I went over to Mrs. Kennard's and was soon sent for. Dr. Austin and Lieut. Bulkley[31] were here. Mr. Bulkley is getting better. He has been at Mrs. Cox's now nearly four months. He is very lively. After they left, Sarah and I went to Mrs. Case's.

JUNE 14TH

Ella's birthday, fourteen today. Ma's children are all getting as large as she. Friday we undertook to clean house. I had put on a dirty dress, no hoops, and an old apron, and went to work in good earnest. We had everything out of the front room. I was scrubbing the floor when here came John Smith. Sarah went out and I had to come in, made room for him on the porch. I did not mind him much; he has been here so often. He only stayed a few minutes, said, "Good Bye," and left for Newton's Regiment, of which he is adjutant. Then came Mr. Bulkley and Dr. Austin. They had to sit out under the trees. Mr. Bulkley was leaving for camps; before they got off, Mr. and Mrs. Dannelly came.

---

30. Mary did not yet know that on April 26 the garrison of fortified Cape Girardeau, Missouri, repulsed Marmaduke's attack. On May 1 and 2 at Chalk Bluff on the Arkansas-Missouri line, Federal forces inflicted additional heavy casualties on the Confederates, ending Marmaduke's Second Missouri Expedition. The Missourian's column returned to Jackson County by May 9. *OR*, 34:285–88.

31. Lieutenant Bulkley was a young cavalryman in Marmaduke's command, wounded at Hartville, Missouri, on January 11 and apparently recuperating in the home of Mrs. Laura Erwin Cox, later Ewing. He was popular with the young ladies of Batesville.

Mary's friends, 1863 (first pose). Left to right: Mary Catherine Case, Lucretia Noland Maxfield, Elvena Maxfield, and Cynthiana Desloges ("Annie" or "Puss") Smith, June 18, 1863.
Courtesy Independence County Historical Society.

Mary's friends, 1863 (second pose). Left to right: Mary Catherine Case, Lucretia Noland Maxfield, Cynthiana Desloges ("Annie" or "Puss") Smith, and Elvena Maxfield, June 18, 1863.
Courtesy Independence County Historical Society.

JUNE 28TH

I never feel like writing except when I feel as I do tonight. Ma and I have had a long and serious conversation. It left [me] in a serious mood, and I am never serious without a shade of sadness. I may say that I never want to write unless sad. If I were an authoress, my compositions would be of a gloomy nature, not gloomy exactly but there would not be that vein of humor through them that anyone would expect to find upon conversing with me. For when in a lively mood I cannot take time to write. It is too slow. My tongue hardly goes fast enough to suit me, but I must write more and talk less, especially about my neighbors, for I am fast falling into the habit of gossiping, a habit which I despise above all others.

This morning I went to Sunday School but did not stay to church. Sarah and Ella and Mrs. Maxwell went. Em Wycough is sick, and Ma went down to see her. Mrs. Kennard came over and we were talking of Martha Wilkinson's wedding. To-night she is married to Mr. Lloyd.[32] At the battle of Lexington [Missouri], in loading a cannon, an explosion took place which took off both his arms, his right above the elbow, the left at the wrist. He came to town the first of May. Everyone felt a great sympathy for him in his misfortune, and the ladies paid him every attention. May 1st he was at the May party and seemed attracted by Nannie and Emma Weaver. In a few days he was going with Cousin Annie. He got in the best society on entering Batesville, but persons like water will soon seek a level, or I might say that they will seek congenial society. Sixteen days ago he met Martha Wilkinson at Mr. Crouch's ambrotype gallery. He waited on her home and as he says showed her his Confederate money (he had $2000). In a week Martha, Sarah Price, White Brickey, and he were on their way to Jacksonport to see Gen. Price. A week this evening since they got back and by this time they are married. Twenty minutes ago a party on horseback and in a wagon passed by going out to give them a chivaree. She is engaged to three other gentlemen, all of whom are drunkards and gamblers but have

---

32. Capt. Richard L. Loyd, CSA.

two arms and, unless they are perfect demons, as amiable as Lloyd. He drinks, gambles, is selfish, cross, tyrannical, and has [no] particle of delicacy in his composition. He has no respect for his bride if one may judge from the manner that he spoke of her. It was not only indelicate but vulgar. But Martha, poor deluded girl, thinks he has plenty of money, a horse and buggy; what more is necessary?

After dinner Ella was on the sofa asleep, Sarah in the front bedroom, Ma and I in her room, all undressed except Ella, when Dr. Dobbins[33] came. What a scrambling time Ma had! After he left Sarah and I had a long walk.

JUNE 29TH

Puss Smith spent the morning here. Mr. Kennard came in this morning in the buggy with Mrs. Wilkinson. We went over to hear about the wedding. Mr. Kennard got the ring out of the bridal cake. We spent this evening at Mrs. Goodwin's, had a very pleasant evening. Dr. Dobbins played on the violin, Eugene on the flute, Puss, Fannie, Lizzie, and Mrs. Aikin on the piano. They are all coming here tomorrow night. I should not be surprised if Cousins Henry and Rilla were to come in tomorrow evening, but I think they might see to what trouble and inconvenience they put us [to] and not come in to stay all night. In such warm weather we would almost suffocate in the little room, as we have to give this one up to them. Cousin Henry is now showing his little, mean, spiteful nature, in all kind of ways. I don't suppose there could be a more unhappy family than the one now residing in Catalpa Hall.

Uncle William and Cousin Annie are over on the Arkansas River, and the last news was that Uncle was sick. Aunt Emma and Henry never could agree. While he was in the army she and Rilla got along very harmoniously, but soon Cousin Henry comes home on an unlimited furlough. In time he hires the substitute and stays at home to fuss all the time. He treats Aunt Emma with positive contempt, frequently speaking of things as "*Mr. Byers*" and making insinuations that she had

---

33. Theophilus Dobbins, CSA.

Emily Burton Wilson Byers (Aunt
Emma), c. 1822–?.
Courtesy Independence County Historical Society.

no right to direct affairs as though she was not his wife, and though a
second wife as much entitled to respect as the first. Aunt Emma has her
faults, and very glaring ones too, but she has now met her superior in
that line.

Aunt Emma told Ma this evening that he (Henry) treated Rilla like a
dog, that he frequently cursed her. I know he is in the habit of swearing,
but I little thought that he would curse his wife, for he really loves her,
as much as it is possible for him to love anyone. Cousin Rilla has such
a proud, fierce spirit and can so little bear slight that I can hardly credit
that he would have the audacity to curse her, for at times he stands in
awe of her.

The last day of June, and a glorious morning. Twenty years yesterday since Ma was married. Last night I took Vena's beau Dr. Fulsome from her.[34] Dobbins as usual was Sarah's attendant.

Soon after we came home, Ma was seized with a pain in her heart, and for some time it was with difficulty that she drew her breath. She has been subject to this ever since I can remember, but the attacks are generally very slight and of short duration. I sometimes fear that it is disease of the heart; yet I can hardly believe it possible for it is now a year since she has suffered from it.

Mrs. Maxwell wishes to continue her French lessons with me, but I don't like it much; she is such a dull scholar, and I have forgotten a great deal that I once knew. I must now go and hear Ella's and Will's lessons.

Just returned from Aunt Emma's. Dr. Dobbins and Mr. Bulkley came up with one of the hospital wagons and Fannie and Lizzie Goodwin in it. Sarah and I got in and off we started, the moon shining bright and the road as rough as stumps, rocks, and mud holes could make it. Here we went, "jolt, jolt this way, jolt, jolt that way, and all for the fun." Mrs. Cox and Em Weaver went on horseback. We had a dance and backgammon, music and conversation. Fannie Goodwin was in such a hurry to come, the evening was not half long enough. Last night we had a soiree or more properly a conversation party.

Fannie and Lizzie spent the day here today. Dr. Dobbins and Bulkley came up, and as we all became engaged in playing chess [and] draughts, they stayed to dinner.

I was so sleepy this morning that it was with difficulty that Sarah got me out of bed. I had washed and was standing before the glass combing

---

34. Dr. James E. Folsom (b. 1838), son of Isaac and Lucy D. Folsom. Mary apparently did this despite Vena's being four years her senior.

my head, in my gown, and hearing a buggy looked out, and there were Cousins Henry and Rilla.

I was vexed immediately for I have got so that the very sight of Henry Smith makes me angry. He had to start to Little Rock, and came in to take breakfast with [us]. He has brought all his powers to bear to create dissension in the families. As Aunt Emma say[s], she got along not only harmoniously but very happily; stepmother and children were attached to each other until Rilla married; since then there is continually some difficulty between them. If they do not have open warfare there is some kind of diplomacy going on by which one may be injured and another revenged. This is a hard word but I think it applicable.

Cousin Henry has come to such a pitch that he says he won't stay there. I don't know where he is going to stay. He has told it that he was coming here, but he has said nothing to Ma about it. We don't want them, bless goodness! We have little enough room now. Ma can't tell them not to come until they ask her, but if they do ask she will tell them they can't come. It is uncomfortable enough when he is here for a few days only, but to be here all the time would be to make a purgatory of it.

He talks so about the Missourians, and they all know it [so] that when he is here not one of these gentlemen who are staying in town come near. Last week he was here all week; with the exception of Mr. Bulkley a few minutes one evening we had not a bit of company, but since he has been gone there has not been a single day but some have been here. Yesterday he did not come to dinner until we had sat down to the table. On finding Bulkley and Dobbins here he would not come to the table although Ma sent for him twice. He is always saying something about Mr. Head being such an intelligent man and of the girls leaving Mr. Head to go off with some of these "fly up the creek Missourians." The other night he came here tight; I never was so glad of anything; now I'll talk Head to him.

Night. This evening Aunt Emma was here. I cannot blame her for hating Cousin Henry, for he talks scandalously about Nannie. He does not come out boldly and tell things but insinuates and throws out hints about what he has seen and heard until a person who did not know him would think Nannie was an infamous woman. I have known Nannie

Wilson all my life, and I would stake my honor on her purity. He even went so far yesterday as to advise Ma not to let Sarah and I visit at Aunt Emma's. Not visit Uncle William's! To whose generosity we owe the bread that we eat daily! But I must leave this subject.

JULY 4TH

We celebrated the day[35] by a picnic at the caves.[36] Eddie Burr[37] went with me. He is very friendly, calls me "Cousin Mary." The Misses [illegible] were there; they afford amusement for all the picnic parties. Mr. Head, Dr. Austin, Dr. Fulsome, Mrs. Cox, and I went farther in the Moulder Cave then any of the others and the dirtiest place I ever was in. Dr. Austin was very attentive today; since I explained about the note he is the same as ever.

JULY 5TH

I was too lazy this morning to exert myself to wash and dress, and the Sunday-School bell rang and I was in an old dress, no corset, my hair very rough, and the *tout ensemble* not very prepossessing. By dint of much hurrying from Sarah, I got ready and we were there before

---

35. Mary and her friends could not know that on this day the Federals won a battle at Helena, Arkansas, and that Confederate forces at Vicksburg, Mississippi, had surrendered, completing the isolation of the Trans-Mississippi West from the rest of the South and, together with the simultaneous victory at Gettysburg, dooming the Confederacy.

36. Independence County history is full of accounts of people visiting caves for recreation. But the caves in the Trans-Mississippi Department also were, for the Confederate Ordnance Bureau, one of the few sources of potassium nitrate (KNO_3; saltpeter; niter), an essential component of gunpowder. In Texas caves the niter came from bat guano, but in the Ozarks it was mostly the product of naturally occurring dilute nitric acid reacting with the limestone of the caves, especially on an impermeable foundation of clay. Johnston, "Bullets for Johnny Reb," 48–50. Confederate women often saved their family's urine for its niter content.

37. Edwin Burr, twenty-one, son of E. T. and Nancy Burton Burr. E. T. Burr was a wealthy local merchant, and his wife a sister of Aunt Emma.

school commenced. I did not stay to meeting. Mary Wycough came up to Em's,[38] and we stayed there until 11 ½ o'clock, when we had one of our old-fashioned days together such as we have not had for a long time. Since Mark came home, Sarah has not been to Mrs. Wycough's.[39] One evening we were at Em's; I was talking very busily (as I usually am) with Em, when up Sarah jumped, saying, "Let's go, Mary." Looking out I saw Mark just starting in the gate, Sarah was starting out the door, bonnet on, gloves and parasol in hand. Mark recognized her, wheeled, and walked up street, leaving us plenty of time to make our retreat before Em had time to recover from the surprise into which our abrupt departure had thrown her. It was the first time they had seen each other since the Batesville Volunteers left—two years ago the 25th of last May. I go to Mrs. Wycough's and shall continue to do so until Mrs. Wycough and Mary show me that my company is not acceptable, even if Mark and I should have an outbreak, which I think very possible, for he never liked me, and the feeling was and is still reciprocated.

After dinner, Mary, Sarah, and I put on our gowns and indulged in a lounge and nap until five, when we dressed and went to walk. We intended to stop for Puss, but Mr. Bulkley was there, and as we had made an engagement to call for Eliza and Mary we knew it would never do. Mr. Case would have preached their funeral sermons when they returned. What! To walk in company with a Missourian! The offense is unpardonable. Eliza and Mary were very anxious to go to the picnic, but *Old Dad* objected. They watched the girls start from Mr. Maxfield's and then had a good cry.

This evening as we went into Mrs. Maxfield's, Barron was coming the other way. Eliza saw him, and thought he was coming in, too. "There's Barron," said she, "Now Pa'll scotch! What'll we do?" But fortunately he did not come in. All the men are so opposed to these Missourians, and all the ladies are champions for them. Missouri gentlem[e]n should be

---

38. Emma, the wife of Dolph Wycough.
39. Malinda Wycough, mother of Dolph, Mary, and Mark.

grateful to Arkansas Ladies, for they are the only defenders they have. The feeling of hatred is almost as intense between any soldiers of the two states as between Federals and Confederates.

Nannie got a letter from Cousin Ann today: Uncle William is able to be up but far from well.

JULY 10TH, WEDNESDAY

Mrs. Case got up a blackberry party, and all of "our set" went. We got a great quantity of berries; I alone gathered in three gallons. We got full of chiggers, and I am going bare-legged yet. It was sundown when we got home, and supper was ready. After supper, Sarah and I fixed a dish of nice berries and sent them with our compliments to Drs. Dobbins and Austin. They sent word that they would be up directly, and, before I thought, they were here. They saw me in my uniform for I was in the door and they at the gate.

Yesterday about eleven, Cousin Henry came; we were none of us glad to see him, Cousin Rilla not excepted.

In the evening came news of our defeat at Helena. Our forces attacked the town, and it strongly fortified and garrisoned with a force of eight thousand and could be reinforced by the river at any time. The slaughter was great: we lost 1800 in killed and wounded, were obliged to leave the field and our wounded in possession of the enemy. Parsons' Brigade suffered most. Capt. Clark of Marmaduke's escort was mortally wounded, Maj. Smith killed, also Mr. Besom. Col. Shelby wounded in the right arm. None of Rutherford's company hurt, although Bob Weaver brings word that they rushed down on the levee [with]in twenty yards of the gunboats and commenced slaying negroes. It is now reported and almost universally believed that the Federals are coming down from Ironton.

JULY 11TH

All excitement has died down. A letter was rec'd yesterday evening from Gen. Marmaduke in which he said that he had heard from his outposts eighty miles [away], and all was quiet.

Our reading club is at length to be organized. We meet at Mrs. Smith's to make arrangements.

Cousins Henry and Rilla are going to the Arkansas River with Cynthia and Job.[40]

Evening. At three this evening we went to Mrs. Smith's. Mr. Bulkley, Mrs. Lewis, Vena Maxfield, Sarah, and I were the only ones there. Miss Sarah Perrin had ironing to do, and Mary Wycough had some work to finish. We decided on Mrs. Maxwell for president and Puss for secretary, and Mr. Bulkley, Eliza, and Mrs. M. for a committee to select the books to be read and the places to meet.

Mr. Bulkley came home with us and would have stayed to supper if Cousin Henry had not been here. He goes on at such a length about Missourians that when he is here they shun the house like we had the leprosy. I don't believe that he is going over on the Arkansas River at all. They will pretend that they are going, get their trunks in here, and here they will stay till the end of time, I suppose, and if he is to stay here always, I don't care how soon that is.

Ed Burr called this morning. He wanted Sarah and I to go down there to spend the day there next week, but we had never been there except to Em's wedding and to call. He said he would bring horses for us. At first we consented, but after he went over to Mrs. Kennard's I remembered an engagement to spend the week at Aunt Emma's and told him of it. If we were in the habit of going to Mrs. Burr's it would be different, but she ridicules everything and everybody and directly would be telling it around that Sarah and Mary Byers came down and spent the day with Eddie.

Gen. Marmaduke is going to send his sick up here, so we will have the hospitals here all summer. Cousin Henry always sneered at Dr. Dobbins, and at Sarah for allowing him to wait upon her, but now as he (Dobbins) has a shot-gun which he wishes to buy, he is a great fellow. I asked him just now how they traded, but the Dr. would not let him have it.

---

40. Cynthia and Job were Henry and Rilla's slaves.

I went to Sunday School and church. It is the strangest weather I have ever known: not cloudy but smoky and cold. It is like Indian summer. Everyone remarks, "what strange weather! Did you ever see the like." Some think it is caused by the battle at Helena, but that cannot be for it is 100 miles from here, and then that would not cause the cold. It is a strange phenomena of nature for which we cannot account.[41]

JULY 13TH

Dr. Dobbins had an engagement to go to church with Sarah, and when he came up he brought Dr. Austin along to go with me. I suppose he was afraid I would go along with him and Sarah. I like Dr. Dobbins very much. He and Sarah are excellent friends. At first he pretended to be very much in love with her, but now it is friendship. I did not know that Sarah possessed such a spirit for mischief until Dobbins drew her out. When they are together you may be sure that some mischief is brewing.

Mr. Wycough has commenced building a shed-room beside the smoke-house in which to store Cousin Henry's things.

Dr. Austin told me last night that Col. Shelby had had his right hand amputated.

Mr. Lee just brought a letter to Leanna from Purnell. He says that he has seen some of the negroes taken by the Federals. They were in a wretched condition, having nothing to carry water in nor make up bread, doing the latter in their hats and carrying the former in their shoes. He advised her never to let anybody, white or black, persuade her from her home, that she is better off here then she will ever be with the Federals. There were 2000 negroes captured at Delhi, La., 200 of which

---

41. More likely the smoke came from the Confederates burning cotton at Little Rock, also one hundred miles away, to avoid Union capture. On September 10 the state capital would fall to General Steele's forces.

were in arms and will be shot: the law of the C. S. [is] to shoot every negro found in arms.[42]

JULY 14TH

Last night, Messrs. Bulkley and Barron called. Not long after, Dr. Dobbins struck up on his violin in front of the porch. Presently he came in and we spent a very pleasant evening together. Ella has come to the conclusion that she is a young lady, too, and when we have company always stays in the room until they leave.

I'm going to Aunt Emma's this evening if I can get a horse to ride.

JULY 24TH

Just got home from Aunt Emma's. I have had such a very pleasant visit, but they have had *such* a *time* here at home. Our *very dear* Cousin Henry has stayed here every night for three weeks. He took a chill just as I was leaving, and for over one week he was not able to leave the house, having a chill every other day. Cousin Rilla worked so hard getting all her clothes washed and her furniture hauled in and packed in the little storeroom that he put up by the smokehouse that she lay down and had a chill, and to cap the climax, Byers took one the next day. What a sweet time they must have had! I envy them their felicity.

Tuesday morning, Aunt Emma came to town to get George's clothes cut. Emma Weaver was out there. Nannie and she had put on their nightgowns when we heard someone knock. I jumped up, ran to the door; there stood an old gentleman dressed in citizen's clothes, with very heavy gray whiskers and mustachios. I invited him in, asked him to take a chair; sitting down, he pulled off his hat and asked in a grim

---

42. In 1862 Confederate president Davis proclaimed "[t]hat all negro slaves captured in arms be at once turned over to the executive authorities of the respective States to which they belong to be dealt with according to the laws of said States." *OR,* ser. 2, 5:795–97. This draconian order was enforced only erratically, but it led eventually to the end of prisoner exchanges and in turn the mistreatment of prisoners, most notoriously at Andersonville, Georgia.

voice, "Can I get breakfast with you this morning?" There was something familiar in the tone. Darting a swift look at him, I exclaimed, "Why, Uncle William!" Then I knew him.[43]

He and Cousin Annie wearied of waiting for Cousin Henry to come, left the negroes in George Ruddell's[44] care and came home. Cousin Ann had stayed back on the hill and let him come on to surprise Aunt Emma. She came soon after, but she had heard in town that he had come.

John has come again. He has been at Aunt Emma's three times. Part of the visits I took to myself. This evening [he] came out in the buggy and brought me some ... [entry incomplete]

JULY 26TH

Last night we went to Mrs. Smith's. They always have such pleasant parties there. Cousins Rilla and Ann spent the day here yesterday. After five they went down street, and Sarah and I went to the Reading Club, which met at Mrs. Maxfield's.

JULY 28TH

There has been great excitement about the Federals coming for the last four days. The hospitals broke up Sunday evening. The sick together with Drs. Barron and Fulsome went down to Jacksonport on the *Kaskaskia.* Drs. Austin and Dobbins left since dinner. I regretted very much to see them leave. I have only been acquainted three months yet in that time had become better acquainted than very often with other strangers after 12 months' acquaintance. Cousins Henry and Rilla left this evening.

---

43. This is probably a tall tale, derived from Mary's love of drama. It is hard to believe that she did not at once recognize her Uncle William despite his new facial hair.

44. Probably George Wesley Ruddell, overseer of William Byers's plantation at Des Arc. The Ruddell family from Kentucky was among the earliest settlers of Independence County, their surname used often for political and geographic features (e.g., Ruddell Township, Ruddell Hill, and Ruddell Mill).

Puss and I were taking on at great length about Dr. Austin when Mrs. Smith remarked that there was great "cutting out" going on for Dr. A. had cut John out, and now Miss Sarah Perrin was about to cut us both out. I had a long conversation with Dr. A. last night and at last convinced him that John and I were not engaged. This is the impression everywhere; he pretended at least that he was convinced. He had heard it several times and from a gentleman and lady who were my friends and knew this to be a certainty. I told him that I had never spoken of that gentleman to but two persons and certain I was that they had not told it. I think that it was Mrs. Maxwell from what he said. I have never told anyone except Mrs. Kennard and Nannie that I rejected John, for I know how mortifying it would be to a person of his proud and independent spirit to be shown in the light of a discarded suitor. I should have held John on for some time if it had not been for Ma.

JULY 30TH

This morning two strips of carpet had to be taken up and shaken. The plastering fell.

Mr. Bulkley left this morning for Louisiana. He has an aunt living in the northern part of the state who wrote to him to come and make his house with her until he recovered or could return home. It is now nearly seven months since he was wounded, and his wound is no better now than it was four months ago. When he told the girls goodbye, he gave all an onion, but no tears would come. We have all become so well acquainted with him that we regretted exceedingly to see him leave.

Eliza Jane sent Dr. Dobbins a pair of socks and told Mr. Bulkley to say that Sarah sent them and another to Barron with Vene's compliments.

AUGUST 2ND

Laziness! Laziness! I am lying on the bed, "en dishabille," with my journal beside [me] trying to write, but this is the way I usually spend Sunday morning after coming from Sunday school.

10 o'clock. Just after dinner, John wrote a note up to me to go to Mrs. Fairchild's, but a cloud came up and although it did not rain yet it was so dark at the appointed time that we did not go. John had a chill on Friday.

Saturday morning, I was at Mrs. Smith's a short time, and when I was leaving Mrs. Smith told me John was sick and asked if I did not want to see him. I told her that I did not care particularly about it and then asked her if he wanted to see me. She went in his room, and when she returned I was on the porch leaving, so she did not say what he said. I think now that he told her to ask me to come in and see him, for she was in his room a short time after I called. I knew very well what he wanted to see me for, as I had had a kind of quarrel with John just a week before, and now he wanted to make up, but I had no notion of being placed in the situation that she placed Nannie in once, that of having been left alone in that room with John to *make up* a quarrel.

John has not been here until tonight since last Monday night; then I did not see him for there was company here, and I was in the house and he on the porch. He and Mrs. Kennard were over here a little while tonight. Just at dusk, Puss and Mrs. Smith came up. Puss told her to console her because she was sick and the Dr. had come. Sarah had been sick all day, but Dobbins came up presently, and she got up and I believe she is well now.

John is going away Tuesday. He and I have several things to arrange before he leaves. He has broken his promise about drinking, and I did not answer his last letter, although I rec'd it two days after he left and he was gone five weeks. We were talking about these things down at Mrs. Smith's one night, and Dr. Austin overheard us. He told me that the next night, when speaking of my engagement to John, which I denied, that he had heard some things that convinced him that there was an engagement existing, and moreover that he could inform me "that the course of true love never ran smooth." Dobbins spoke, too, of my *lovers' quarrel.*

Lucretia "Lutie" Noland Maxfield (1846–80), 1863.
Courtesy Old Independence Regional Museum, ICHS Collection.

AUGUST 3RD

This morning, feeling like walking, I went to Mrs. Maxfield's to get some bobonet.[45] While there, a gentleman brought a letter to Lutie from Capt. Lawrence,[46] who is sick at Mr. Thomas' at Sulphur Rock.

Mary Case came home with me and stayed all day. This evening John sent up to know if I would go to Mrs. Fairchild's this evening as we did not get to go yesterday. I did not wish to leave Mary after bringing her home with me, but she and Sarah had to go to the singing class at five, so I went. We had a merry ride and a very pleasant visit.

I have promised to answer John's letters when he goes back to camp. This I know Ma will not like for she don't approve of the correspondence nor never did.

But John will never court me again, and I have no reasons for declining the correspondence. I like John very much but as for loving *him*, bah! There is one Smith in the family now, and I had ocular demonstration of the felicity a marriage with one would bring. But I don't believe that John is as mean and picayunish as Henry.

Ma fears I will learn to love John and says she would rather lay me in my grave than see me married to him.

But of that there is no danger, for as I told Col. Gordon when he was warning me, "not to fall in love with any of these soldiers," I am proof against all such foolishness. Eliza sent Mr. Trone a pair of socks accompanied by a note signed, "Chief of Staff." He thought I sent them, so the soldiers who brought Lutie's letter told me.

AUGUST 4TH

This morning Ma and Mrs. Wycough went up the country to Mr. Hall's, whose wife, they heard, had calico to sell. Sarah went to take her music lesson. Soon after I had a call from Mr. Stevenson of Marmaduke's escort. It is so warm that I am so lazy that I cannot do anything. I must come out of this or Nannie's corsets won't be finished this week.

---

45. Bobbinet (bobbin net, or machine-made lace).

46. Capt. (later Maj.) Robert J. Lawrence, CSA, a member of Colonel Shelby's staff.

Night. Mrs. West and Jennie and all their children were here this evening. They came to have their ambrotypes taken.

Mr. Bulkley came this evening.[47] He brought Sarah and I a box of sardines and one of oysters, a present from Dr. Austin. Sarah and I had intended to go to Mrs. Smith's tonight, but after Mr. Bulkley came we knew he would be there so we concluded not to go, but it was much against Sarah's will, and it so happened that it was very well, for Mr. Stevenson called and spent the evening. I got acquainted with him at Aunt Emma's. He is a slow, lazy, good sort of a fellow, has very little energy.

I have not been anyplace today. Ma did not get anything. It was a mistake about her having goods; it is strange the stories that we do hear.

AUGUST 5TH

Yesterday morning I ironed and in the afternoon went to join the reading class, which met at Mrs. Perrin's. Mr. Bulkley came home with us, stayed to supper, then we went to Mrs. Case's. Mrs. Aikin wanted us to go to her house, but we had made the engagement. I had much rather gone there, for Dr. Wallace was there.

Cousin Ann had a chill yesterday, and I think I will go out there this evening to stay with her. We made an engagement to go to Mrs. Maxfield's tonight, but I do not care anything about going. I don't know what is the reason, but I have not taken any interest in anything for the last week. I feel dull, stupid, and careless. I stayed last night with Mrs. Kennard, and that is one reason that I feel so dull: her room is so close. When I came, they were all in bed asleep, the candle was burning. I undressed and went to bed without waking a single sleeper.

Night—11 o'clock. This morning I learned that Mary Wycough had returned and immediately went down, intending to return before twelve, but it was five before I started. This evening at four, Mary and I went to see Elvira Denton.[48] Tonight we all went around to Mrs. Maxfield's. Bettie Cullins[49] and Delia Neal[50] were there.

---

47. Evidently, Mr. Bulkley abandoned his proposed move to his aunt's in Louisiana, perhaps unable to get past Federal lines.

48. Elvira Denton, nineteen, was the eldest daughter of Mrs. Neely.

John went away today. Last night he made an engagement with Mrs. Kennard to come over and see me, but she not telling me I went off down to Mrs. Case's. He told her he would come this morning; I waited until nine, and he not coming supposed he had given out going and went to Mary's. At ten he came up, so I missed seeing him. Of this I am sorry for I wanted to see him before he left.

Cousin Ann is still sick. I promised Aunt Emma to go out early in the morning.

AUGUST 12TH

I came from Aunt Emma's this morning. I have had a very pleasant visit. Maj. Page was out there the evening I went. Monday morning, I had dressed in my calico, faded in the back and [with] no corset, when Mr. Barron came out. I did not mind him much but before he left came Capt. Lawrence (Lutie's sweetheart) and Mr. Bulkley, and there I was and had to stay. About ten here came Nannie and Capt. Price. They stayed to dinner, all except Barron; it did not make me more entertaining nor more comfortable to know that I had on the most unbecoming [dress] I had. Capt. Lawrence is very attentive to Lutie. I do not know whether he means anything serious; I presume not, but he esteems Lutie very highly. As a proof of this he never mentions her name in camps, and in his correspondence with her pretended that it was me.

Mr. Trone came up Friday morning, came out to Aunt Emma's to see me Monday. Dr. Austin is in town also; they had a *sardine* supper at Mrs. Perrin's last night. I am sorry I missed it, for from all accounts it was a pleasant party.

---

49. Catherine Elizabeth McGuire "Bettie" Cullins, twenty-one, widow of James A. Cullins, CSA. She lived with her aunt, Mrs. F. W. Desha, south of White River in Greenbrier Township.

50. Margaret Delia Neill, fifteen, daughter of Col. Henry A. Neill and Dorcas Stark Neill, Mary's future in-laws. The Neill tanyard was in the Alderbrook community in Greenbrier.

Aunt Emma made me a present of a new *hoop;* she bought three, gave $50 apiece, the same for two muslin dress patterns and 12 spools of thread.[51]

This morning Sarah has sent for me very early; soon after coming in I went down to Mrs. Weaver's after Cousin Annie's chessmen. Came up home and went down to the store, bought Sarah a pair of slippers, gave $6 for them.[52] The reading class met at Mrs. Maxwell's, and at three Capt. Rathbun[53] came up according to [an] engagement to go down with Sarah. We did not have as merry a time as we do sometimes. Capt. Rathbun read some from Moore; he is a beautiful reader. If I ever marry I hope he will be a good reader, the man I marry, I mean. I think that shall be one of the requisites.

Our troops are falling back to L. R. The Federals are supposed to be advancing from both Helena and Ft. Smith. Our troops are fortifying rapidly, determined to resist.

AUGUST 13TH

This morning I got out my sewing with the expectation of doing a "big day's work." Before I got fairly started, Mrs. Wycough sent word that she would be up presently to spend the day. Soon after, Maj. Lawrence on his way to Jacksonport stopped a few minutes. After he left came Dr. Austin and stayed until three. We or rather I got up an advertisement for Mr. Bulkley, who was "lost, strayed, or stolen." Lutie and Mary came up this evening, and tonight Puss, Delia, Miss Sarah Perrin, Dr. Austin, and Mr. Bulkley were here. They stayed until twelve, and I have promised Ma not to write exceeding 10 minutes, so I have not time for anything more than a mere statement of facts.

---

51. Payment was in Confederate money, which had fallen greatly in value by this time.

52. Payment for the slippers probably was made in U.S. currency.

53. Capt. George Rathbun, Confederate provost marshal in the Batesville area.

AUGUST 14TH

We have had a splendid rain to-day which was needed very much on account of the dust. Dr. Austin and Mr. Bulkley left again this morning, but I think the last-named person will be back in a few weeks, as the Federals are supposed to be advancing on L. R. from two points and will be resisted. He will await at Searcy until the fight comes off.

Ma and Sarah are both unwell. Ma spun four cuts[54] day before yesterday and has been able barely to sit up since. Sarah has the sick headache.

Mrs. Mix was here a little while this evening. She is a very pleasant lady; we like her very much.

Dr. Austin still insists that I am engaged; I cannot convince him otherwise. I would give most anything to know who told him so: one of my "best friends," he says, told him so, confidentially. Sometimes I think it was John himself. When I deny it most positively, he says he does not doubt my word at all, but that I take the privilege all Ladies have of denying such things. He tells Puss of her engagement, too, and says he is convinced of it. Miss Sarah Perrin told me last night if I wished to convince him I must not blush so when told of it. When I denied blushing, he said if I did not now I did when he first spoke to me of it. "That," I replied, "was because it was so unexpected, being the second or third time I had ever heard it."

I have grown old rapidly in the last four months, more particularly in the last two. I can realize now what the authoress of "Rutledge" says: after a girl has crossed the threshold of womanhood, she makes rapid strides nor can she ever turn back and become the girl again.[55] This I know from the fact that were I to receive twenty offers, I could never feel as I did the night of Em Burr's wedding, standing on the porch when John asked me to marry him. It was so unexpected, although he had been waiting on me for a year and corresponding with me for three months, and I knew he was trying to make me believe he loved me but

---

54. A "cut" is a unit of yarn length that varies by region and yarn type. The "American" or "Philadelphia" cut for spun woolen yarn is 300 yards.

55. *Rutledge* was an American Gothic novel of 1860 written by Miriam Coles Harris (1834–1925) but published anonymously.

had never told me so. I tried to pass it off as a joke, and when I could not do that told him I would tell him in two days. I wished to put him off without answering, for I liked him too much to reject him yet not sufficient[ly] to accept, but in three days it had to come.

He did not want to take the answer then but would wait; probably I would change my mind when he came again. While he was gone I did not answer his letter and when he returned told him a story. I do not think he will write, for he will think that I shunned him before he left. Puss wrote Sarah a note yesterday; on the back she wrote, "John started on a scout as soon as he got to the regiment," so that may account for him not writing.

AUGUST 15TH

The Reading Class met at Mrs. Maxfield's this evening. Sarah did not feel like going, and I was late, for I lay down to take a nap and it was so warm that I did not succeed for some time. It was three when Ma waked me. After taking a bath and dressing, it was four when I got there. Maj. Lawrence was there for half an hour. We read Irving's "Sketch Book," or rather a portion of it.

Every one seems confident that the Federals are at Des Arc. I feel very anxious on Uncle William's account, for he is very feeble and to travel this hot weather in his condition would, I fear, kill him. Sarah had a note of thanks from Dr. Dobbins; it was enclosed in a letter to Miss Sarah Perrin.

AUGUST 16TH, SUNDAY NIGHT

I went to Sunday school this morning. Eliza told me first thing of the fight at Searcy Landing. A gun boat came up the Little Red, captured the *Kaskaskia*, and chased the *Tom Suggs*, but she escaped.[56] What more

---

56. On August 14, 1863, the USS *Cricket* steamed up the Little Red River and, contrary to Mary's entry, captured two Confederate cargo steamers, the *Kaskaskia* and the *Tom Sugg*. This essentially ended Confederate river transportation in northern Arkansas and impeded the flow of supplies to Southern troops east of the Mississippi. *OR*, 34:479–86, 511–12.

transpired we could not learn except our forces went down on both sides of the river as the boat was returning and recaptured the *K*. In the affray, twenty-four were wounded, among whom was Maj. Shanks. Col. Gilky was killed.[57]

After school was out I came home and, taking a lunch, prepared for church. Mr. Garthwaite did not preach a very interesting sermon, or at least I have forgotten all about it. I do not remember the text; it was a portion of the 144th Psalm. Some of the congregation went to sleep, among the number Mrs. Maxfield. This afternoon was spent in sleeping and eating and so ends today; nothing accomplished. Our President has appointed next Friday fast day.

AUGUST 17TH

This morning was a dull one. Dinner time came: no better. About three, Sarah went down street; presently Cousin Ann and Uncle William came in. Ann has received a letter from Cousin Rilla. As Bill Ruddell[58] starts in the morning, I commenced writing immediately. After they left, Sarah returned from singing school with an *invitation* to a *storm party* at Mrs. Weaver's. Ella, Willie, and I decided to go. Sarah thought she would stay at home with Ma who has such pains in the calves of her legs and her feet that she has been in bed nearly all day, but while we were at supper, Mrs. Smith and Puss came in. As Puss was going, Sarah changed her mind and we all went. A great many were there, big and little, had music on the violin and some great dancing. Ma is now impatient for me to go to bed and put out the candle, so I will write a description of it some other time.

---

57. Lt. Col. Charles A. Gilky, 12th Missouri Cavalry, under Shelby's command. Estes, *List of Field Officers, Regiments, and Battalions in the Confederate States Army*, 40.

58. Bill Ruddell's relation to George Ruddell, if any, remains unknown.

Nancy "Nannie" Manning Wilson, c. 1842–?.
Courtesy Independence County Historical Society.

AUGUST 18TH

Today Sarah and I paid the long promised visit to Fannie Goodwin. Everything was very pleasant. Charlie walked up home with us. Tonight Will Maxfield called; I was very gla[d].[59]

AUGUST 20TH

Yesterday morning I ironed. Nannie came in and asked me to go to Mrs. Smith's with her. After we started I found this was only a pretext,

---

59. Maxfield was home recuperating from a wound to his nose and eye, suffered during a skirmish in May prior to the Battle of Helena. Odd that Mary does not mention it.

Crouch's Daguerreian Gallery being her destination. She imparted to me as a profound secret that she was to be married to Carroll Wood[60] October 12th, that he had asked and gained the consent of both parents the day before, but she wished to surprise every-body and was going to keep it secret. I inquired what she would do if Wash came before October. That, she said, was "played out." Wash was lazy, was dependent on his father, who had lost all his property, and could not marry now, that she was of age (21) now, that her [step]father had placed her property in her hands, and that she did not wish to be dependent on him any longer.

Wood was of a gay disposition, just suited her, and she should marry him. He loved her. I don't think she loves him yet. She will never marry one whom she has known long, and she says Wood is "immensely wealthy," so probably it is for the best. She wishes me to help her make some preparations.

Cousin Annie came in last evening and stayed all night. Capt. Wood has not asked for Nannie nor does not intend to say anything to Aunt Emma until the day before, so Nannie told her. Cousin Ann is not right sure that Carroll Wood is not flirting.

Sarah went out to Aunt Emma's yesterday so I am alone tonight. Mary Wycough promised to stay with me tonight but did not come.

AUGUST 21ST

Fast Day, appointed by President Davis. There was service at both churches; I went to the Methodist. Mr. Hickison preached against dancing and frolicking and going with and, as he expressed it, "kissing and slobbering" over the soldiers. There were but few there, but those few were disgusted.[61]

Tonight there is a party at Mrs. Aikin's. I wanted very much to go, but Mamma thought it would not be showing a proper respect for religion,

60. Capt. Carroll H. Wood, CSA.

61. Indeed, the Rev. Mr. Hickison's tone does seem strange, preached on a day appointed for patriotic fasting to honor those same soldiers.

so instead Ella and I went down to Mrs. Perrin's and stayed an hour or so. Soon after we came home, John Warner[62] came up to go to Mrs. Aikin's with us, but we declined going. Most of the young ladies he said were going from there to church.

AUGUST 22ND

This is Quarterly Meeting. Tonight we went to church. A Mr. Cox, a Missourian, preached a very good sermon, but he had received his cue from Mr. Hickison and slammed at the people about dancing, raked the parents about letting their children act as they pleased so that neither God, themselves, nor the devil reigned supreme in their hearts. The Reading Class met at Mrs. Wycough's this evening. Mrs. Maxwell delivered a very good essay; we are to read criticisms on it next Wednesday but I fear we will make sad work of it.

Col. Shelby is in town, boarding at Mrs. Neely's.[63] Sarah has come home; Ma and she are keeping [up] such a chatter that I cannot write.

AUGUST 24TH

The doors and windows are all shut. I have drawn on a merino sacque. Strange state of things for August. Last night was warm. The morning was bright and foretold a hot day, but before nigh the wind was blowing a regular northeaster.

I did not [go] to church yesterday morning. I was lazy, and it was the day for communion, and a collection was to be taken up, and the services would be so long, so I stayed at home and partly wrote my criticism. Mr. Foster and Mr. Shepherd and Mrs. Maxwell came home with Ma to dinner. Mr. Shepherd is the Jacksonport preacher. I like him; he is an Englishman, preached last night and again tonight. We did not go

---

62. John T. Warner, about Mary's age, would become a Confederate soldier, then a steamboat captain and engineer, and four times mayor of Batesville.

63. Shelby stayed at the home of his widowed cousin, Margaret Neely, while he recuperated from the wound he sustained at Helena in July. Mobley, *Making Sense of the Civil War in Batesville-Jacksonport and Northeast Arkansas*, 126.

tonight; Willie had a chill. Will Maxfield came up a while this evening. Will is a Baptist but one of the greatest jokers about here. This evening Sarah was speaking of "getting religion," as it is termed,[64] and said if she ever got religion it would be at home, not in a crowd. "No," remarked Will, "I do not know that it is necessary to be in a crowd." This was said in a low, dry tone. I roared with laughter. If conference is here they will worry us until I should not be surprised if they got me to go to the "mourners' bench." If I go, Sarah will follow suit, I expect. I know she will not go before me. The other night at Mrs. Weaver's, she wanted to dance yet first came and asked if I intended to, then said she would not. Seeing that she wanted to, I told her to "go forward" if she wanted to, that I never intended to dance again but that need not keep her from it. She minded me and danced every set. It is only with regard to things that are or will become public that she is so conformable to my wishes or rather with my actions, for like most persons easily persuaded by strangers, she [is] as stubborn as a little mule with the family.

Wash has come, and I don't know what Nannie will do.

AUGUST 26TH

I am out of patience, have an engagement with Eugene. He came. I have been to church, done something that I [have] never done before. Mr. Foster asked all those who wished those preachers to pray that they might go to heaven to come forward and take them by the hand. I was among the number. I did not want to go, thought for some time that I would not. Lizzie Goodwin asked me to go up with her. I would not, but after all had gone thought that the prayers would not do me any harm, yet I do not think that they will prove very beneficial, for though I wish to go to heaven, yet I have never wished to "get religion." There will be preaching tomorrow and again tomorrow night, and I know Mr.

---

64. Mary refers to the Methodist practice of going to the mourners' bench before the altar and proclaiming oneself a sinner who wishes redemption. Family members, friends, and even exhorters from the congregation might join them there for encouragement.

Shepherd will ask me to go to the altar, yet I do not intend going. Mary
Wycough and Mary Case have been going forward since Monday night.
Fannie Goodwin went up tonight and tried to get Lizzie to go. Lizzie
would not but asked me; if I had gone she would. Mary Wycough is
really serious. I was there this morning and talked with her.

AUGUST 27TH

We had better establish a hospital and send for a surgeon; every one of
Mrs. Kennard's family except the baby had a chill either yesterday or today, and Ella and Willie had one apiece. Ma cannot leave them to go to
church, so I cannot attend tonight, yet I would like to. I have spun two
cuts today.

AUGUST 29TH

I feel badly this evening. Mrs. Smith has been talking to me about seeking religion. I don't know what to do yet. I feel it my duty to seek God. I
cannot live forever yet do not want to become religious. My mind is in a
conflict. I cannot tell what to do.

Ma has never said anything to me upon the subject except to ask me
if I expected to get to heaven without religion. I sometimes think that
if she had told me to go to the altar the night after Mr. Shepherd was
up here, I should have gone, but then when I think of the way I have
received her counsels, I do not wonder that she said nothing for she
knows that what my reason say[s] do, I will.

I have been talking with Ma on this subject; she says do exactly what
I think right, do as my judgment dictates, but not to try to seek religion
unless I feel an earnest conviction and will seek until I find it and then
attach myself to some church and live up to its rules. She told me that
she knew me well enough to be convinced that what others said against
it would have no influence with me. How little she knows her daughter!
Yet I fear nothing but the sneers of Aunt Emma, these I do not fear
either, for I know that once [I] convince her I am in earnest, she will say
nothing more. I don't believe that I am sufficiently convicted, but one

thing I am certain of: I will read my Bible more and pray. I will try to seek religion at home for I don't like the altar.

Nine o'clock. Sarah and I expected to go to church, but just as we were getting ready to start, Mr. Stevenson came in. He had been here this evening, but we were not at home so he called again tonight by particular request of Drs. Dobbins and Austin, who are at Searcy.

There was a man here yesterday from Newton's Regt. He brought letters for Mrs. Weaver and Mrs. Smith. Mrs. Smith's was a very short note; she showed it to me this evening by way of reparation to me, I suppose, for not receiving one. I could not help but think this evening when she was talking to me about being a Christian and of her wishes and prayers for John that probably she knew my influence over him, that that was why she felt so anxious for my welfare, but I tried to silence all such feelings as unworthy of a Christian. For this I am going to try to make up my mind to be so, conclude as Mary Case and Mary Wycough have done; they have both professed religion and joined the church.

Mr. Bulkley is seventeen miles below Little Rock, laid up with his wound.

AUGUST 30TH, SUNDAY NIGHT

I have just come from church. I don't know the reason that Mrs. Smith takes such interest in my spiritual welfare. I have no right to judge, but sometimes I think, as Sarah said to me tonight when I asked why she was so anxious about me particularly, "Oh! She is converting you for John." But then would she be willing for her son to marry a portionless girl? I cannot tell. She thinks now that I exert an influence for good over him. I do not now, but I did once. He almost abstained from drink and I should have believed had done so altogether had it not been for an accident. She has found my one vulnerable point, a regard for the good opinion of the world. As she told me last winter that she heard an old gentleman say that he would rather his son would marry Mary Byers if she had but one ring on her finger than any girl he knew. I know she meant Col. Smith, but I am not going to marry John. I could get him by merely saying the word but will not. I like him better than any of my gentleman acquaintances and might in time learn to love him a little but never enough to cover the multitude of faults that I know he possesses. Besides, when I marry, I wish it to be someone on whom I can rely to be "my staff and my guide."

I read over what I wrote last night and find that I am farther from believing than I was last night.

Delia McGuire is dead, died on Friday 2 o'clock, a year and a few days since Mary's death. Delia was happy, a professor of Christianity, a member of the Methodist church. How uncertain is life! How certain death!

John Warner wrote a note to Sarah in church tonight to know if she would not go with him to the altar. She refused, [and] he went alone. Eugene Goodwin says if I will go with him he will go tomorrow night. Mrs. Smith wants me to go to Ebenezer[65] with her tomorrow. Mr. Stevenson came home with me tonight; I told him I believed these people would worry me into going up to the mourners' bench.

AUGUST 31ST

It is done. I have been and come back. I went with Mrs. Smith today. The sermon was good; I felt it. At the close he spoke of Bunyan, in the Pilgrim's Progress, of the city on the hill, of the straight and narrow way that leadeth unto life. He who kept in it would get there, meet his kindred who had gone before. The congregation was much moved, I among the rest. I cried as I had never done before at my own sins and wickedness. They called mourners to the altar. I was standing up crying at the time. Mr. Foster came up singing and crying and asked, "O! Don't you want religion—the religion of Jesus Christ—in your soul?" I could only reply by my tears. "Come then, and go to the altar. I will go with you." I shook my head; I could not go.

After dinner I went to see Mrs. Hickison. Tonight, although I have a very bad cold and a headache, I went to the church. Mr. Hickison preached from the text, "What if a man gain the whole world and lose

---

65. Ebenezer Methodist Church, about five miles east of Batesville. It has since been relocated as the modern Moorefield United Methodist Church.

his own soul," or, "What shall a man give in exchange for his soul," when they called for mourners. I asked Ma if I must go. I determined to abide by her decision. She told me to do as I pleased but that she believed I wanted to go, that I might go up there, kneel during the prayer, and then, if I wished, come back. I did so. When kneeling there, my old faith in presentiments came to me. I felt that if I did go I could not pray or if I did pray and get religion that my faith would be weak. I could not stand. I came back, yet since I came the word[s], "He who putteth his hand to the ploughshare and looking back is not fit for the kingdom of Heaven." Yet I am not sorry I done it; will I ever be . . . [entry incomplete]

SEPTEMBER 2ND

Yes, I am now. I have only wrote this in order to ease my mind; it is said, "Confession is good for the soul." I believe it. Already I feel my heart lightened, but will not the old heavy feeling come back as soon as I cease writing? I am going to church tonight. I have felt all along that, if I could tell Cousin Ann of my intention previous to going, I could kneel at the altar and feel perfectly happy. If I had gone up Sunday night or Monday at Ebenezer, I would have been blessed by this time, but Mr. Foster says I steeled my heart against the spirit of God. This may be.

I am going to Aunt Emma's tomorrow. I should have gone on Monday if I could have got my shoe mended. If I feel when I return as I do now, I shall overcome my repugnance to the "mourners' bench" and at the first opportunity kneel there. Now, troubled heart, peace, be still. Will Maxfield told me yesterday that he believed I would get religion. I took a reasonable view of it, but be sure I did not "run reason in[to] the ground." Lute Maxfield feels just as I did before I was awakened to a view of my sin and transgression. I have felt during this meeting that we would both pass through unconverted and be made firm friends. The girls say that I am trying to keep Lutie back. Perhaps I have been, at least I have not been sorry when she stayed, but now I shall say nothing to her except if she feels it her duty to go, to do so, to believe that now is the appropriate time and not to wait for a future and more convenient opportunity.

Fannie Goodwin says I must not harden my heart so that finally I will cease to feel at all, but I must see Cousin Ann, talk with her. The churches doubt and perplex me. Until yesterday it was none but Methodist and Presbyterian; now, after my conversation with Will Maxfield, conflicts have gone on in my mind about the Baptist. I must join some church, but which one? I like the Methodist best, but then there are some of its rules that I very seriously object to. I have thought, thought, thought that it would be a positive relief to stop thinking, but to do that must lose my intellect. A casual observer of human nature soon perceives that as my pride, my point upon which I can be flattered until I scarcely know myself.

11 o'clock. I have returned. The conflict is ended. I feel at peace. My old religion has returned. My religion? What is it? Mere hard-heartedness. Today if any person had asked me, "Is man a free moral agent?" I should have replied, "Yes." Now I doubt it. I startled Lute tonight by asking her if she really believed there was a God. Do I believe this? No. Yet, doubts will arise in my mind, and I never read one page of infidelism or heard a disbeliever converse. Lute also has settled down into the old lethargy. I was in hopes she would not, but tonight although Mr. Foster's sermon was good it produced no more effect upon her than it did on me. He mentioned it tonight in his sermon. By "it," I mean of a young lady who, while the tears were running down her cheeks, *tears* that a knowledge of her sins had caused, bracing herself against the spirit of God. Last night it would have brought me to my knees; tonight my lip curled—with what? I suppose he will cite that circumstance all over the circuit.

SEPTEMBER 3RD

Tonight I went to church, went to the mourners' bench, but, to begin at the beginning, this evening I had awaked from my nap and was lying on the sofa reading when Belle[66] came in and said, "Miss Susan [Mrs. Smith] said please come down there." Mrs. Smith said that Puss believed she had experienced a change of heart, that she felt so happy she thought she

---

66. Mrs. Smith's servant.

would send for me and see how I felt by that time. I told her my heart was so hard I could not feel nor pray, that I had not prayed since Tuesday morning at Ebenezer. She said it was the groaning of a spirit too great for utterance. I did not think so. Miss Sarah Perrin came in; she thought the same. I told them my repugnance to going to the altar yet felt it a cross that I would be obliged to take up before I got religion.

Lute came home with me. We had stayed away together from the altar and agreed when one went the other would also. But tonight, when Mr. Hickison preached from the text, "The harvest is passed, the summer is ended, and you are not saved," I said nothing to her but as soon as the invitation was extended, before they commenced singing, I started. I could not stay back, or I could have stayed but feared I would get out of the notion. Lutie and Sarah followed. I feel much calmer, happier. I do not wish to deceive myself yet am almost constrained to believe I have religion.

SEPTEMBER 10TH

I returned from Aunt Emma's today.[67] I had come to the conclusion that I did not have religion, but Mrs. Smith came out. She thinks I have.

SEPTEMBER 12TH

Tomorrow morning I start to Mr. McGuire's to attend Delia's funeral. How strange it seems that she is dead. When last I saw her she was so lively and more beautiful than I ever saw her, but she is gone, departed *forever*—what a sound! Am I prepared to die? I cannot tell. This question crowds my mind continually to the exclusion of nearly everything else. Thursday night one week ago, when I asked myself this question I answered in the affirmative. I felt such a calm I thought it was religion, but I have almost come to the conclusion that I was mistaken. Mrs. Smith, Miss Sarah Perrin, and Mrs. Kennard are confident that I experienced a change of heart.

---

67. Mary did not know that on this day Little Rock fell to Federal forces.

There is one thing which I have determined upon, that is, not to repose the confidence in Mary Wycough that I have hitherto done. For years I have hardly had a thought that she has not shared, but for the last year Mary has almost ceased to come here unless she wanted something, which has been very seldom. She hardly gives me credit for one good thought, that is, when she is talking to me; I know not how it is when I am the subject of conversation.

'Tis four weeks since John left. He has not written to me, to his mother but once. He thinks that I treated him shamefully. Well! Let it rest so. I do not love John Smith, yet his attentions were very agreeable to me. Why this was I could never tell, for he is not a person whose companionship was interesting to me. I never appeared to such disadvantage as when conversing with him. All the worser elements of my nature were called in[to] play. I have a greater influence with him than anyone, but at the bare idea of a union with him my soul recoils with horror. Why is it then that I feel his neglect? It is my wounded pride I believe, but I will banish him from my mind forever. His name shall never be in my journal again. Now as I said once before, "Troubled heart"; "peace, be still," but the cause was entirely different.

SEPTEMBER 14TH

There have many changes taken place during the last three weeks. My feelings have undergone a complete change. Three weeks tomorrow since Mr. Shepherd came up to talk with me. He went away and pronounced me an infidel. Both he and Mr. Hickison told this in Jacksonport. Now I have professed myself a believer in Jesus Christ. I was not perfectly satisfied that it was religion until tonight. When they would have made me believe it I almost repelled the idea, but tonight Vene and I went up to the altar, knelt there. I did not feel one bit of conflict. Everything was peace and quietness, but I am convinced that it was the Lord's blessing, yet it is not so clear, so strong as I would have it. There will doubts arise in my mind even as I write, but I will banish them as machinations of Satan. But can I only have such faith as Delia McGuire, then will I be happy to say when dying, "I walk through the

Elvena "Vene" Maxfield (1842–81), 1862.
Courtesy Old Independence Regional Museum,
ICHS Collection.

dark valley of the shadow of death, I fear no evil, for Thou art with me,
Thy rod and Thy staff they comfort me."

Mr. Bulkley died of his wound in Little Rock at Dr. Kirkwood's Sept.
5th.[68] He also died happy.

SEPTEMBER 15TH

Tonight for the first time in life, religion made me happy. Mr. Hickison
preached an excellent sermon from Ecclesiastes 11:9: "Rejoice, O young
man in the days of thy youth," etc. Vene came to church with the determination of giving up forever. She felt that religion was not for such as

---

68. He may have died September 13. L. Maxfield, "Lucretia Noland Maxfield
Journal."

she. She would be damned, she felt. Others had gone up to the altar, others no worse than she and been blessed in a short time. I begged, persuaded her, if not for her sake then to please me, to go up this one time; she went. I believe she has been blessed. When they were calling mourners I went to Sarah. She had told me going down that she did not feel like going, consequently should not go. I felt that she must want to go. I went to her, held out my hand, she grasped it immediately. I feel that she will be blessed soon. There are many things that I would write, but it is late and I must read my Bible and go to bed.

SEPTEMBER 19TH

How strange are the ways of the Almighty! A report of the Federals broke up our meeting, the preachers leaving town for fear they would be captured, the Secretary of War having ordered that every Methodist or Presbyterian minister shall be imprisoned until the close of the war. I very much regretted that our meeting should, or did, close so suddenly. I have been very happy this week, but today was reading of the different kinds of faith in "The Lady of the Manor,"[69] and had feared that mine was *temporary* instead of *justifying.* Yet I feel this is one of the machinations of Satan and will overcome it. I have not yet decided about joining the church; I must soon decide.

SEPTEMBER 22ND

Sarah is still sick, consequently I have more to do. I ironed this morning, but I have now resolved that I will quit shirking the work of the household. It is wrong. There is not much to do, and if each does his part all will go on smoothly. I have never been sensible of the influence that I exerted in the family until the last week. I very frequently am petulant, and this breeds discord in the family. The last week, all has been order,

---

69. *The Lady of the Manor* (1823–29) by Mary Martha Butt Sherwood (1775–1851). Sherwood was a prolific and influential English evangelical Christian writer of children's literature.

peace, and harmony. I will always try to remember that "A soft answer turneth away wrath." I stayed with Mrs. Mix last night. Her baby is very sick; I do not think it will live. She has so much trouble, has lost her only daughter, her husband during the last year, and it looks cruel to us mortals to deprive her of her baby also, but the Lord chasteneth in order to purify, and this may be necessary to incline her heart to Him.

I received a letter from John Smith yesterday. I hoped that he would not write again, but he has and again makes confessions of love, yet at the same time, considering what has passed between us, says it looks like foolishness. I cannot understand him; he must love me. I read all his letters over Saturday and wondered that I never perceived it before: there is the same strain of deep feeling pervading them all. No! I am wrong. It is not deep feeling; of that he is incapable. Until he addressed me I considered this as flattery.

Now I am in a scrape. I thought from Mrs. Smith's manner she was aware of John's feelings for me, and last night as I was going to Mrs. Mix's I met her and Puss. She took my hands in hers, drew me toward her, then enfolded me in her arms and kissed me, telling me that she had received a letter from a young gentleman telling her "to take good care of Mary." I made some reply, I don't remember what, when she asked me who it was. Then I saw my error—but too late—when I told her John, I supposed, she laughed and said now she had the care of me she would be always kissing me. I told her that I considered myself capable of taking care of myself and that I did not know that anybody had that right to commit me to another's care. She said sometimes people took *rights*. I allowed that they did.

Now what to do I know not. They consider me engaged to John; that is evident now. I do not wish to deceive them but can't do otherwise for I can't come out plain and tell them that I am not. John must make a confidante of his mother respecting me. I can't do anything. My hands are literally tied. But perhaps the Lord will provide some way to extricate me from this Slough of Despond, but this has learned me a lesson. If I ever have another offer and if I intend to accept it, I will do so or say *no* flatly no for this is too much like playing with the lion's paw in the fable.

SEPTEMBER 23RD

Mary Wycough spent the day here. "The Reading Society" met at Mrs. Perrin's this evening. Sarah is still sick, and I could not attend. Eliza, Vene, and Puss were up this evening. They were talking about baptism. Puss is a Baptist in belief yet cannot bear the idea of becoming a member of the church and being *dipped,* as she expresses it. Vene is a good deal of a Baptist. I have nearly renounced "infant baptism." I cannot tell what to do today. My heart has been farther from God then it has been since I was convinced of the new birth. I have pretty serious doubts tonight as to whether I have been regenerated. I must be humble and charitable. This evening I expressed it as my belief that Mr. Kennard was not a good Christian. I wonder that the words, "Judge not, that ye be not judged," and "Now, hypocrite, first cast out the beam out thine own eye," did not rise up before me. How much need have we of prayers of humility! Of charity! Of faith! Also I am far from God, I fear. I can never hold that sweet communion with him that some enjoy. Will Maxfield came up tonight to talk with me regarding baptism and the close communion. He come[s] up frequently.

SEPTEMBER 24TH

Sarah was much better until sundown, when her fever began to rise. She has considerable now. The girls were speaking of spending one more day in the woods before the Federals come, and tomorrow was decided upon as the day, but Mrs. Mix's baby died today, and I cannot go on Sarah's account. So it will be deferred. I have spent this week at home and have not been anywhere except to Mrs. Mix's.

These are indeed times of trouble. Mr. Ruddell started down to Double Trouble last Saturday and got within twelve miles when he met Federalists who searched him and took his money and letters, among which was one I had written to Cousin Rilla, and ordered him to return home which he did without delay. He knows nothing farther from Cousin Henry than we before heard: that is he is in the woods. This is indeed the time that we know not what a day will bring forth.

This morning Mrs. Smith came to see Sarah and again tonight. Col. Shaver, in company with thirty-six men, came today to take charge of these deserters that have been coming in so rapidly since the fall of Little Rock. They brought ammunition, and as these deserters say they are willing to fight at home to defend their own firesides, they will now have an opportunity. John Smith will be here in a few days. I suppose he was to have come with Col. Shaver but did not get his papers all arranged. I wish he would come; I want to put an end to this matter. I don't see what pleasure it can possibly be to a young lady to flirt; I shall never attempt it again. If I can get safely through this scrape, I shall be thankful, for if I do, and do not suffer in John's opinion, it will be owing to God, for I have done nothing to elevate but everything to degrade myself. But on this subject I dislike to think, for I know not to what this may bring me. My character will suffer if my name is connected with John's much more, yet such is his apparent respect for me that he never speaks but in the most appropriate manner in my presence.

Mrs. Mix sent up for me to spend tonight with her. She is *so lonely,* but Sarah was entirely too sick for me to leave.

I am now reading the "Lady of the Manor," a series of conversations on confirmation. It is an excellent work. I very much fear that I am one who cries, "Lord, Lord," without doing the will of The Father. I am selfish and proud, proud of my personal appearance. It would be difficult to tell how often I have looked in the glass today. Oh! How weak is man! This text I like and must remember, "God resisteth the proud but giveth grace to the humble." Tonight for the first time for three weeks Sarah and I openly disagreed.

The girls have been neglecting "The Reading Class" sadly of late. Only five members present, only half.

SEPTEMBER 27TH

This morning for the first time in four weeks I went to Sunday School and Church. Mr. Garthwaite preached an excellent sermon from the text, "No man having put his hand to the plough and looking back is fit for the Kingdom of God." It appears to me that he has improved lately. The last three sermons were really *good sermons*. I used to find fault with his delivery, but today I liked it. He handled the text skillfully. It strengthened me. His hymns are always appropriate. I am going to let the baptism question alone for the present, and [on the] 21st of October Conference will commence. During that time the doors of the Methodist Church will be opened, and I will be taken in. I want Sarah to profess religion by that time, and together we will be admitted.

Why do so many visit the sick on Sunday? We have had company all evening. Yesterday, no one was here.

Tomorrow the candidates for Congress speak. If Sarah and Ella are well enough for me to leave, I will go, but I hardly think now that I can for Leanna goes to the branch to wash.

SEPTEMBER 28TH

This morning, Sarah, Ella, and Willie were sick. I thought that I was not going to get to go to the speaking, but at eleven they were all so much better that Ma said I could go. Mr. Head spoke first of the condition of north Arkansas. [He] begged the citizens to remain true to themselves, to their country, that all would be right in the end. To organize immediately and assist in driving Lincoln's myrmidons from their country. While he was speaking I was much encouraged and thought as he did: if our citizens would only have the faith that he has, the works would soon follow, and every Federal would be driven from the state by Christmas. But there are so many who stand one foot on one side of the line and the other on the other side, waiting to see which will be victorious before they declare their sentiments. Now as the United States is in power now and likely to remain so for some time, they now come out strong Union. The majority of the men in north Arkansas are Federals.

A "Memphis Bulletin" gives an account of a battle with Bragg and

Rosencrans in which the latter was badly beaten, and says if a fuss is raised with foreign powers, the C. S. will undoubtedly gain her independence in the smoke.[70]

I have a slight headache tonight.

SEPTEMBER 29TH

This morning while I was sitting on the front porch waiting for the irons to heat, Mrs. Smith came up in the buggy and asked me to go to Aunt Emma's to see Sam, Oliver [Redd], and Dick Redd[71] who are sick out there. While we were there, John came home. Not finding his mother, he came up to Mrs. Kennard's, told her to tell me that when he put on his clean clothes he would come and see me. Tonight he came. I don't think I will have much trouble to discard him. He has found out that I do not love him and is tired of paying his court to a stone. He looked handsomer tonight than I ever saw him. It agrees with him to be away from here. As soon as he comes home, he gets with Henry Egner [and] Dolph Wycough, to drinking, and is in bad health.[72]

Will Maxfield came up to see me this evening. He come[s] very often of late.

OCTOBER IST

I have just returned from Mrs. Smith's from a soiree. We were to go there last night, but it rained. John was not there. Will Maxfield and Will McGuire were here this morning, and I made an engagement with Maxfield for tonight. He has got a great notion lately of coming to see me. I don't like him. He is a very good young man but by no means interesting. I never had a beau that I liked except John, and now to him

---

70. Although a Confederate victory, the Battle of Chickamauga (September 19–20, 1863) between Maj. Gen. William S. Rosecrans, CSA, and Gen. Braxton Bragg, USA, had no real effect on stemming the Union tide or realizing the forlorn hope that England or France would come in on the side of the Confederacy.

71. Probably employees of Uncle William's.

72. Egner was twenty-six years old and Wycough twenty-seven and with a family. John Smith was only eighteen.

I have *bidden farewell*. Will Maxfield wants to be very polite and generally overdoes the thing. Tonight he turned over the music for Puss and
then turned it back again after she had played one verse. He is so very
awkward: in speaking of himself in connection with another, he always
says, "I and _____," instead of "_____ and I," and many other things
entirely ungrammatical. Perhaps I am fastidious, but I like gentlemen's
society, not awkward and overgrown school boys. Mary Case appears to
like Will M. very much.[73]

OCTOBER 2ND

This morning I went to see Eliza Jane, who had a chill day before yesterday. This evening Mrs. Kennard sent for me and gave me a letter from
John. I was surprised and on opening it read as follows:

Mary,

After what has passed between us, I may be wrong in writing you as I now do. But Mary, *as you know* and as I have told
you, *I love you*, and with all my heart I have tried, in vain, to
forget I had ever loved you. But I love you the more each day
that passes. I love you simply for your matchless purity and
goodness—and to ask that you would love me in return, I cannot. Would to God I were worthy of being loved by such [a]
one as you. Although I feel myself so unworthy, I would ask
that you would accept my proffered hand, not now but at any
time in the future. Only to know that I could one day claim
thee as "my own" would make my happiness complete. I would
make any promises you might require, which would, if broken,
of course release you. I shall *never* cease to love you.

Yours,

John

---

73. The two Wills were home recuperating from wounds suffered at Helena—
Maxfield in the nose and eye and McGuire in the leg. Will Maxfield and Mary
Case would marry in 1866.

I had hoped from his silence that he was content to let matters remain as they were for the present. I am beginning to love John Smith. This I know, for the tell-tale blood dyes my cheek whenever he approaches, but I will stifle it for it would not bring happiness. I am so tired of being poor and I never expect to have as wealthy an offer again. All of his family want it to be a match. I say all; I don't know about Puss, but Mrs. Smith told me the night I professed religion she loved me like one of her own children and told Mrs. Kennard that both she and the Col. would rather John marry me than anybody they ever saw. But I think how unhappy Mrs. S. and Cousin Rilla are and of all that I have heard of John and think I will not.

OCTOBER 4TH, SUNDAY NIGHT

I have spent this day at home and in a way that may not prove unprofitable to me hereafter. I have been led today to see how near I came to breaking the Seventh Commandant in my thoughts concerning John. I was inclined to think I loved him yet would not own it but was sensible all the while that he was drawing my thoughts from the Creator, that giver of every good and perfect gift, that I was becoming dissatisfied with my station in life, sighing for something higher. But by the blessing of God I have been enabled this day to perceive that had I accepted him I should have broken the Fifth Commandment, which is, Honor thy father and mother that thy days may be long in the land which the Lord thy God giveth thee. For Ma is very much opposed to it, said she would rather lay me in my grave than marry me to John Smith. And the Sixth, thou shalt do no murder, for it would be worse [than] natural death, it would be spiritual and very probably eternal death to unite myself to him. I answered his letter yesterday. He has not yet returned so has not received it. It was,

John,

I received your letter this evening, and it is but just that I should reply frankly to you. For you would confer a great honor upon me, the greatest a man can confer upon woman, and I would that it was in my power to receive it, but as I once told you, I do not love you. Why it is, that I do not, I cannot tell; I do not know. It is not as you say on account of your unworthiness. There you do yourself injustice that I will not allow. But John, ask yourself your own heart if you could be happy with one whom you were aware did not love you. You could not. It would be impossible. Great as is my esteem for you, I do not think that alone is sufficient.

OCTOBER 7TH

Nannie is married, and the Federals have been in during the last two days!

Monday at 12, Little John[74] brought me a horse to go out and help Cousin Ann, for Carroll had come and they were to [be] married at three [on] Tuesday. I went; she was in the kitchen making cake. I went to the parlor and with Oliver Redd's assistance cleaned the parlor nicely.[75] Then we cleaned the hall. After dark Cousin Preston came out and reported the Federals within two miles. Then one of Carroll's [men] came. All was confusion for a few minutes except "the groom"; he was an iceberg. In a very businesslike manner he proposed to "the mother" that the parson should be sent for, and in an hour Mr. Kennard and Sarah were there and the knot was tied.[76]

NOVEMBER 15TH, SUNDAY MORNING

While waiting for the church bell I will write. We are again alone. Cousin Rilla and Byers have been here for three weeks and have . . . [entry incomplete]

---

74. A servant from Catalpa Hall.
75. All the slaves had been sent south to Double Trouble the previous year.
76. See Appendix 2 for further accounts of the wedding.

1864

A new year! How will it be spent? I hope it may prove the year of years
to me. The Federal army occupy our town now. They came Christmas
Day.[1]

The Reading Class met here this evening. During the six months that
we have attended it, many changes have taken place. Mrs. Maxwell, our
president, has gone to Ohio to her relations, left her husband fighting
for the C. S. and she [is] now under the protection of the U. S.[2] I glory
more and more each day that I am a rebel and I hope always to be one.
Mary Wycough has become the wife of a Methodist preacher. I incurred
her displeasure by objecting to the match and so missed an invitation to
the wedding.[3] Mr. Bulkley is dead. Miss Sarah Perrin is confined to her
bed; it is very doubtful if she ever recovers. The class is now limited to
four houses an[d] seven members, as Sarah is now at Grand Glaize with
Cousins Preston and Rilla.

I want this year to be one of constant improvement to me. I will soon
be seventeen. I feel that I am backsliding from my God, and the feeling
causes me no pain in comparison with what I expected to feel. Oh, for
an humble and contrite heart, a heart from sin set free, for it is sin that
is separating me from Jesus, drawing me from heaven, down I dare not
think where. I can now feel my utter inability to change my own heart,
but I have His word and read His promise, "For neither death, nor life,

---

1. Col. R. R. Livingston's 1st Nebraska Cavalry, 11th Missouri Cavalry, and 2nd
Missouri Artillery had surprised Confederate soldiers celebrating at a Batesville
Christmas party. Mobley, *Making Sense of the Civil War in Batesville-Jacksonport and
Northeast Arkansas*, 147.

2. A later report says that Mrs. Maxwell traveled to Virginia to visit her husband,
a Federal prisoner. L. Maxfield, "Lucretia Noland Maxfield Journal," Aug. 15, 1864.

3. Mary Wycough was twenty, whereas Mr. Shepherd was forty-three and not
popular with Mary's set. Ibid.

nor angels nor principalities, nor powers, nor things present, nor things to come, nor height, nor depth, nor any other creature shall be able to separate us from the love of God, which is Christ Jesus our Lord."

JANUARY 4TH

The weather is extremely cold. Thursday, the last day of 1863, it snowed, and New Year's day the thermometer was 15 degrees below zero: the coldest weather ever known here. What a fine time we would have had if the Yankees had not come, for Will Maxfield promised the first snow to make a sleigh and take all our girls sleigh riding. But the Feds are here and Will is paroled to report daily, and all we can do is hover over the fire and wish them at the North Pole, for every time they come it turns cold.

I am troubled because I have no way to make money [out] of them. We would take boarders, but none have applied. To some people it is a harvest to have the Federal army here but it is loss to us. They have burnt the fence[4] and turned the stock on Mama's peach trees that she labored so hard to set out. But we were never intended to be rich, for nothing that we have ever undertaken proved profitable. But probably

---

4. This was the picket fence separating the Byers home from the Federal camp occupying the other half of the block. A century later Mary's son Ernest Neill recalled visiting the site of the Federal campground next to his mother's home:

When I was a boy I used to pick up unfired bullets, minie balls they were called, on the ground. The cartridge used in the muzzle-loading rifles was a sharp-nosed bullet like [in] a present-day cartridge, with its butt end hollowed out somewhat so powder would occupy it. Attached to that was a waxed-paper sort of bag containing the powder, the whole thing making a cartridge.

The gun was loaded by tearing off the paper from the end of the cartridge where the powder was and ramming the cartridge down the barrel. My supposition as to why so many bullets were found there was that, in handling the cartridges, the paper end containing the powder became torn and the powder wasted; the bullet was then of no use and was discarded.

Ernest Neill to Neill Phillips, Jan. 24, 1962.

prosperity would harden our hearts, and we have always had enough to eat and wear, and that is as much as anyone can use.

I want to see Sarah very much, but she cannot get home now. She was never away from home so long, six weeks. I believe I love her better than I do Ella. She, poor child, I'm afraid will never love me much. I have to scold her so much lately. She has such a habit of exaggerating everything she relates of which I am trying to break her, and my temper is so fierce and I have so little charity that I do not reprove her in a gentle manner.

Sarah and I used to quarrel, but during the last two years we have gotten along very amicably, but she and Ella jar constantly. Usually Ella and I get along very well, for although she quarrels with the other children she very rarely does with me. I believe she is crying now because of my rough reproof. Oh! God give me a more compassionate spirit for the weaknesses of others! For I want them to love me and think they will never do unless I am worthy of it.

JANUARY 5TH

The more I resolve to do better, the worse I do. Housework is my abomination, and since the weather has been so cold I have neglected the house sadly. Mamma has been in the kitchen as Leanna's baby is but three weeks old today. This morning I was grunting about hating to clean it and Mama offered to do it. I consented. After she had finished she asked if I was not ashamed of myself to let her clean a room for me to sit down in when I knew she had so much to do. I was ashamed, but I was so glad to get rid of cleaning the house that I never thought of her. Mrs. Sherwood was right when she said that self was the idol necessary to be dethroned before we could worship our Lord as we should. I can only say with the poet: "The dearest idol I have known / What e'er that idol be / Help me to cast it from thy throne / And worship only thee."[5]

I am afraid I shall never subdue the old Adam. He is continually breaking out.

---

5. From "Walking with God," in William Cowper, *Olney Hymns* (1779).

Mr. Pierson,[6] our preacher, and Lutie and Mary Case were here this evening. I had a snowball with Mr. P. He is not a talented man, but a good one I think and a pleasant one.

FEBRUARY 28TH

This is Sarah's birthday: Nineteen! It scarcely seems possible, she very small and childlike but rather self-willed.

We now have Cousins Henry, Rilla, and Byers here, and I cannot tell how long they will stay. It is very uncomfortable to have them for we have so little house room, and then Cousin Henry is so despiseable that I have the most contempt for him than any man I ever saw. He has no mind for anything except money and the gratification of his appetite. I never saw a man eat so much. He has eaten enough today for an ordinary man three days. I am fearful lest he become sick here that I wouldn't have happen for anything for he can out-grunt anybody. Cousin Rilla, Sarah, and Will[ie] still have the chills. Henry let out last night what brought him here. He has come in [through] the Federal lines to escape the conscript, for the Confederate Congress has annulled the bill for substitutes. I wish they would conscript him. He was in the service about three months and has hired two substitutes, but both have gone to the Feds. We have had no open quarrel, but there is continual sparring. If it was not for Cousin Rilla, Mama would soon have him leave. I never saw any person with the audacity that he has, coming without an invitation when he knows that we are dependent upon Uncle William, who is daily growing more feeble and the Federals are gradually stripping him of all he possesses. When I think of all his meanness and imposition and how he speaks of Uncle William, I am surprised that I can treat him with civility. For Mama's sake I try, for if we make them mad, he will injure us all in his power. He would scruple to do nothing. Carroll Wood would give him but his just desserts if he should [give] him a cowhiding, for he has made the foulest aspersions on Nannie's character, and many who are strangers to Nannie's

---

6. Rev. Mortimer B. Pearson, Methodist Episcopal Church, South.

wild impulses and love of admiration really believe there was something criminal in her intercourse with Col. Shelby. He began by insinuations and as an evil seed will always take root he gradually spread the conviction throughout the country and Nannie's fair name sacrificed to gratify a love of revenge for which he thought he was justified on account of the advantage gained over him in their quarrels.

I have been in no Christian mood today. I have not been to church this year. There is no service except that by the chaplains and that I will not attend. I heard one preach Miss Sarah Perrin's funeral, but that was an extreme case or I would not have been there. John Miniken was killed in a fight between Rutherford and a Fed Scout.[7]

MARCH 1ST

I don't know what we are to do, for Henry Smith seems determined to live here, and we all despise him more and more each day. I wish I was more like Puss Smith in one particular, that I could live in the house with and never speak or take any notice of him whatever.

None of the girls have been here since he came except to the Reading Class, nor will they come for they all despise him. Cousin Annie stays away on his account, and besides we have no room for her so long as he intrudes himself. The Federal officers will not extend to Mama that protection with him here that they would were we alone. Ma is going to ask Uncle William what she must do, and if it will not offend him she will tell him he must find another boarding place if he intends staying here long, but he is one of those sneaking characters who evade a direct question and yet catechize others freely. I expect nothing else but he and I will have a quarrel before long, and I will tell him that his room would be better than his company for it has been preying on my mind for ten days now and I can contain but a little longer. Only for Cousin Rilla's sake have I forborne so long. He calls all these poor, low, tired suggins[8] liars whenever it suits him, and twice since he has been

---

7. The skirmish at Waugh's Farm; see Appendix 4.
8. People of low class, here used affectionately.

here has he openly doubted my word. Poor Papa opposed Cousin Rilla's marriage, and had he known how much trouble it was destined to bring upon his family he would have opposed it more strenuously. If Pa had lived I should have been a different girl. I could now have boasted an education, the best a northern college could give.[9]

We had a letter from Auntie.[10] They all insist upon our coming north. I expect we will be compelled to go before the war is over, for conditions here are daily growing worse, but I believe if Henry Smith was away I could stand all other trouble better. How glad and grateful I am that I was not bound to John, for he was a Smith, and when that is said all's said that is disagreeable. John came home after Little Rock fell, got in a fracas with Henry Egner, and shot a man named Taylor, a cousin to Turpin, who was murdered so foully in prison by the Federals, and fled the country. At last accounts he was in St. Louis.

MARCH 6TH

Wednesday the hired boy of Uncle William's came in, in the ox wagon, bringing me a note from Cousin Annie. The boy got me a pass—I had intended to stay two weeks, and tomorrow we were to go up to Mrs. Fairchild's, but Friday Mr. Kennard sent me word that his father was sick with the measles and he wished me to come in and assist him in the school, so my plans were changed, and yesterday (Saturday) Cousin Annie and I went to Mrs. Fairchild's and returned this evening. What a delightful place it is to visit! They are [the] happiest pair I know. They have been married about twenty-two years, yet are as fond of one another's company as they were during the honeymoon. They are very hospitable.

Tomorrow I commence school teaching. I do not expect to like it very much, yet I need money badly, and Mr. Kennard promises me $25 per month. I am not as well qualified as I would wish to be before com-

---

9. Mary never did attend college, but she would send all her children, which was unusual in those times.

10. Her mother's sister, Ensey, living in Ohio, probably near Xenia.

mencing to teach the young idea how to shoot, but here I will have only
the primary department. I expect I shall have to pursue this occupation
for a livelihood, for Uncle William's health is very poor. I will need a
large stock of patience I know. Sarah went home with Cousin Annie;
when Mr. Harpham gave her the pass, he said that the next time she
wanted one she must take the oath; several ladies took it yesterday.[11]

MARCH 7TH

My first day at school-teaching passed very pleasantly. The children
behaved well. I do not want to whip them. Lute was up awhile tonight.
She was much surprised that I should teach school. There is a ball, or
as the ticket expresses it, a "Complimentary Soiree" at "the Exchange
Hotel," tonight, the third that the Feds have given.

Three steamboats are at the landing. The cotton speculators now have
an opportunity of sending off their cotton. Eighty bales were burned at
Jacksonport yesterday. I wish Cousin Henry was going on one of them
for [he] is hardly endurable, with his meanness and his gluttony. If he
could read a few pages of you, old Journal, I don't suppose he would
trouble us with his company long. I wish he could; I know we must
make him mad before he leaves, and the quicker over with the better.
Mama had letters from Aunt Ensey and Will Neal today; the latter is
Aide-de-Camp of someone stationed at Vicksburg. She answered them
this evening.

MARCH 8TH

Nine years today since Papa died! Nine years of mingled joy and sorrow. Nine years has Uncle William been faithful to the trust reposed in

---

11. After the fall of Little Rock and the almost complete occupation and subjuga-
tion of northeastern Arkansas, all citizens were expected to take the loyalty oath to
the Union in order to obtain amnesty and to go on with normal life. Many Confederate sympathizers utterly refused to sign the oath. Reuben Harpham was a Unionist and tailor who by 1864 was county clerk. He had daughters about the ages of
Mary and her friends, who seem to have treated them coolly.

him by his dying brother. He has shielded us from every ill that was in his power. Sarah and I are both grown now, and Uncle's health is now failing. I fear that he will never be well again. We must try and support ourselves. This would not be such a task if we were free from all burdens, but Henry Smith, he is the meanest man, the biggest liar, the greatest scoundrel that ever crossed my path, and I am grieved to say it. Cousin Rilla has not lived all these years with him without being contaminated. She gave Ma a bedstead more than a year ago when she was going to buy one and now has taken it away from her. She has stooped to a *lie!* Yes! She has lived with him until her mind and soul have become warped. The higher pursuits of life have become distasteful to her, at least when he is present. When he is away, she is pleasant and obliging. Never were people imposed upon as we have been. Between them and the negroes I cannot see how Ma is to live; they are worrying her life out of her. I hope they will leave and I may never more behold them. Henry told that what he spent while living at Uncle's would have supported them two years. He allows nothing for the inconvenience he puts people to. O! when I think of him I wonder how I hold my tongue! I have forborne for Cousin Rilla's sake, but now I have found out her duplicity, I care nothing for her, but for Uncle's sake I will bear it a little longer if I can. He has become so dictatorial I don't see how I can. There is no happiness here now. Our home, which I used to think the happiest in the world, can be scarcely endured. Oh! God, deliver us!

I don't speak irreverently, for I am powerless; in Him alone rests my strength. I cannot pray the clause, "Forgive us our trespasses, as we forgive those who trespass against us," without a shudder, for I cannot yet forgive Henry Smith, and if we come to want, I shall blame him for bringing it six months sooner, for I believe it is his intention to stay here until he uses the last thing we have up. "The blood-sucker," he is indeed "A bloody and deceitful man," but I grow more furious as I proceed. I don't expect he will give me time to put on my clothes before he will be in in the morning giving me the benefit of his *delightful long-sought-for* company.

Will Maxfield was up to see me tonight. I like him much better than I used to; he is *southern*, [even] if he has taken the oath. Now an order is issued that every man must take the oath of the President's amnesty proclamation and vote at the coming election or be treated as an enemy, an alien! Our poor country, to what are you reduced? The inhabitants of Batesville are the lowest, the most deprived of creation, the so-called inhabitants, but I would call them squatters, "*the refugees.*"

MARCH 9TH

It has rained steadily all day, so we could have no school. I have finished several pieces of work that had been commenced sometime and had a quarrel with Henry Smith. It originated in my speaking of the law of the Confederate Congress respecting the taxation of the money. He denounced the government for everything mean and, as he generally does, wound up about Missourians jayhawking. This is his standby, for in an argument I always have the best of it, for he has not the mind to prove anything conclusively by argument. He knows too that I do not approve of that any more than he does, and when he gets on that strain I will stop merely to get rid of his sing-song repetitions. If I ever marry, it must be to a man with a mind above dollars and cents, and a brave man, too, for I am disgusted with cowards. I said yesterday that I hoped the Feds would draft every man who goes within their lines for protection from the conscript. It made him mad in a minute, and tonight I remarked that it was a great oversight in the government not to have made him Secretary of War. But I begin to despise myself for my petty meanness. He is too contemptible to notice if he would not force himself upon your attention, and I have always made it a rule to be second best at nothing that I attempt.

MARCH 11TH

Today I did not succeed so well at school, for the novelty of the new teacher has worn off, and the children tried my patience sadly. I struck three of them, but they only laughed, and I am not dignified enough for a teacher, for I would laugh and then they think they may do as they please.

Tomorrow it will be one year since the review and prize drill of the

Missouri troops camped over the river. Oh, what a pleasant day that was, the ride on the bright sunny morning, the gay officers, and then the first dinner in camp, the brilliant speeches, the witty retorts, then the races. It was a day long to be remembered. I formed some acquaintances that day to whom I am indebted for many pleasant hours since. But so many changes have taken place since then. "Smiles have been given, tears have been wept." "Friends have been scattered like roses in bloom, some at the bridal, some at the tomb."[12]

MARCH 12TH

This morning I expected to call on Fannie Goodwin and return the commentary on Job and get one on Peter, but I felt too indolent.

This evening Mrs. Aikin came up, and Vene, Lute, and Mary. Tonight Will Maxfield came up. He gave me a graphic description of the escape of Gen. Morgan from Columbus. Some of his escapes were very narrow.[13]

Henry is so disgusting; he always talks and shows off his affection for his family when there is company present. Tonight he lay on the sofa holding and kissing Byers. I intend to tell him of it.

Tomorrow is Sunday; I wish I could go to church, but I have said that I would not hear a Federal preach, and I won't when I can possibly avoid it.

MARCH 13TH

Today I went to Bible class. I miss church so much. The long mornings pass slowly away, and I make little or no improvement in spiritual grace. I am not going on from regeneration to justification, from justification to sanctification. My trials are beginning, but instead of rejoicing in tribulation, I repine or rebel. I will try to be patient, but Henry

---

12. From "Joys That We've Tasted" (1843), a popular song by F. D. Benteen.

13. On November 26, 1863, Brig. Gen. John Hunt Morgan and his officers had tunneled out of the Federal prison at Columbus, Ohio. Stewart Sifakis, *Who Was Who in the Civil War* (New York: Facts on File, 1988), 457.

Smith would make discord in Eden, I fear, for there is a great deal of
the serpent in his composition. Three weeks since he came and no more
towards departure. I am wearied out. I will now have to bear on and on
until I can bear no more, then the explosion will come, for he will be
like the negroes: will not leave until he is driven off. Ma has been trying
to get the negroes for a week. I think probably she will succeed in getting Purnell conscripted.

My mind will not dwell on spiritual things long but returns to the
carnal and dwells on poverty and the accompanying sisters vice and
crime.

MARCH 14TH

There was no school this evening owing to the death of one of the
scholars, one of the numerous "refugees." Tonight a Federal officer, Maj.
Pace[14] of the 11th Missouri Cav., called to get board. Ma has concluded
to take him if they can agree on the terms. I don't think either Henry or
Rilla fancy it.

MARCH 15TH

The Federals are still here, and this month is half gone. In February I
said I felt it in my bones that there would not be one here by April. Our
boarder is as pleasant as a Fed can be, but he thinks my prejudices are
too strong to allow me to enjoy myself as much as I might. He goes on
a scout after rebels tomorrow; I hope George Rutherford will "gobble"
him up.

Will sent me a can of Pine Apple today, and came tonight when he,
Cousin Henry, and I tried to impress it on Maj. Pace's mind what a
cautious yet daring leader Rutherford was. Sarah has not yet returned.
Cousin Annie and Mrs. Cullins crossed the river with clothes for soldiers Saturday.

---

14. Maj. Lewis C. Pace, USA.

MARCH 16TH

I am mad again tonight. Henry Smith would worry a great deal better person than I am mad. Maj. Pace went on a scout today after Rutherford.[15] This evening Mama had another application for board, from a Lieut. Was[h]ington. The house is so small that we will be crowded, but we must have money. I wish they were gone, every rag of them. This was a pleasant place for officers to board, and if we were alone we would make it so again. I was unloading myself of a little of the hate and contempt that has accumulated when Mama said, "Maybe a better day would come." I replied that I wished it would dawn soon. The cloud is still dark, black, and will be as long as Henry Smith stays. I know he has no idea of leaving, for he had eight loads of wood hauled, costing him $2 1/2. He will think that would pay all their board one month.

I have never met a Federal officer that I would not rather have in my house then Henry Smith. He wants my embroidered slippers, but he'll not get them.

MARCH 18TH

I fear I will never be such a sincere heartfelt Christian as Mama. She never talks of religion; she acts it every day, every hour of her life. I may be farther famed, my deeds and charity louder, but never so truly charitable. She gave evidence of it tonight in speaking of the negroes who have become so insolent and idle that it is impossible to bear with them longer. Tonight, Mama told Leanna she would give her until Monday to make up her mind to go and go now, or stay and go to work as she must if she remained. I do not know what they will do: go, I hope, for though I am unused to work, know scarcely anything about it, yet if they leave we will have provision enough to do us this year. Then

---

15. The scout led by Maj. Pace went hard after Rutherford, traveling 206 miles and capturing six Confederates. U.S. War Department, *War of the Rebellion*, ser. 1, 34: 640–41. The contrast between the civilized banter at his boarding with the Byers and the serious business of his scouting is striking.

Cousins Henry and Rilla will leave, too. I think there will be no one to wait on them, for I won't. Mama hates to see them leave, not for herself nor us but for their own sakes, for they must suffer. Most anyone wouldn't care how much they suffered after treating her as they have, but the idol self seems completely cast down from the throne, and Jesus reigns alone. Much repentance is needed before I reach her standard.

MARCH 22ND

A new era in our lives. We have now entered into a real workaday life. The negroes have taken advantage of the President's Emancipation Proclamation and departed. We are all chief cooks and bottle washers. Maj. Pace came this evening, and as I invited him in the kitchen to supper told him of it. He expressed his sorrow for he wished them to cook, for he is very anxious to board here. We will still keep him, Mama and Cousin Rilla cleaned up the kitchen nicely. It is really a pleasant room with a lounge in it; it reminds me of a story of Mrs. Sherwood's, "Rich in the kitchen, Poor in the parlor." We are in a pecuniary point of view from $1500 to $2000 poorer tonight then we were this morning. That is valuing negroes as they were in 1860, but as they are valued in 1864, their food and clothing, better off, and then are rid of their doctors' bills and insolence. The last had become unbearable. Now if the second family were off we would be alone and lonesome. Maj. Pace and I quarrel, just as Lieut. Crabtree and I did.

MARCH 24TH

O! I have been mad tonight. I came home in the rain to meet that old major at the gate. Last night at supper I was frying batter cakes, and this evening he asked why I was not at the stove, then threw back his head and with an exulting laugh remarked, "Ah! You southern ladies have to come down to the work, ha, ha, ha." From that we got on the slave question and the system of government of the aristocracy. One word led to another until I became angry. "Yes," he said, "Under your government, no widow's son can hold office, none except those who have the almighty nigger or broad acres of land or the son of some aristocratical jackass." I replied, for I had now reached the boiling point, "We are accustomed to having gentlemen speak in a respectful manner in our presence," and a good deal more in the same way. I could have knocked him down. I used to think Nature made a mistake when I was created a girl, and now I know it. I should have been dignified, coldly polite, excruciatingly polite, but my warm southern nature will not permit me. I wish I was womanly, dependent; there is something so lovely about a dependent woman whose dignity, whose true womanhood is her protection. Maj. Pace apologized several time[s] until I told him to forget it and I would, but I never will. He is a Northern Methodist preacher, a perfect mono-maniac on the subject of slavery, but I must control my temper and my tongue, for we are now in their power, and it is absolutely necessary that we have boarders.

MARCH 29TH

11 o'clock. Will has spent the evening with me and promises to send me a pair of squirrels. We are excellent friends. He spends two or three evenings of every week here. Sarah has gone to Grand Glaize again with Cousin Annie to see Preston. I fear the girls will get in some trouble about *passes,* for the[y] borrow them from smaller children, for none over fifteen can obtain a pass without taking the oath. I get along tolerably well teaching school. The children are rather unruly, but I must be firm. It is tiresome, and since we have been doing our own work, more so, for I scarcely get through at home before it is school time. I am on my feet so much that at night I am very tired.

Cousin Henry bought a turkey yesterday and today I offended him by not doing as he wished about taking it to the prisoners, but if he wants turkey messages carried he m[a]y carry them. I will carry the provisions to Capt. Hancock. I give it to Henry every opportunity, and in a war of words I have decidedly the advantage.

MARCH 31ST

One year ago today I went to a review of Gen. Marmaduke's division. Emma Weaver was then flying around with Confederate officers, with three stars on her collar. "Little Weaver" was a toast. Mounted on Rebel Redd, Oliver's present, armed with sword, pistol, and bugle. Tonight she gives a "little dance," a "select party" for the benefit of Uncle Sam's noble nephews, for according to Dr. McClelland, she is the only lady worthy of attention. I cannot accept the very kind invitation; the night is too wet.

Last Saturday, Maj. Pace brought a beautiful flag which had been presented to him by the ladies of St. Joseph [Missouri] and asked me to mend it for him. I did so on condition that he obtained me passes through the lines when I wished them. He seems anxious to gratify me for he only returned from a forage scout last night, and this morning left again to escort the commissary wagons from the boat at Paroquet Bluff.[16] But before leaving, he went to the Provost Marshal's and made arrangements for me to get a pass to go to Uncle's Saturday. Mama was out yesterday. Uncle William said he was lonesome to see me and would send for me Saturday. I have been there so much this winter, and if it was not for the school would be there most of the time now. The girls— Puss, Eliza, Vene, Sarah, and Cousin Ann—are having such a nice time. Betty and Vene have gone again to Rutherford's camps. The other girls are engaged in smuggling something to our boys. If the Federals only knew of the dispatches that fly as if on the wings of the morning, they would double their vigilance, but the women would outwit them, for they do everything now. The men have all taken the oath and voted for the new government.

I am becoming wicked I fear. I despise the term backslide, or I might say I had fallen from grace, but I am in hopes not yet. The question, "Am I prepared to die?" strikes me very forcibly. I fear not. I possess none of the Christian virtues, unless it is faith. My charity cannot be found nor my humility, and although every day it is, "Forgive us our trespasses as we forgive those who trespass against us," yet I always feel delighted when I am tormenting Henry.

---

16. This bluff is on the right bank of the Black River, two miles northwest of Jacksonport. The name derives from the many parakeet (paroquet) birds found there, a nuisance to the farmers. Robert Craig, "Berkeley Bluff and Paroquet," *Independence County Chronicle* 51, no. 2 (July 2010): 5.

APRIL 4TH

I returned from Aunt Emma's this morning. The rain prevented me from coming yesterday. Maj. Pace's pass carried me through. I am going to be ever so good and get another. Tonight we talked very pleasantly about the war. I let him say what he pleases, and he is very careful not to say anything which could offend me. I think I made him respect me a little more by the manner I talked to him in our little "difficulty." He treats me with due deference.

Sarah and Cousin Annie have not come yet. Uncle William is getting uneasy about them. I think they are enjoying themselves and waiting for clear weather. The Federal papers give accounts of several disasters lately. The attempt on Richmond was an entire failure. Uncle William's mind dwells on the war continually. He reads everything relative to the war and watches the movements of both armies. Maj. Pace kindly let him have late papers that came by the mail. Tonight puts me in mind of old times: newspapers, books, and periodicals lying around, or to speak more correctly, all the family gathered around the little table, each with a paper, eagerly devouring the contents.

Cousin Henry is now plotting to separate our family from Uncle's. Cousin Rilla is lending her aid. Last summer he attempted it but, as he did not have her active cooperation, failed. By now she has become angry with us and forgetting the months she has remained under Mama's roof, partaking of her hospitality, sometimes grudging I must confess, and as soon as Cousin Annie comes home she's going out there to set Uncle by the ears again. It is my nightly prayer that God will deliver us from them, for in this instance we are powerless.

APRIL 6TH

This evening Mr. Kennard had a spasm caused by the bone pressing on the brain. I taught alone. I am weary, dull, sleepy. I want the negroes back. It is no fun to do the work week after week and have the *enlivening* prospect of having to do so all your life. I blame Henry Smith for it a great deal, and then I thought if the negroes were gone he would pack up and leave, but he is here for the summer, I plainly see, unless Mama will make him mad by telling him that she cannot keep them longer. I have offended them, how I do not know, but they barely speak. I am very tired working for them. We would have one third less to do if they would only remove the curse that has been hanging over us since last October. We must have trouble of some kind so long as we are inhabitants of Earth, and probably this is the lightest the Almighty could inflict upon us, but this is not the kind which chasteneth in order to purify but renders more evil, wicked.

Will Maxfield sent me a beautiful pair of pet squirrels this evening by Cousin Henry. I am going to call them, "Pet Frisky," and "Diogenes."

I believe these Federals are going to remain here all summer. Two transports and a gunboat were up three days ago and took off all our prisoners confined in the court house.

APRIL 8TH

Tonight we went to Mrs. Smith's. I thought of John more tonight than I have for a long time, thought of him not as the murderer, the exile from his home, but as he was last summer, when he came home and I had not answered his letters. It was at a soiree at his home; Dr. Austin had gone with me. Many were there; gay and lively we all were. John had spoken to me about my "shameful neglect" as he termed it. I told him the true reason I had not written: he had broken a solemn promise made me not to drink. That night he begged forgiveness for that breach and renewed his promise, by an oath he would, but I would not permit him. I would not have him perjure himself. He talked long and earnestly and, fickle boy that he is, he felt it then. Poor boy! His mother heard he was coming home. I hope he will not, for much as I would like to see him and persuade him to return to his regiment, I do not want him for his mother's sake to come here, where no one can extend him the hand of friendship.

Mr. and Mrs. Shepherd[17] came up yesterday.

---

17. Mary Wycough Shepherd and the Reverend Shepherd.

APRIL 12TH

This is the anniversary of a pleasant day to me. This day began very sorrowfully. Last night I sat up with Em Wycough's children, who have the measles.[18] At nine as I was going to school I stopped and saw Eddie die. Poor mother! Tomorrow her firstborn will be laid in the grave. The spirit has returned to God who gave it. Nothing left but the remembrance of his sweet childish ways, of the ceaseless prattle.

Will sent me a new book, "Woman in White," a strange, fanciful, interesting story.[19] I am absorbed in it. The old passion has come back. I am restless to finish my book, but tired. Nature asserts her claims and demands that I seek repose in sleep. Marian Holcombe is a noble woman. She says, "A woman condemned to patience, propriety, and petticoats for life." I like that book. Mr. Fairlie wishes a reform in children, thinks Nature's only idea was the formation of a ceaseless noise machine. But will I ever become so absorbed in fiction as to forget our private troubles, for my contempt for Henry to slumber, for my sense of injury received from Rilla to heal, for my hatred for that Missouri 11th band to cool, tonight it is gayer and livelier than ever because of the presence of the "*Batesville belles*" at Col. Ward's headquarters.

APRIL 14TH

My book is finished! I can take some interest in housework, in other reading, have some time for sewing, which I have not had since Monday, when I commenced the interesting work. All my old enthusiasm returned. I became absorbed.

This morning little Lutie Wycough died, two children within two days. It is said all have crosses to bear, each person's is that which will prove most beneficial to him. Will the loss of his two children stop

18. Samuel E. "Eddie," age seven, and Sarah L. "Lutie" Wycough, age four, children of M. A. "Dolph" and Emma Bevens Wycough, were among the many to die of measles during the war.

19. *Woman in White* (1860), one of the first mystery stories, was a hugely popular novel by English author Wilkie Collins (1824–89).

Dolph's headlong gallop to perdition? If so, his children will not have died in vain.

Yesterday Sally Allen[20] told me she was going to bring Capt. Williams up to see me, by his own and oft-repeated request. I told her this morning I would rather she would not, as I did not wish to form any acquaintances among the Federals, but from her reply I expected them tonight. They did not come; I am glad of it if they do not intend coming at all, sorry if it is their intention to come some other time. For tonight for once the house was rid of Henry. Rilla always makes it convenient to be undressing Byers in here about the time I am expecting company. Tonight she kept him in here as long as possible in his nightdress, but finding that, try as she might, she could not annoy me in that way tonight, she finally put him to bed. I know as Capt. W. did not come tonight, when he does come I will have to submit to some mortification from these insolent intruders, for I can call them nothing else, in our home.

I wish Ma would tell them to get another boarding place. I have tried for six weeks to prevail on her to do so, but it only wounds her to have me speak to her of it. She always say[s] she hates to. I wish it was my house for a week, I [would] tell them to leave and kick their trumpery out after them.

APRIL 15TH

This morning I arose with the determination of telling Henry that he would be obliged to shift quarters, but did not have an opportunity of doing so until this evening, when my mind was so engrossed with the thoughts of Price defeating Steele at Rockport and of the evacuation of our town that everything else was banished.[21] Sunday morning, the Missouri 11th [and] Nebraska 1st leave for Jacksonport where *they say*

---

20. Probably the fourteen-year-old daughter of Dr. John F. Allen.

21. Mary evidently refers to the Camden Expedition, March 23–May 3. Steele's army would have passed through Rockport, near Malvern. Clements, "Camden Expedition."

they are going to establish a post. The Arkansas 4th, commanded by Col. Stevens, remains here.[22]

After supper, having composed myself for reading, I was interrupted by Will. He called to take me to Mrs. Perrin's, that lady having invited "the girls" to come around some evening and get acquainted with her boarders. On Wednesday, the Reading Class met and deputized Sarah and Vene to wait on Mrs. Perrin and inform her that we would go nowhere that we would be expected to meet Federals, and tonight we went, thinking after that notice that she would say nothing of our intention to her boarders, but false hope! She told, and Lieut. Santee was there, whether at her invitation I am not able to say, but as he is said to be a very quiet, unobtrusive man, I expect it was. Lute and I were talking very busily when he came in. I drew myself up, very dignified I thought I was looking, when Lute asked if I had lost any friends lately. Instead of being dignified I was woe-be-gone. Then we both wanting a drink [of water] went out the back door, slipped around the house, and came up here and stayed half an hour. Going back we found the Fed gone, but he returned. Our leaving had not had the desired effect. The Lieut. thought he was in a hotbed of rebels, for we talked secesh strong among ourselves, only addressing him two or three times during the evening, but he heard every word.

---

22. Mary may have been mistaken in the command structure: Lt. Col. John W. Stephens commanded the Eleventh Missouri Cavalry, and Col. Elisha Baxter the Fourth Arkansas Mounted Infantry (USA). "Col. Livingston's command in Independence County was rapidly approaching the same circumstances in which Gen. Curtis found himself during his occupation of Batesville in the early summer of 1862. He had scoured the adjacent counties west of Black River, and his wagon trains were attacked on every expedition. White River between Jacksonport and Batesville was too low for navigation of transports, and the problem of hauling stores from boats at Jacksonport was becoming increasingly difficult. To add to his responsibility, about 500 Union refugee families had come to Batesville for his protection and sustenance." Watson, *Fight and Survive*, 105. As a result, Livingston took 1,400 troops from Batesville to Jacksonport, leaving behind Colonel Baxter and a garrison of 450 men.

This morning I was so sleepy that I could scarcely arise and with haste got the room arranged before Maj. Pace came in to breakfast. We have two boarders now, a Capt. Rouch. Tomorrow they leave for Jacksonport. The Major and I are on very good terms now. He has been trying to prevail upon me to attend the party tonight in honor of their departure, but didn't succeed. He does not know how to take me, asked Sarah if I really meant what I said about the Federals, [if I] was in earnest! He then appealed to Cousin Henry, but as Cousin Henry never can say anything to the point, he told two Feds who came in that he could not keep up with me then. He asked if I would not marry a man of Northern principles if I loved him? "Yes," I replied, "*If I loved him*, but how could I love him? How could I?" He laughed and said he did not know how I could.

At "Reading" we discussed Mrs. Perrin's conduct, inviting us to her house and making appointments with Feds to meet us. After Lute and I left she remarked that, "Miss Mary was as great a rebel as ever." He had perceived it, perceived what every Federal can perceive in five minutes.

Will was up again tonight.

Am I always to be a trial, a heartache to my mother? I have thought she loved me more than the others or that she agreed with me *oftener* than with them. I have always heard that the most troublesome child, the worst one, was the best beloved. This evening Leanna came up while I was at school. When I came in I noticed Ma's face was swollen, and Sarah says, "We have had a visitor." "And you've been crying again," I said to Ma. Then she went out, and after she came back I was asking questions about Leanna. Mama said [I] ought to have remembered how she felt about the negroes. If I could not feel I should not have an utter disregard for the feelings of others. That I, her child, had less respect for her than the nigger. I had really wounded her.

She and I feel so different about them. If I had known she was so much attached to them and would feel their departure so, I should have opposed her ever saying anything to them about leaving. I shall always blame Henry Smith and family as the cause of it, for Mama was so worried about both them and [the] niggers that she must get rid of one, and the niggers were the only ones she could get away. I wish she would make the others leave. She will work, work, and wait on them, and let them stay here, and a pack of lies and their board bill unpaid will be all the return she will get. I wish she would make them leave. I should have done it before now if it had been my house.

APRIL 21ST

Tonight we were at Mrs. Case's, but the evenings are very dull. There was considerable laughing, but the conversation lagged. Last summer when there were as many gentlemen as ladies, the evenings passed away very pleasantly, with music and conversation. Conversation with gentlemen is more lively and more improving than girls. Unless as in our Reading we are employed with reading and work, we will get in the saddest habit of all, that of gossiping.

APRIL 25TH, MONDAY NIGHT

Saturday, I went to Aunt Emma's, afterward to Mrs. Fairchild's. It was raining. We were riding fast when my saddle, which was girted loosely, turned, and down I came on my face in the sand. Lelia ran over me, but I was not hurt. Not waiting to tighten the saddle, I mounted again and started off in a gallop. Just as I got to the gate, the saddle turned backward and there I fell on my head. From this fall I had the headache for twenty-four hours. If it had been rocks instead of sand I would never have risen. We went home in the rain, when I made the old mare gallop all the way for pitching me off.

This morning I came home to find old Mr. Kennard very sick. Mr. Kennard unable to leave him, I taught today, and this evening dismissed the school until next Monday.

Mama has said nothing to Henry yet, not even attempted to get out to see Uncle William. I have been trying for eight weeks to get her to go, for she will do nothing herself towards getting them off. Now Rilla and Byers will be here until doomsday, I reckon. He pretends that he is going to Texas, but I don't believe it, and here Mama will work for them, inconvenience herself, subject herself and us to all kinds of annoyances, and not an effort to get rid of them.

APRIL 29TH

This week has flown by. I have worried several times, "growled," Sarah called it. I am tired doing the work. I wish the Federals would conscript Purnell, then Leanna would come back. The negro has a hard time; she has to wash every day. Mrs. Mo[o]re says [that] if she had her own way, she would come home now, that Purnell is always grumbling because she does not make more money.

Mr. and Mrs. Fairchild have gone to St. Louis. Sue Brearley has run off with Cromwell, a sutler, after selling 200 lbs of sugar and some dishes of Mr. Lyon's. We have long known that she was a woman without principle, without virtue. Carroll Wood proved that beyond a doubt, but to steal from her uncle, go off as mistress of a man who is an entire stranger, is dreadful, awful. She is so ugly that she must expect to be deserted soon. O, woman! Call your pride to your assistance. If you have no respect for relatives, for religion, think of yourself, making yourself a thing to be sneered at, derided by everybody, your name a forbidden word in decent society, entailing upon yourself a lifetime of misery, an eternity of woe. A mighty work is to be done: reclaim the lost, the ruined of society, to one of whom our Savior said, "Go and sin no more." How can anyone fall so low, be a slave of such degrading passions. Sue Brearley did not return my call when she first arrived, and afterward offered me a slight in her uncle's house. I am glad I never visited her. Many suspect Mrs. Lyon of principles as base as Sue's, but not I.

APRIL 30TH

This night one year ago, Dr. Dobbins called here for the first time, accompanied by Mr. Bulkley. It was the beginning of an acquaintance which brought much pleasure. Now Will Maxfield is my only beau, but a very attentive one. He furnishes me with books. I have read more light literature within the last month than in the preceding twelve, but I must stop and read something more solid, for I have already injured my mind and memory. This evening I went to see Lute Maxfield. Vene came down from Mrs. Glenn's,[23] exulting in the knowledge that there were 1000 Confederates across White River. I place no confidence whatever in it. Puss and Eliza took the oath to obtain passes to go out to see Will McGuire, who has returned from McRae's[24] camps to make arrangements for a trip south to Price. Will could not swallow the "Amnesty" oath, so he decamped. Will Denton was killed last Friday, April 23rd.[25] This ought to bring Elvira to her senses, a brother-in-law, now a brother killed, and she attending Federal balls, giving an egg-nogg party to which the bluecoats were invited. It is a shame, a disgrace to Batesville that the girls will act so.

MAY IST, SUNDAY MORNING

I determined this day to have a self-examination to review my past feelings, my present ones, and what a falling away, what a long list of delinquencies might be charged to me. Our Bible lesson (Peter I) spoke of the Christian graces, that we must add to faith, virtue; to virtue, knowledge; to knowledge, temperance; to temperance, patience; to patience, godliness; to godliness, brotherly kindness; to brotherly kindness, charity. That is, all these things abound in us; we will not be barren nor unfruitful in Jesus Christ.

Mr. Hickison came up to see Mr. Kennard, and Mrs. K. heard the lesson. She did not press it home to us as he would have done, so we would appear blind as those who have forgotten that they had been purged from their sins. The Sabbath is the best of divine institutions.

---

23. W. W. Glenn was a wealthy landowner in Washington Township. He had children around the same age as Mary and her friends, whom they visited occasionally. The Glenns would own Catalpa Hall for a time after the war.

24. Brig. Gen. Dandridge McRae, CSA.

25. A member of the "Pop-Corn Company," Will Denton was said to have died at the action at Fitzhugh's Woods near Augusta, but that engagement occurred on April 1.

Without it, where would we be, floating down the river of life, into the ocean of eternity without any stopping place where we might receive the necessaries for such a voyage. "Remember the Sabbath, to keep it holy." Tonight Will M. came to supper. We had a pleasant evening, as we always do if they leave us to ourselves. Then we generally talk of such books, papers, histories as we have read, of the Christian religion and its application to wants of man. None of the family appear to take any interest in such conversation and when they are all here, some reading, others playing, others listening, I cannot talk well; neither can he. Sarah has just been speaking to me of the loud tone in which I speak. I often wish for the soft, low voice, that sweet attribute [of] woman, but, alas, not such [a] masculine one as I [have].

MAY 2ND

This morning Ma initiated me in the mysteries of washing, or, more properly, introduced me to the wash tub. I got along well but do not like it on account of my hands. My hand[s] will not be ladylike. This evening I visited Lizzie Goodwin and Mrs. Allen. The latter although very quiet in her manners is an incessant talker. It is a nice place to visit. I saw Leanna today; she looks worn out, thin. Purnell will prove a hard taskmaster.

MAY 4TH

This morning I attempted to go to Aunt Emma's but failed in getting a horse. I have been out of school for nearly two weeks and have not been there. Tonight it is believed Mr. Kennard will die. I cannot realize that it is so. Death seems like some far-off monster whom we were all using precautions to keep at a distance. Although we do not dive into the depths of science in order to find the Elixir, of what strange flights the mind of man is capable. Yet look around us; how commonplace is all.

Bulwer's "Strange Story" was read with dispatch and some interest yesterday.[26] Some time when my mind is more sobered I will re-read

---

26. *Strange Story* (1862) is an occult fantasy by Edward George Bulwer-Lytton (1803–73), a popular English novelist and politician.

it to better advantage, understand what it is that the author wishes to impress upon our minds. Tonight I was trying to bring mine back to sober thought when Lute came in; she and Will have just gone.

When we feel that we are Christian, we feel that we are near death's door, that it is only through the mercy of an all-powerful being that we are saved from instant destruction. But when we forget that we have been purged from our sins, have fallen into the old habit of letting fancy run wild and assisting her in her flight by wild romances, then it is that death rises before us only as a vision that we have seen sometimes during our lives, that must be realized sometime in the future.

MAY 9TH

Mr. Kennard died Thursday, was buried Friday. After the funeral I went home with Cousin Ann and returned yesterday evening, commenced school today. I am very tired of school teaching, wish I could collect what is due me now for I want to make some purchases.

I never feel like writing unless I feel depressed, and tonight I feel unusually so. The girls have spent the evening with us, and it was spent in retailing small gossip, an evening lost, lost forever and leaves a sting behind, for memory goes back to the time Mary Wycough and I were friends before Mary Case had supplanted me in her affections, before her heart was [made] captive by one who has shown himself an enemy to me. I blame him alone, for if the girl would allow me, I would love her as much as ever. Mary! Deceit did not once form a part of your character. It is not your nature. You are only warped to better assimilate with your husband; when you met me you told me you bore me no ill will, that you knew my objections to your union, that you were confident when you met me all would be well, that we had been friends too long for me to back bite you. I looked down into your truthful eyes and believed you. I believe you yet; if aught of distrust of me springs up in your bosom [it] was implanted there by the one whom you have promised, "to love, honor, and obey." If anything there was to my detriment in the letter written to Mary Case, it was dictated by the same one. We speak of tearing a love out, trampling it underfoot, not crushing it, not smothering it, but eradicating it, leaving no traces except on the surface.

Mary Catherine Case (1847–1940), 1866.
Courtesy Independence County Historical Society.

But when this love began years ago, grew with our growth, strengthened
with our strength, there will come much labor, much pain before all is
removed, and the fires of jealousy springing up are the first notice we
have that the old plant has left offspring behind.

MAY 10TH

Today [at] twelve it was raining so I went home with Lute to dinner.
When I came home this evening, my head aching, throbbing, almost
bursting, it was to find Sarah and Cousin Rilla had walked through the
rain and mud to warn Uncle William that the Federals had threatened
his life. Mrs. Smith came up and told Ma his life was not safe until he
took the President's Amnesty oath. Probably not then, but this affords

a pretext for withholding the protection of the United States from him. Sunday, young Ward, only 17, was shot in his father's dooryard. Murder is the watchword, extermination the battle cry.

MAY 22ND

I have been sick, had a light attack of bilious fever. During the time the Feds have gone,[27] a few Southerners have been in.... [entry incomplete]

MAY 31ST

So much has transpired during the last five days I have been too busy to write. Gen. Shelby's brigade has come and gone. Such a happy, happy time, meeting old friends. They came dashing across the bridge Thursday evening, making such a noise everyone thought "Feds." Arkansas 2nd from Yellville, on they came through town, never halting a moment, hurrahing for Jeff Davis, Joe Shelby, the Southern Confederacy, bidding everybody welcome "Shelby's company." Nobody believed but what it was a ruse to throw the people off their guard to get some pretext to burn the town. When they came, they halted at our gate, wheeled, formed into line to wait for the column to come up. Some dismounted, came in, tried to make us believe they were Shelby's men. "Well!" exclaimed one, "Yonder's Old Joe himself. Now will you believe it?" There at the head of the column stood Gen. Shelby, familiarly called, "Old Joe." Then came Maj. Lawrence riding up. What shaking of hands and joyous welcomes all around! They had made forced marches from the Arkansas River, hoping to surprise and capture the garrison at this place. Col. Gordon came presently, then Gus Stevenson, Maj. [Jeremiah] Cravens, Oliver Redd, Barron, Dr. Dobbins, Austin, one after another until twelve o'clock, when arrivals ceased. Some stayed to the supper which we in the hurry and excitement could scarcely cook, some only a few minutes, but

---

27. On May 20 Baxter's garrison and the refugees left for Jacksonport. Mobley, *Making Sense of the Civil War in Batesville-Jacksonport and Northeast Arkansas,* 167.

all so well, so joyous and happy, the happiest evening I remember having ever passed.

After being surrounded six month[s] with Federals, all communication cut off, and then when we least expected it to have all our favorites come, was too much for me to bear and keep my brain cool. During the two days they were here I most truly lived upon excitement, for I neither ate nor slept and was going constantly cooking, for many soldiers came, serving for them, walking, visiting, talking, "and all for the soldiers." It seemed like the days of Auld Lang Syne, only Mr. Bulkley was sadly missed. Dobbins is more frolicsome than ever and just as much in love with Sarah, I think, although [he] stayed the greater portion of the time at Mrs. Smith's. Dr. Austin is as dignified as ever, Gus as lazy, nobody has changed, nothing except our poor little town. Saturday at 11 Theodore Maxfield came up and reported six transports aground at Grand Glaize; at two they were off. We hated sadly to have them go. We were making preparations for a general "smashup" or "shebang" up here. All of our Missouri acquaintances and "our girls" were coming, but "'twas ever thus from childhood's hour" &c.[28] All were gone by five; old Maj. Blackwell and Gus were the last to leave.

I cannot write near all that passed.

JUNE 1ST

Rain, rain, rain. This evening we contemplated a fish-fry and supper on the bayou. It was proposed by Will. None of us cared anything about it, but it would not do not to go, as Will leaves for George Rutherford tomorrow. If we refused he would think it was because no Missourians were here. He is jealous and would not go to Mrs. Smith's the night of the soiree, or "sorry" as he *very* native-like pronounces it. He is touchy on the Missouri question, but he might be satisfied, for during the last six months we have all paid him our court most assiduously. Mrs. Smith compares us to *one rooster, seven pullets.* Monday evening I went to Aunt

---

28. This quote comes from *The Old Curiosity Shop* (1841) by Charles Dickens (1812–70).

Emma's with him, rode his new horse, "Byers." The girls have assigned him to me as my captive, told our friends of the Brigade of my conquest. Maj. Lawrence came up yesterday from Magness (he is quartermaster) to superintend the building of thirty boats for pontoon bridges on White and Black River[s]. The transports had gotten off the bar and down the river before the[y] got down; their forced march all night was for naught.

Major called yesterday evening, but Sarah and I were away. I was sorry, for there was a child's party at Mrs. Kennard's in honor of Nell's eighth birthday. I would have invited him. The supper was excellent, and we enjoyed the evening so much. He would have enjoyed it, too, for he [has] a lively disposition.

The little ones came over here after eight. Puss gave them some music. They had a little dance; at nine we took them home.

Bob Case sent me his photograph.

Night. 11 o'clock. Tonight the young people came up, but it was a dull evening. Will Maxfield, Theodore, Will McGuire were the only gentlemen except Col. Gordon. Lute and Maj. Bob did not come. I think we ought to stop these parties; they are wearisome or I am changed. Last summer I enjoyed them but now I tire of acting all the time. Such foolish conversation: love, matrimony, broken hearts, declines, and all such romantic stuff. A long conversation I had with Dr. Dobbins about John I enjoyed. We were serious, earnest; that I liked, but frivolity, levity, how tired I am of it. We are living to no purpose, life without an aim, in the world and of it, professing Christ yet by our actions denying Him. I must break it off.

These times put me in mind of one year ago. I was younger than now. I feel old in heart and ignorant in mind. John rises before me in all his youth, pride, and beauty, but my blood courses no faster through my veins. I am almost devoid of feeling. I want to feel, know, and enjoy myself with someone; myself, not something artificial.

JUNE 6TH

I had been too busy, too much occupied with company, visiting, for writing. Dr. Austin and Mr. Stevenson returned Thursday. Cousin Annie came in the same day, and since then we have been out or engaged until 12 or 1 o'clock every night. Dr. Dobbins was her[e] Friday night. We went to Mrs. Aikin's, the neutral ground on which the up- and down-town girls meet. The division is greater now than ever since "the down-towns" went with the Feds, we had all the beaux except two, and those talked to Puss and Cousin Ann until the girls' jealousy was fully aroused. We got sour and sneerful looks. We left early and went to Mrs. Smith's, where with the Doctors and Gus we spent two hours more pleasantly than the first of the reading.

Will Maxfield has annoyed me no little, and I have been imprudent and inconsiderate. He took into his head to be angry and jealous at Mrs. Kennard's because I had endeavored to dress myself becomingly—to meet Missourians, as he said so scornfully—that I would do nothing for an Arkansas boy. My wrath was aroused, but I considered his narrow-mindedness, bigotry, and pedantry, and controlled myself and disputed with him, he speaking earnestly, I lightly and rather jocosely, until he became angry; then I grew worse. The attention of the company was drawn upon us when we ceased. After that he took it upon himself to be angry or to have the sulks.

The first time I tried to joke him on indifferent subjects until he recovered his wonted humor, for probably I had not shown quite enough deference for him considering my position and my silent encouragement, but all to no purpose. He was grum, as he expressed it. Next, during our ride he was jealous, uneasy, could not, would not enjoy himself. He went away today. I am not sorry, for though he is a faithful attendant he has really become disagreeable to me, with his bigotry and pedantry. Probably his want of refinement goes as far as anything else. For although I am rough, yet I appreciate refinement and true sensibility.

Will has a loyal heart, and I must be careful and not wound it. For this reason I am glad he is gone for since he has shown his narrow views respecting woman, her rights and privileges, I want to have as little to do with him as possible. I told Cousin Annie Sunday evening if there was anything in him to make a flirtation interesting or even amusing I would give him a good flirt for presuming to be angry because he suspected I looked more approvingly on others than himself. But I could not do it; he never flirted, could not understand the game, it would be painful to him and redound none to my credit. What self-ishness! What egotism! A woman's heart is a strange compound. If Will had been another, how my heart would have leaped at his evidence of attachment!

JUNE 7TH

Sarah made a revelation to me this evening, one I was expecting but not so soon. She engaged herself to Dr. Dobbins last Friday night, just one year from the time he revealed his love. It does not exactly please me, although I have known some time that Sarah loved him more than anyone else. He appears to love her, but these soldiers! How they flirt! Dr. Dobbins said nothing to Mama, nor has Sarah yet told her. This I do not like. The engagement was too sudden; Ma will not approve, I fear, and if he does not return soon, walk straight up, confess his love for her child and ask her consent before she hears of the proposal, much less of the engagement, he may as well walk overboard.

This is my test of him. I like him, yet have not confidence enough in him to give him my little sister.[29] He must ask Mama, and quickly, or I shall distrust him and sow the seeds of distrust in Sarah's bosom. But I feel that nothing will come of it, that there will be a painful scene at home. Mama will be wounded deeply at the want of confidence in her daughter, for I do not believe she suspects that Dobbins is serious. If he acts to suit me, I will try to [win] Mama over to his side, for I have considerable influence with her and will use it all for Sarah's good and happiness. But I feel some trouble approaching, have felt it since I knew of the engagement. Sarah does not love him as I would wish to love the man I expected to marry. I asked if she really believed he was in earnest. She replied that she believed so, but if he was not it would not kill her. Little one, you are on dangerous ground; beware. I hope my prophetic

---

29. Actually, Sarah was two years older than Mary.

fears are groundless.

Old Mrs. Kanice guessed pretty well when she told our fortunes, for Sarah's and Puss's beaux have come and gone and left vows of fidelity behind them. Puss has been engaged for three years to Capt. Duffie of [the] 6th Arkansas. Now, if all signs are true, she favors Maj. Cravens. The fortune teller said she would be married in six weeks but I think she meant engaged. I can find out if this is true in a few days and why the long engagement is broken off. I must go and stay with Lute one night this week and ascertain if the Major [Lawrence] left her free. I expect not; she has not been heart-free for some time. Shelby's Brigade is making sad havoc of the girls' affections, those on White River. May all terminate happily.

JUNE 9TH

I am serious now, looking life firmly in the face and asking myself the question, "What am I living for?" "What aim have I?" I cannot be living for the good of my fellow men, for I cannot remember having ever done anything that in the scale of man's justice would compensate for the sins of one day. Have I ever done a good action, one that was prompted by no motive save love to God and my fellow man? No, I am a weak, vain, selfish creature, living almost without God in the world.

My religious impressions are almost effaced by the lust of flesh, the pride of life. My temper is almost without control, and my thoughts continually building chateaux en Espagne. The busier my hands are, the quicker fly my thoughts to the boundless realms of fancy and hard is it, as 'twas this morning to stoop over a tub of steaming soapsuds and rub, wring, and wrench for nearly two days. My air castles were peopled with the dark Ethiopian race, and grumbles went up against the Feds for taking the only legacy Papa was able to leave his children. I am sleepy; my journal receives none of the interest[ing] period that is now passing.

JUNE 24TH

Weary, weary of woman's slanderous tongue, of man's depravity, I have
returned from the dinner given the "Pop-Corn"[30] in Mrs. Perrin's yard,
wearied and dispirited. Two weeks tomorrow I went to Aunt Emma's to
spend a week. On Tuesday Mr. Kennard got up a fish fry at the mill to
which many went. It was intended for a family party (Mrs. Kennard['s]
and ours) but all the "reading class" was invited. Will, Theodore, Lieut.
Morgan, Mr. Russell, were the only beaux. We did not once think of
McGuffin's company of little boys; we have never regarded them as
grown. They were deeply offended. Miss Emma Hynson, Jennie Egner,
and some others still stinging under the smart received while Shelby's
brigade was here (it was generally known they went with the Feds and
were treated accordingly) urged the boys on and with other mischief
makers repeated with great exaggerations things that were lightly spoken. They had given us the names, "Our Circle," "The Exclusive Rebels,"
[and] "Southern Flower." From all accounts, we for the last ten days
have been the chief topic when "The Mess" has its social reunions, so
they term themselves, Mark Wycough being chief. There are several stories afloat about our being unacquainted with the "Pop-Corn," saving
ourselves and families for Missouri officers who will appreciate them,
and many, many things too trifling to be worthy of attention, yet irri-
tating, annoying when we know they proceed from those who will not
flinch under a falsehood and who are urged on by all the evil passions:
envy, jealousy, hatred.

---

30. The Pop-Corn Company, later Company A, Twenty-Eighth Arkansas
Mounted Infantry, was organized in Batesville in September 1863 by Capt. Samuel
J. McGuffin. It was made up largely of boys as young as fifteen and called the Pop-
Corn Company because of its members' youth, size, and energy. The unit mostly
operated in Independence, Jackson, Woodruff, White, Izard, and adjacent counties.
In the summer of 1864, it was made part of Colonel Crabtree's regiment in Maj.
Gen. Sterling Price's army. Some of the company members who are mentioned by
Mary in her journal are: John T. Warner, the Wycough brothers, E. R. Goodwin, R.
P. and Abe Weaver, the Rev. John Rice, and Will Denton. The unit fought in skir-
mishes at Waugh's Farm and Fitzhugh's Woods.

We attended a party at Mrs. Aikin's which was very pleasant. Gus was up, and as all went smoothly, Mrs. Smith and Mrs. Perrin proposed giving the soldiers a dinner. Everybody in town was invited to contribute and attend. Everything promised to go merry as a marriage bell. Dinner came, the table groaned under the loads of beans, peas, potatoes, beets, chickens, and every thing that could be procured in this scarce country. The "Pop-Corn" did not appear—Em H., Jennie E., [and] Mrs. McGuffin made excuses for them—had been on a two-days' scout, danced all night the two preceding nights and this morning had to graze their horses and were tired and sleepy. After dinner, Dr. Allen was hand[ed] a package directed, "To the Managers of 'Our Circle.'" Upon opening it there was found a dead squirrel and the accompanying note: "Here is the opinion of the Pop-Corn, with compliments, but being unacquainted cannot attend." I, who with my usual curiosity had followed Dr. Allen and Will out into the yard, was the only lady present when the package was opened, and seizing the note read it and hand[ed] it to the gentlemen who now collected Capt. McGuffin, Mr. Kennard, and one or two others with Will and Theodore and the Doctor. I was angered, my pride was raised. I felt wounded, insulted, and acting under these feelings, turned and looked all around. All were surprised and silent. "Capt. McGuffin," I said, "we feel highly honored by the compliment your boys have paid us." I must have said it proudly, scornfully, for my voice trembled. I turned and walked rapidly to the office where the "Exclusives" were and related what happened. We concluded to take no notice whatever of it, show our contempt for such ill-bred fellows who are not worthy of bear[ing] the name of Confederate soldiers.

JUNE 25TH

Tonight at 10:00 I am tired, both in body and mind. This morning the usual Saturday's work was to perform, and this evening "Reading" met at Mrs. Maxfield's. Sarah, Lute, and I comprised the class, Eliza, Vene, and Puss having gone to Col. Neal's across the river, as it is rumored that Bett[ie] Cullins and Lieut. Morgan are to unite their destinies tomorrow after [the] 11 o'clock service. This brought on a long discussion on marriage, its rights, privileges, pleasures, and pains, with Will

Maxfield, who came up tonight. He is wearisome. I could not enter into all his cases of supposition, and when I could, I wouldn't. I felt disgusted with him at times. He is stubborn, conceited, and jealous, yet he has many excellent qualities and will render the woman he marries happy, if she is not a person of fine sensibilities. He is accommodating and is now making my embroidered slippers; I fear he will ruin them. I am tired of these stories with which the town is floating concerning the girls of "Our Circle" and the soldiers: all, all false. Mark Wycough, Mrs. Aikin, Em Hynson, are the principal persons in fabricating the tales, and they and their satellites repeat with embellishments. What a place for scandal this is! Twice Mark Wycough has offered insult to our family. I scarcely think he will offer it a third time. He was the *gentleman* who wrote the note. The rupture between the families is made. [Illegible] and Will are the only ones who visit since Mary's[31] very *ladylike* and unnecessary letter to Mary Case, wherein were stated her reasons for not returning our calls. I had assailed her husband's character, not only as a gentlemen but a Christian minister who is helping to build up the church of God. I had remarked to Mollie Bevens, and she like a kind friend repeated it, that in five years we would have to plant flowers over Mary's grave.... [entry incomplete]

JUNE 26TH, SUNDAY

This day I appointed for a thorough examination of myself, my inmost thoughts and feelings. The search was short, for wickedness, worldliness, and love of self seem to have almost as undisputed [a] sway over my heart as it had before I professed myself one of the called of God through his son Jesus. I shudder when I think on what a brink I stand. If I fall, my second state is much worse than the first, but generally I feel a security or more properly an indifference that is more to be dreaded than any of the wiles Satan throws around us. I cannot think of heavenly things; today my mind would wander from the sermon. I would think

---

31. Mary Wycough Shepherd.

of Sarah and Dr. Dobbins continually. I rely upon myself too much, I must remember that when I would do good, evil is continually with me. My confidence must be placed in Christ, who is ever ready to uphold [us if] we only call upon him, inspirit and in truth. It is almost a year and I have united with no church and have added none of the Christian graces to my character.

Evening. The Bible Class was very interesting on account of Mr. Hickison's absence, yet the evening I trust was spent beneficially. Arrangements were made for organizing the Sunday School. I think of commencing school again. It is very warm, but I believe I would be happier if constantly employed and I need all I can make. If Mr. Kennard could have paid me all ($50) at the time the school closed, I could have bought much that we needed. I got $23 worth at very reasonable rates. I would not be surprised if Sarah marries this fall, and she will need many things.

Maj. Cravens and Dr. Dobbins were up last week while I was at Aunt Emma's, came at 11 o'clock at night and left at 3 next day [for] camp 45 miles away. They got a pass to go to the Glaize. Gus told them the girls were there; not finding [them] they came on, nearly killed their horses.

JUNE 27TH

Today Mama and I washed. I was very tired. Will came up tonight; the conversation dragged and I kept thinking how tired I was and wishing he would go, when he asked if I would not walk. I consented, although I felt what was coming. He told his love in few words. His breath came quickly, he seemed gathering energy for the avowal, and in low tones it came. "Well, Mary, I have learned a lesson in life you have taught me. I love you; cannot I hope for a return?" I could not evade this if I had wished. I could not pass it off in a jest for he seemed more noble to me than ever I had seen him, offering the sincere devoted affections of a heart that had never been moved by the "tender passion" to me who had often wounded him, flirted only to provoke him to jealousy. I can trifle with a trifler but not with a *man,* one with whom love is marriage and, as he assured me, whose every thought should be to promote my happiness. I told him kindly but firmly that I did not nor could not hope to love him, tried to soften the blow, ameliorate the pain by offering my friendship, but cold is any return that woman can make for an offered heart when she cannot give herself to be guided, directed by him as his one pearl of great price, and she in return love him, watch him, influence by kind words and gentle endearments, so that when they lay down to die he may say he is better for having lived with her.

But I could give Will nothing more, for at times he is repulsive to me and it is only when I pity him that I can see his good qualities. It is said that pity is akin to love. Will says he *will* hope will think that in time he can gain my affection, and what could I say but reiterate my expressions of gratitude and friendship and sorrow for paining him. Thus we parted. I do not know how it will end. I feel sorrowful, sad. I cannot express my feelings, though. I may bestow my affections upon some one who will not prize them. Careless, indifferent, my life may be miserable. Here is one who I know loves me, who will always provide liberally for me, treat me kindly.

Why not say the word, promise to marry him? Say the word? 'Tis easily done. It will lighten his heart. It will be doing a kind action; then I listened to the promptings of my heart. I felt, as your wife, I will be provided for, but I must be a machine, attend to the duties of the household. You will be proud of my intellect but it must be confined to home. You must not have a thought above me, recognize me as your superior, obey my behests in all matters of dispute, yield to me as to [one] whose judgment surpasses yours. You are my wife. This would be easy if I believed it, felt it. By not doing so and seeing how he was moved, I felt the truth of Miss Landon's beautiful words, learned long ago, more forcibly than ever:

> It is a dreadful thing
> To love as I love thee; to feel the world—
> The bright, beautiful, joy-giving world—
> A blank without thee. Never more to me
> Can hope, joy, fear, wear different seeming. Now
> I have no hope that does not dream of thee;
> I have no joy not shared by thee;

I have no fear that does not dread for thee;
All that I once took pleasure in,—my lute
Is only sweet when it repeats thy name;
My flowers, I only gather them for thee;
The book drops listless down, I cannot read
Unless it is of thee....[32]

I could scarcely forbear repeating them aloud, so much I felt them, for him, but the old story must be told again before my heart responds.

JUNE 28TH

Today it was reported that Mr. Ruddell was to give a barbecue and have a dance to-night. Cousin Preston came up and said if we would go he would get a wagon and take us. Sarah and I did not want to go unless some of the girls were going, but they had not got back from the country, and we would not go alone: the only ones from "Our Circle." Cousin had gone when Mrs. Burr, Cousin Rilla, and Ann came. Then I wanted to go, sent to Mr. Lacefield's, got a horse, and went. I had decided with Ma that it would be better for us not to go, for the "Pop-Corn" might say something insulting, and it would be a rude affair, but when they came I forgot all these things nor did I remember them until Ma said she wished they had not come. I found she would rather I had not gone, but I was ready, the horse at the gate. I started, but mad with myself, feeling that some unpleasant[ness] would occur, murmuring against my want of stability, *me* who felt that I was really a Christian who only Sunday was making such good resolutions, now going to this "Shebang." It was inconsistent.

I was miserable all the way over, but on arriving found Mr. Ruddell knew nothing of it. They had made no preparations whatever, there

---

32. After "The Ancestress" (1850), by Letitia Elizabeth Landon (1802–38), an English poet and novelist popularly known as L. E. L.

were two tallow candles in the house; the remainder was wrapped in total darkness. Country girls, country beaux in profusion, no fiddlers, no water, no nothing. The old man and woman both mad. It was "un grand affaire." We waited two hours, but the fiddlers had four and eight miles to come and had not arrived. We, wearied out, completely sold, left. I was truly glad; never will I act as tonight. I will make a decision and abide by it, have stability. I have the reputation of great force of character; it must be founded. John Warner came out, hitched our horses, and tried to make himself agreeable to me, but I remembered the insult offered only Friday and did not force my *acquaintance* upon him. Lieut. Crisp had some words with one of the "Pop-Corn" about me today; I do not know exactly what. Theodore is a noble boy. He say[s] the boys are ashamed of themselves; well they may be.

JUNE 29TH

Tonight Mrs. Aikin gives a party to the officers. She invited us, but we did not wish to go. Hall and Crisp came up and insisted on my going, as Sarah pleaded a headache and was not presentable. I made many excuses and finally got off.

I have told several I was a member of the church, a Methodist. It is not strictly true, although I did consider myself as much a member as if my name was on the book. I intend to joining [at] the first opportunity. I had been happier since Sunday than for many weeks. I felt I was doing right. Cousin Rilla had gone to Aunt Emma's Friday, and we were having a quiet, happy time at home, the family alone, but last night I acted so wrong in going over yonder and now they have come back. Byers is four times worse than ever he was, as his mouth is sore. He can have that for a pretext for any kind of capers he chooses. I never was so tired of anybody as I am of my kin folks. Cousin Henry is at Little Rock. I expect any day he will come over; then what a time we will have. Sarah has some idea of marrying this fall and going to the Doctor's father's in Marshall, Texas. She had better remain single for it would be inconvenient for us to have him here, and nobody wants their relations to live with them so long. As an argument to prevent this I shall tell her that his stepmother and sisters would hate to have her. She would be as annoying to them as ours are to us. Relatives are very dear when at a distance, but close proximity brings out deficiencies. Everything conspires against me.

This evening the girls made an arrangement to go to the caves. I was not present or should have opposed it bitterly. The weather is oppressively warm. Will and Theodore and Will McGuire the only beaux, and there has been so much going around—picnics, fish-frys, parties—that I am sick, tired of the whole of it. I wish it would rain tonight and tomorrow so we could not go. Besides, there is so much talk about us that I want to be perfectly quiet and let it die down. By tomorrow it will be going the rounds that "The Exclusives had a cave party, nobody out of the set invited." This together with our non-attendance at her party will make Mrs. Aikin more angry than the fish-fry. I dislike this. I do not like cliques. I want to go where I please, but everything works against me. It is down, down, down, spiritually and socially. I am worried. I believe I will commence school Monday. Perhaps if my mind is constantly employed I will regain my accustomed equanimity.

JUNE 30TH

We had a joyful day. Dr. Allen was the life of the crowd. I was worried because they would go today and would not assist Sarah one bit in preparing dinner, but it far surpassed my expectations. Theodore drove the wagon; he is a careless driver. I sat on the seat with him. We were talking continually and would not notice the horses, when bump! We would go against a tree stump or log. Such jolting and such fun! I like Theo more each time I am in his company. He is so kind, accommodating, and has such a fund of humor like Lute, not like Will always trying to say something witty and learned and making a failure. We broke down coming home; he enjoyed it more than all the day's fun. I did not talk five minutes to Will today. He is repulsive to me now; I can scarcely tell why. I am going to try to prevent him renewing the conversation of the other night. I have to be very careful how I treat him; he is now more touchy than ever. With Theodore you can say and do anything.

Today, practicing pistol shooting, I carelessly held my pistol downward and shot it off, the ball passing through my dress in entering the

ground about six inches from my foot. They were very much frightened.
Tonight. Mr. Kennard came up from Shelby's Brigade, bringing news
of the capture of a gunboat and another so disabled it had to be towed
off.[33] (I scarcely ever write news of the war, for we get it so irregularly, so
confusedly that I never think to write it.)

Mr. Kennard brought Sarah and Puss a note of thanks for a cake sent
by Gus. I did not think until tonight that Sarah cared much for Dr.
Dobbins. When the note was brought she seized it eagerly. "O, pshaw!"
she exclaimed in a disappointed tone, "'Tis from Dr. Austin. Nell, run
over and ask if your papa did not bring me another letter." None came.
Dobbins was asleep. The poor child was grieved, mad, and disappointed.
If she had been alone she would have cried. She *loves* him. She said she
did not care, she would like to receive a letter but it did not hurt her
not to get one, then came in looking so badly I was sorry for her and
mad at Dobbins. Could he be trifling with her? I whispered to her, as
Cousin Rilla entered, to laugh it off. She jumped [up], proposed to read
us all Dr. Austin's letter, that was better than all, then laughed, sang,
thrummed on the piano as though she was not suffering in the least, but
it did not last long. Throwing herself on the sofa she told me she was
mad, she never wanted to see him again. Puss got a letter, and she didn't.
I commenced telling her how I would treat him now. I'd show him a
thing or two, when womanlike she began to make excuses for him. She

---

33. After the Camden Expedition, Shelby was ordered to close off the White
River. He returned to Batesville as Mary reported (May 31) and, after two weeks'
rest and recuperation, pursued "jayhawkers, boomers, and deserters," including "the
notorious Bill Williams, who commands a company of hybrid deserters, negroes,
women-ravishers, and Federals." At Buck Horn (modern St. James, Stone County),
Shelby's men charged, routed, and scattered them, killing forty-seven and capturing two, who were shot next day. "Young girls and old women met us the next day
and called down Heaven's blessing on my command for what they termed a glorious and a righteous deed." Shelby went on to destroy the gunboat *Queen City*, sink
the gunboat *Naumkeag*, and engage four other gunboats at strategic DeValls Bluff,
below Des Arc, thus impeding Federal traffic on the White. Mobley, *Making Sense
of the Civil War in Batesville-Jacksonport and Northeast Arkansas*, 172; *OR*, 34:926–30.

believed he had written [and] Mrs. Kennard was teasing her. She has loved now; now her heartaches will begin. Now is the time for hope and despair to reign alternately. Little Sister, I had hoped you would be spared trouble of this kind. Why must woman ever love? it brings so much unhappiness. Sarah was soon relieved. Dr. Dobbins was camped below. Mr. Kennard saw none of Gordon's regiment. Now she is happy and sleeping tranquilly. No doubt he will visit her in dreams tonight.

JULY 1ST

It is twelve o'clock, and I have just returned from Mrs. Smith's farewell party. Will, Theodore, and Will leave tomorrow. Eliza had a long conversation with Will, gave him some kind of encouragement and I must needs hear the story over again. I'll make her tell me what she told him. She ought to be ashamed of herself; she knew I was joking when I told her all that was necessary was for him to ask me. He asks me for some assurance that I reciprocate his love. Assurance? Indeed! He has more of it now than anybody I know. If a woman was to tell me, "No," four times, I would not ask her the fifth. He thinks he could win the affections of the princess of Austria. He will still hope. The other night I was sorry for him; tonight he has made himself so ridiculous I don't care who knows it. Cousin Rilla had her head at the window and heard the story. She pronounces him foolish, but he don't know how to court. I could do better myself. I told him tonight. I was afraid he'd whip me, that I was cross, ill-grained, capricious, jealous, that we would not agree one week. Mary Case would just suit him.

JULY 2ND

Today I went down to have the school-house cleaned out. Dr. Allen and Mr. Kennard are taking an interest in my school, getting me the requisite number of pupils (25), when I shall refuse to take more. Will called to tell me good-bye. He asked me not to forget him. I feel relieved now that he is gone. I hope ere he returns he will have conquered his passion for me. I feel sorry for him. Although I have never loved deeply I have sufficient experience to know that unrequited love is painful; very, it must be, for jealousy is dreadful, even when you know you are beloved. The girls received letters from the brigade. The "Pop-Corn" have made enemies down there by 'pressing Puss'[s] horse. Dr. Dobbins writes they will return the horse or annihilate the whole Pop-Corn tribe, especially that slime-faced "Limber Jack" (Mark). This name Puss gave him when Gus was up here. This evening Gen. Shelby sent up orders for the horse to be returned, which were obeyed; soon after they 'pressed it again. I do not know how they will satisfy the General; they have violate[d] his especial order. Sarah is playing, singing; all the rest are talking. I cannot think, much less write. Dr. Dobbins and Maj. Cravens will be up next week. I will then be in school but as I have no lover it makes no difference. Eliza has something to tell me; I want to hear it; it is relative to Will.

JULY 3RD

Today has been very quiet. I went to church but was nearly asleep during sermon. I could not get interested although the subject—the resurrection—was very interesting. Tomorrow is the 4th, the anniversary of American Independence. Last year we had a pleasant pic-nic at the caves. Vicksburg surrendered and the battle of Helena was fought. Grant was very anxious to enter Richmond tomorrow but from present intelligence he will have to wait some time. Sarah and Ma have been talking about the wedding. Sarah wants Mama to hire but she thinks we are not able. So many or rather several have got their negroes back; I do wish we could get ours—no one needs them worse—but I never expect to see them again. We have never heard of them since they left Jacksonport. I am so tired working, so much to be done. Mama has to work so hard. I hate washing worse than anything else. Cousin Rilla heard from Henry: he is going to Texas, is now [at] Little Rock.

JULY 5TH

Gus has just left. I am tired, sleepy, would have been in bed some time ago but for him, yet I am not sorry he came. I refused to accompany Dr. Dobbins and Sarah to Mrs. Smith's, saying I did not feel like going. I wanted a quiet evening. I am tired of the little parties where there are three or four ladies to a gentleman. I had not really enjoyed myself at one party this summer, consequently have failed to be interesting, for 'tis only when my face is lightened, my eyes sparkling, my tongue racing, that I am in the least attractive. I don't like parties where the girls must make the advances. They are irksome to me.

My school commenced yesterday, and today I had eighteen scholars. I will have a full school; the step is taken. I am a schoolma'am. I know that in the South school teachers are not so highly esteemed as in other countries, but I am among near and dear friends and am going to keep up the intercourse. I am too sleepy or I would write of Dobbins' arrival, of Ma's and Sarah's disagreement, my school, Sarah's ring, and much else.

JULY IITH

Warm, warmer, warmest. Thermometer up to dear knows where. Matters are progressing swimmingly. Dobbins and Gus left this morning. I have been up so late every night that I have not had time to note events as they passed and now am writing, and expecting Maj. [Jeremiah] Cravens and Annie. Maj. Jere came this evening. He is very much disappointed because he did not arrive before the Dr. left. He was expected yesterday, then they would all have remained three or four days. Such times as we would have had! This week has flown, and I had been busy during school hours but in the intervals and evening have talked as much as a common talker would wish to in a week.

Dr. Dobbins imparted to me his intention night before last, when we went to Mrs. Kennard's, to propose to Mama for her daughter. Yesterday morning early he came up, and, behold! Lucia Lowe was here and stayed all night, accompanied us to Mrs. Aikin's, and spoiled our pleasant tete-a-tetes after coming home. Dr. Dobbins was very much worried, kept telling me she was sleepy to invite her off to bed. He is one caution, said he would have had all matters arranged with Mama, been ready to be married next fall, but for her. There she sat. He came up from the brigade for that purpose and now will have to make another trip week after next. Jere has gotten ahead of him. He came up and tomorrow will put on a starched shirt collar, walk right up to the old man and request or demand, I know not which, the hand of his daughter.

I cannot realize that Puss and Sarah are really in earnest about marrying. Such things sound queer. Sarah married! Imagine her a wife? Impossible! I do not like the idea of losing my sister, but if Ma does not strenuously oppose it, he says I must say, "Brother Theophilus," this fall. But Ma will object to Sarah marrying soon. She will evade Dobbins in order to prevent him asking her.

Tonight there was a party at Mrs. Aikin's again, but I was obliged to decline, for aside from objecting to meeting the "Pop-Corn" I was sleepy, was compelled to go to bed as soon as breakfast was over in order to be wide enough awake to teach. Puss has her horse back, and Limber Jack remarked in Dr. Dobbins' hearing that he supposed Puss Smith would be satisfied now she had got her *old mare* back. He also talked to Lucia Lowe for Sarah's benefit. Afterward Sarah made several remarks respecting him, all of which she, Luce, will repeat, for she is a regular scandal monger. Dr. was vexed because Sarah went where the *honorable gentleman* was, says [he] will never go in that crowd again. Mrs. Aikin is attempting to be peacemaker; she cannot succeed. I as the most tractable was invited yesterday to dinner. She gave me an excellent dinner. I will go again, but I cannot say that I can be brought by her into that happy state of feeling to "Love my neighbor as myself." Adieu.

JULY 10TH [SIC]

How thankful I should be for the many kind friends I am blessed with. First on the list comes my dear little sister. I love her more each day, or probably 'tis because I now think of losing her. Dr. Dobbins has found out her worth, and this fall I think the first wedding will take place. I love him dearly. He is just such a person as I shall like for a brother-in-law. I talked very seriously with him when here but not so much as I should have liked. It is a grave matter to place the happiness of a favorite sister in the keeping of another. I, although two years younger, generally direct her, always advise her. I have become so accustomed to it that I should not know what to do without her and think often will she not miss me? My assistance? When another calls her by the endearing name, "Wife,"

I have thought of her so much of late that I am becoming accustomed to thinking of her as married. Not until I talked to the Dr. could I realize they were in earnest. They love one another, will be happy; I feel it. Sarah has changed much, improved much since her acquaintance with him. Now she is self-possessed, but not forward, frank, joyous, yet her childlike confidence, outbursts of feeling still remain, but I write of her scarcely knowing what I say. It may be repetition of that which is written every night.

Then come[s] Cousin Annie, my own cousin, I value her more highly than any of my cousins. I am her confidante, poor Annie! She still love[s] Stevens although five years have passed away since his mysterious disappearance. Time alone will reveal if we ever know what became of him. I believe he was murdered. She has many admirers, has had more affairs than any girl in all this country. She is frank with them, and her warmest friends are rejected suitors.

Puss comes next. I love her, but she is more selfish. I cannot feel so devoted to her as to Lute. I am now in confidence of all. Major is up now. He asked Col. Smith's consent. He granted it; now the "cruel war" is the only obstacle to his happiness. Puss confided to me the whole story of her engagement to Capt. Duffie. She insists that she still loves him as much as ever, but this new love has sprung up. It exceeds the other in fervency. If he (Major) had never appeared she would have married Duffie and bee[n] happy with him. He is mild, confiding in disposition, as she last night expressed it, "With Mr. Duffie everything I do is right. He don't know I can do wrong, while with Jerry I can't have my own way at all, not even *now* will he do as I wish, yet like a fool I go on loving him more and more." Puss has found her master, yet the yoke is light. 'Tis sweet to be submissive to him, yet she is in trouble respecting Capt. Duffie, who has been wounded, lost part of one foot, and gone to his parents in South Carolina. She fears he cannot understand her motives and think[s] 'tis because he is now a cripple. She will not break off her engagement; the first intelligence of her falsity he will receive will be the announcement of her marriage, which will take place this fall [upon] Major's returning from Missouri.

Oh! The love affairs! Lute, during our long walk on the bank of the river this evening, related her experience. There is so little affectation about that girl that when with her I almost despise myself. I do not know that I am affected, yet there is such a simplicity and archness about her that I envy her, and compared with her I feel twenty-five. She says she does not love Maj. Lawrence, as yet has given him no answer. I know she does love him or will love him. She, if I am not widely mistaken, will be another of the Batesville girls who will belong to the "horse stealin' and fightin' brigade."

The Circle is in love with the exception of Mary Case and myself. [Of] Vene I am not quite certain either. When will the impression wear off that I am engaged to John? I am hearing about it now from all sides. Lute herself told me she heard it from Mrs. Hickison, Eliza, and many others. All the officers think so. Dr. Dobbins questioned me seriously about it. He says I am changed from the gay, thoughtless girl the every emotion of whose heart was plainly visible on her face, in one year, to the thoughtful, dignified young lady who though talkative, yet repels every advance, who attracts yet whose demeanor shows the most dignified politeness is all she will allow. I have repeated his words though attaching no importance or even credit to them.

If changed I am it is owing to a higher power than John, who as he thinks has caused this. I hope I am more sedate than one year ago. I want my thoughts one year from now to be many, many more times removed from the things of this world than now. I do not understand myself. I feel a listlessness now about these little parties and company. Is it because I am detaching my thought from the world? I fear not, but owing to some physical cause. Today I attended church. Our preacher is now married to an old acquaintance of mine, Mary Moore.

JULY 12TH

I have just seen Sarah and Florence[34] off after the other girls; all are going to Aunt Emma's to spend the day. Dr. Austin came up last night.

---

34. Probably Florence Neill, sister of Mary's contemporary Delia Neill.

He has been sick. If able, he and several officers will dine with the girls today, and I have just seated myself to write until the bell rings for school, where I must hear all those children spell, "baker." Such days as today will be I want to be out[side]. The day will be lovely, the sun shining bright, the sky so blue, trees and grass so fresh from the recent shower, a breeze playing the vines and shrubs around Catalpa Hall, the place of all others I love best.

Last summer I was happy there, Nan so gay, and I was more careless then. But now they say I am changed. I ought to be, but the old wicked heart reigns still I fear. I have so little patience, forbearance. I was completely worried out with Will[ie] yesterday, sent him home with a note to Ma; she punished him and sent him back; he will do better now. I hate to punish him; he is not really bad but full of mischief and, as I am teacher, takes so many liberties. He is very industrious but has no taste for learning. He takes after Ma's family. I wish our only boy was a Byers. He will never astound the world; he cannot walk in his father's footsteps. All three of the brothers were eloquent lawyers.[35]

Night. Tonight Dr. Austin came up or rather he was here when I came in. I had been calling on Mrs. Pierson, afterward called on Puss. I thought Dr. Austin would never leave. I would gape, gape, stretch behind my fan, then break out in some new subject, but one or two questions and answers on both sides would complete the remarks on any subject: love, war, woman. I do know that women's tongues can make more mischief that all the armies of Lincolndom. Now Aunt Emma today must needs tell Eliza much that Mrs. Aikin should have said respecting her and Puss, but I really believe the woman is innocent of it, but no argument could now convince either to the contrary. I would like to go away where I could hear nothing of these feuds until they died away as they must necessarily do in a short time. We were so quiet, so happy until lately. So far nothing as yet touched me personally, but as Mrs. Smith told me this evening they might find the vulnerable

---

35. Uncle William, Pa, and Uncle Thomas Byers, the last not otherwise mentioned in Mary's journal.

point and attack me. I would be powerless. I must to bed and I have promised to quit writing and answer Sarah's question, "What do you think of my marrying in November anyhow?"

JULY 13TH

I'm getting along very well with my school. I now have twenty-five pupils, am very busy. I keep a switch and occasionally give a rap. I am tired of parties, of company, of everything but rest and sleep. This evening I refused an invitation to Mrs. Aikin's on the plea of indisposition. It was nearly the truth.

Cousin Preston came up from Coleman's command this evening. The brigade commanded by Gordon moved across White River last night, intending to tear up the railroad.[36] The doctor wrote a short note [to Sarah]: he regrets that he now cannot make a visit this week, but in ten or twelve days they will return, when he will visit her and try and prevail upon her to take those vows upon her which will make them forever one. He is exceedingly anxious, as they are making preparations to cross the Arkansas. I tease and worry the poor child almost beyond measure. She is now almost wholly guided by me. I wish I could decide whether 'twould be best for her to marry before the war is over. Jere and Annie will be married soon, and she is beginning now to make preparations.

JULY 14TH

Sister and I went down to spend a quiet evening with Puss when Dr. Allen and all the girls came in. Our quiet chat had been interrupted a few minutes before by Capt. Pollok.

School teaching is much more fatiguing than I first supposed. I have many scholars; when night comes I wish for some quiet nook where I

36. Probably the short section of the Memphis and Little Rock Railroad constructed in 1862 between Little Rock, on the Arkansas River, and DeValls Bluff, on the White River. Hodge, "Railroads." On August 24, Shelby's men destroyed ten miles of track. Mobley, *Making Sense of the Civil War in Batesville-Jacksonport and Northeast Arkansas,* 177.

could read, write, and think of everything, interrupted by no one, but it is best not so or I should soon fall into the old day-dream life from which I am not yet aroused.

Poor little Sarah is in trouble. Puss is making her arrangements, and she knows not that she will be allowed to marry this fall, and she has no trousseau nor the means of getting it. Being in the guest or bridal chamber at Mrs. Smith's deepened the train of melancholy reflections that have been saddening her all day. She feels now more bitterly than ever the sting of poverty—no, not that, for we are not that much reduced—but she contrasts the positions of the brides-elect, and although she has not confessed it, tonight as usual she has thought, "If Pa had lived I would not have been situated thus." I may be wrong; she is sleeping now. She said a few moments ago that she felt she would never see Dr. Theo. again. I laugh at her, but this railroad raid is a dangerous enterprise.

JULY 15TH

What do people talk about when it is not of themselves? I know that self is my idol, that I am egotistical and formed the resolution that henceforth my conversation should be on something or somebody other than Mary Byers. At home I am the same; the old affection will show itself, but with someone like Dr. Austin who cannot be persuaded to talk of *himself* I am at a dead loss. Most persons can become enraptured—no, interested—in themselves and dilate upon [their] acts, speeches, and all that is necessary is to be good listeners and catechisers. I am fretted with myself. I neither sing, play, dance, or ride, nothing to make me attractive except, as some remark, my brilliant conversational powers, and now they have deserted me. What am I to do or be I cannot tell. Tomorrow I shall go to Cousin Ann's to be petted and recover from this weight which at first appeared light but now is rendering me.

JULY 18TH

This morning I came home, found we had two guards. Small's reg't had threatened to tear up things in search of Henry's concealed goods, as he was still [with]in the Federal lines. Cousin Preston requested Lieut. Soper of Shanks's reg't to send up a guard. They are quiet, gentlemanly, one especially, Mr. Overtin, this I learned before I was in the house. The first words Sarah greeted me with were, "The Doctor has come." And sure enough, presently up comes Theophilus. School was very pleasant today. I accepted Eliza's invitation to dinner, and as I had a very interesting book, remained twenty minutes after the scholars had gone. Perceiving the sun was getting low, in haste I closed the house, hurried home.

Eugene Goodwin was here. He had told Sarah yesterday that he was coming to see me this evening [but] she had neglected to tell me. Puss, Dr. Dobbins, Cousin Preston were here, and I felt livelier than I have for weeks. My old self had returned. I enjoyed the conversation, took considerable part in it. Cousin Pres was *primping* for the party. I went to look at the time, [but] my watch was gone!

I studied, yes, in my haste I had left it on my desk. I called Ella and almost ran down. It was gone, so many soldiers passing, someone had taken it. Oh misery! What should I do, perplexity of perplexities! Uncle William's, too, I had lost more than my old school was worth. O my, I was nearly worried out of my senses. I ran to the neighbors to see if the children had noticed it; no, no one had been there, Mr. Isbell promised to acquaint Lieut. Rutledge with the facts. I described the watch to his son; if these soldiers had it, if I would be perfectly quiet, I would have it in a few days. I came home but seeing company in, ran in the back door expecting to see Ma worried as much as myself, but no, she laughed, called Wil[lie], told me to beat him. He had brought it home and would not tell me, just to tease me.

My spirits were in the ascendant in a minute. I came in, talked to Lieut. Soper and others and spent the happiest evening that I have spent in company since the night Shelby's brigade entered Batesville. Sarah went off down to Mrs. Smith's with Dobbins. He intended going over to Mrs. Aikin's for a little while. She would not agree to go, would spend the evening with Annie. I was mad at her. If Dobbins must be with Annie so much he might go. If they ever marry she must entertain him without Annie. If I had him I would teach him a thing or two. It must be me and me alone or take somebody else and leave me "bloom-ing alone." The song, "Whole hog or none," suits me. I can't bear to be half-way.

Sarah has a habit of inviting all "our girls" up every time there is a man in town. I enjoy the evenings best when the gentlemen call and we are alone.

There, I have stopped for an hour to talk to Sarah and the Dr. They do not know whether to marry now or wait. He is not going to ask Mama's consent this visit, I don't believe. When he is here I am reconciled—yes, pleased—that Sarah should marry him, but when he is away I would much rather he would never return.

Sarah and [I] are so different. Now she is engaged, acts and acquiesces to his wishes as a wife of one year. Probably she is right, but I would be constantly trying my power. Mayhap I would try until I lost all, and wrecked hope, love, and happiness.

JULY 20TH

A busy day! Dr. Dobbins called to say goodbye before the breakfast dishes were put away. I went to school mentally vowing to give Sarah a good talking [to] at twelve for allowing matters to proceed so far with-out him consulting Ma. I do not like it a bit, if I feel towards [him] as I now do, if it still increases, I shall endeavor to interpose. Does he think Ma will throw [her] child in *his* arms? That as she knows of the betrothal and does not interfere he feels an *honor* conferred upon the family? I believe he does. I thought this morning until I was really angry. I could not decide whether it would be best to "let off" at Sarah or preserve my wrath until I could pour it out on his head. When I got home here was Henry Smith. All was forgotten in my vexation at this, but I have been expecting it. We were too happy, life must needs be little more embittered and more especially now that we have strange com-pany. He must come. The soldiers all hate him, shun the house like a smallpox hospital. When he is here, it is too much. He is double trouble. Now we cook but two meals and then but a little variety when we have it, but he is a slave to his appetite and now it will be Cook! Cook! Cook! Ma will be sick, I know, for she lets Henry run over her, and there is additional work now that the well has failed. He brought Nannie home; she is enceinte, and proud of it. I thought she would be mad. It seems so strange. Dr. Austin has just left, and I must to bed, to be able to rise at five and prepare breakfast.

JULY 21ST

I am worried out tonight; the children tried themselves today. I would have given anything if I had never commenced teaching. I prayed last night and this morning for renewed grace and made the determination not to worry about Henry until he provoked me to it and that I would be patient with the scholars and win them by kindness. These things sound very well in a book but give me fear in the school room. I done very well until evening, but then I gave way to fancies. I knew that Sarah and Dr. Austin had gone to Cousin Ann's. I thought of everything but the little troublesome brats. All went wrong. I came home feeling cross and hungry. I met Gus; he and Dobbins had come. The latter had better throw up his commission and settle in Batesville. Matters do not please me at all. I prognosticate a storm soon. Sarah now is in favor of marrying soon, poor child! Where would we put her? Was there ever any set of girls put to the same straits for house room. I would give anything for a couple of rooms. It is worse and worse every day. If Henry Smith stays here two years longer I think we will all move into the kitchen and give up the house entirely. Now Cousin Rilla is better situated than any of us, but ruminating on these things only puts me in a humor to make affairs hurt me worse than they ought to. O, my!

Tonight Will[ie] was lying right before the door; Ma would not shut it on account of the heat. I sometimes wish nobody ever would come here; it is no pleasure. I am so wicked. I believe in apostasy now certain. I care for nothing nor nobody. What a difference between the present time and one year ago! Then I did not even make my bed; now I have not time to rest. I never knew before what it was to get up tired in the morning. Now I ache, and what must Ma do? She has not so good health as I, and much more work to do.

Tonight both Doctors and Gus spent the evening here. Theo spoke to
Ma; she was kind but firm, bids him wait until the war is over. Poor
Sarah! She had been thinking all the time that something would transpire that she might marry this fall. We very frequently spoke of what
she should have and wear. She is most heartbroken tonight she thinks
Jerry and Puss will marry soon, and she can't. She just now confessed
with tears in her eyes that she dreaded it. She fears she should make a
fool of herself. She has surrendered her whole heart to him. She consid-
ers herself as truly his as if [a] priest had already bound them. Coquet-
ries she knows nothing of. I must talk to Ma tomorrow, present the case
in a different light to that in which she has viewed it. She must not be in
the way of her child's happiness. Gus and I talk *it* all over. Everybody's
love affairs, Lute's, were under discussion tonight. I hope she told the
Major *no* plainly, unmistakably (I told Gus that she had before now),
for he is now engaged to Mrs. McClure, a second and improved edition
of Mrs. Cox. I must warn Lute in some way yet be cautious. To meddle
in love affairs is dangerous, squally business. I could not bear that they
should think Lawrence flirted Lute, and I know she will tell him *no* if
she has not already.

Tonight I am tired, worn out, even "Little Maude" sung in my ears does
not raise my spirits, but I have heard music until I care something for
it now.

Dr. Dobbins, Mr. Stevenson, Will Redd left this morning. I feel
towards Theo like a brother. He is a dear, good fellow. I do not feel that
he will ever be my brother-in-law; something will transpire to prevent
it. I told him last night that if he did not return to marry her she would
die [a] maid, her energy is so feeble.

OCTOBER 6TH

Two months and not one entry in my journal.[37] Tonight I have read all
written since April. I scarcely recognize myself. So many changes have
taken place, so much transpired that would have been interesting to my
children. It is for them (if I ever have any) that I now write, and for
myself when I grow old and wish to refresh my memory of my youth, its
joys, pleasures, sorrows, and pains. If I die young it must be destroyed.
There are some things here that Ma [and] Sarah must never read. My
expressed inmost thoughts they must never scan. Why do I write this?
Do I expect to die soon? I hope not. For two months I have been sick.
Looking over my journal I find that during July my wish, my constant
wish, was rest, sleep, [and] quiet. I awoke unrefreshed, passed the day in
school and at night returned wearied out both body and mind. I could
think of no cause for it. It was physical debility. I was weakened by a
disease that I scarcely felt, never noticed, but outraged Nature asserted
her claims. July 28th I dismissed school with a violent headache, came
home, was put to bed with a chill. For two weeks I lay ill with bilious
fever, recovered in one week, was down again. Thus it is the slightest
exertion, a walk in the sun, anything but perfect quiet brings on headache for days. Fever follows, up one week, down the next. A walk to
Cousin Rilla's throws me into fever. I am worthless at present and will
be so until spring and probably worse than worthless, a burden if I do
not get better, regain my strength. I dread the winter, I fear a cold, a
settlement on the lungs then will follow that dreadful disease whose

---

37. On September 13, Maj. Gens. Sterling Price and James F. Fagan with their
Confederate forces had passed through Batesville en route to rendezvous with General Shelby at Pocahontas and then march on into Missouri, Kansas, and then back
to Arkansas in the final, disastrous Confederate thrust in the Trans-Mississippi.
Price was to return with only about half of his troops. Ibid., 188; Civil War
Sites Advisory Commission, "Price's Missouri Expedition [September–October 1864]," Civil War Battle Summaries by Campaign, www.nps.gov/hps/abpp/
battles/bycampgn.htm#Trans64.

seeds I have inherited.[38] I who used to be tough as leather am weak as a child. None could out-walk me, few equal me in a foot race. [Now I] am compelled to be perfectly quiet, not even permitted a walk to Mrs. Smith's, but this will not last long. I shall get well; I feel it. I am writing too long; I must to bed. The evening walk with Puss (now Mrs. Cravens) has wearied me.

OCTOBER 7TH

This morning, Sarah came in from Aunt Emma's and spent the day, returned this evening. She is looking very well, although Dr. Dobbins has been in Texas two months. He was recalled by the death of his father and left in company with Cousin Henry. July 30th his father died very suddenly and left his business unsettled. His wife and daughters wished the Doctor to come down immediately. Sarah received a letter written from Camden. He thought he would not be able to return before the last of November in order to go south with the army on its return from Missouri. Mama finally gave her consent for them to marry this fall, if he spent the winter south, but owing to the condition of Col. Dobbins's estate I expect the wedding will be deferred. Puss and Maj. Cravens were married Aug. 11th. I was just recovering from my first attack and had gone to Aunt Emma's and missed the wedding. The army was expecting to move south immediately and Maj. C. was not willing to leave Annie single. They were married "on the run" as the soldiers express it, the Federals being at Grand Glaize and expecting them here within a few hours, but fortunately they retreated.

Soon after Cousin Henry left, Cousin Rilla determined to go to housekeeping. On the 24th she moved. Our family is once more alone. We have been very happy now have plenty of room and a negro in the kitchen, a contraband captured by Gordon's reg't on a raid on the government plantations [on the] Mississippi River. She is a raw field hand

---

38. Mary apparently has malaria but fears tuberculosis, which took her father.

but willing and good-natured and a great assistance indeed! I scarcely know how we should have gotten along without someone, for Ma, Willie, Byers, and I were. . . . [Missing text and at least one page between this and the beginning of the following entry.]

OCTOBER 27TH[?]

. . . Sarah went out next day and came in this evening.[39] I had not returned from Willie Crouch's funeral (he was burned to death night before last). When she came, I got her to go out again, for I did not wish to go, but very unwillingly. Since then I have been ashamed of my selfishness, making her give up to me.

Mr. Shepherd is stationed here this year. How will Mary [Wycough Shepherd] like to be in a town [in] which she desires "no association whatever" with the principal girls in it, the only ones with whom she ever associated. Before the end of the year. I predict she will be friendly with all save Puss and myself. I except Puss because she said when she heard Mary's scathing letter read that she would never trouble her again, and she meant it and will abide by it. With me Mary will never desire an acquaintance, since I "without foundation traduced and maligned his character" and he "a minister of the gospel who is helping to build up the church of God" and "am worse than criminal." But still in my heart I love Mary and if she wished it could not refuse a reconciliation, notwithstanding all she and her husband have said and the manner [in which] she treated me. Our affections make simpletons of us unless backed by strong determination and great pride; neither do I possess. Mary is enceinte; may she be blessed in her child, and tragedy is occurring in Jacksonport in which if I mistake not, Shepherd's name will be connected.

---

39. The date for this partial entry is estimated from the mention of Willie Crouch's death. E. Maxfield, "Elvena Maxfield Journals," Oct. 25, 1864. On October 19, Federal troops—a party of scouts from the 2nd Arkansas—had passed through Batesville for the last time during the war. Mobley, *Making Sense of the Civil War in Batesville-Jacksonport and Northeast Arkansas,* 201.

OCTOBER 30TH

Another Sabbath has passed; no Sunday School, no church. I visited the hospital this morning, carried them some apples. Only four wounded are there now. One died Thursday, a Mr. Armstrong, reminds me of Mr. Bulkley. Old times come up. Delia Neal is again in town. She, too, will miss him who was the life of the circle and her particular admirer.

I seldom speak of spiritual things now, alas! Seldom think of them. Has the world possession of my thoughts? Will I in one more year record that I have backslided? I hope not, where would my hope be? Not in heaven, the Christians' home.

This morning a Miss Hodges who went off with the Federals in May and returned three months ago called at the fence as she said, "on purpose, purposely," to tell us that a Major that boarded with us when "*Mr.*" Livingstone[40] was here, requested us to call and tell us he was here and give his respects, that [if] she did not he would never do her a favor while he lived. Presumptuous old Pace, what do we care if he is living or dead or for his respects? Three times he has sent them.

---

40. Col. R. R. Livingston, Federal commander of Batesville.

1865

MARCH 21ST

Five months have passed, a new year been ushered in, and not one line during all this time have I written in my journal. The winter so much dreaded is gone, spring has come and with it no news of peace. Still war, war unto the death.[1] At home every[thing] remains as usual as it has been for ten years. All together, all happy, but with me the same longing for a change, for travel, not for an extended sphere of usefulness, for I am now a comfit tree in the garden of the Lord, but a selfish longing, a desire for that which is not for my good, or I would long since have received it.

Later. I have looked for the girls until, like Sister Anne on the watch-tower,[2] I am weary. I spent the afternoon with Vene and Lute, and they with Mary, Will, and Bob were to spend the evening with me. Sarah is at Aunt Emma's, Puss with Major, and Eliza in Memphis. Our circle is small but more closely connected than ever. Will Maxfield has been

---

1. On November 8, 1864, Lincoln had been reelected president, ensuring that there would be no negotiated peace. By December 15, the war in northeast Arkansas essentially had ended as local soldiers, furloughed by Price because he could not feed them at his new base in southern Arkansas, failed to report back for duty. Fortunately, in northern Arkansas the crops, mostly raised by the women, were bountiful. Watson, *Fight and Survive*, 139.

2. A reference to *Vanity Fair* (1848), by English novelist William M. Thackeray (1811–63).

paying his addresses to Mary Case since our Charade on Jan. 5th, but with indifferent success, I think. Theodore come[s] up very seldom, but we see the girls often.[3]

3. The Civil War drew to a close during the next few months. Confederate forces east of the Mississippi surrendered in April, while Southern commanders west of the river surrendered in late May and early June. Around May 26, Capt. Hans Mattson and two companies of the Third Minnesota Infantry occupied Batesville. Finally, on June 5, Brig. Gen. M. Jeff Thompson surrendered his 6,000 Confederate troops at Jacksonport, officially ending the war in northeast Arkansas. Watson, *Fight and Survive*, 155, 157–59.

Epilogue

In 1866 Mary and Sarah opened a school for boys and girls in the upper room of the Soulesbury Institute.[1]

Sarah was married in 1868, not to Dr. Dobbins but to Edward M. Dickinson, a merchant in Oil Trough. She outlived her siblings, passing in 1935 at age ninety.

In 1869 Mary married Robert Neill, a former beau of Lutie's and son and brother of the "Col. Neal" and "Delia Neal" mentioned in Mary's journal. As first sergeant of Company K, 1st Arkansas Mounted Rifles, Robert was wounded—and his brother Job killed—at the Battle of Wilson's Creek (Oak Hills). After returning to duty, he was commissioned captain; captured after the battles of Shiloh, Tennessee, and Richmond, Kentucky; and interned at Fort Delaware. In 1869 he and Mary were married. They had ten children, seven living past infancy, including the editor's grandmother, Clare. Robert became a lawyer, was appointed brigadier general in charge of the Arkansas Militia, and after re-franchisement served in Congress (1893–97). He died in 1907. Mary became a leader of the Women's Christian Temperance Union, which despite its name advocated total abstinence from alcohol. She lived until 1918.

Ella married Mary's former beau Bob Case in 1867 and bore him thirteen children.

Willie became a store clerk and eventually married Nellie of the well-to-do Fitzhugh family in 1906. He ran a laundry, published the *North Arkansas Pilot,* and died at age eighty.

Ma died at sixty-seven in 1891.

Vene Maxfield married Thomas B. Padgett in 1868 and died at age thirty-nine in 1881.

---

1. Griffith, "Aaron Woodruff Lyon," 57.

Lutie Maxfield eloped with George Wilson in 1872 and died at age thirty-six in 1880, probably from tuberculosis.

Will Maxfield did lose his eye. He married Mary Case in 1866.

"Puss" Smith married Maj. Jeremiah C. Cravens (one of the "darned Missourians") in 1864. Mary missed the wedding—see the entry for October 7TH. Major Cravens became a lawyer in Springfield, Missouri, and Puss's parents joined them there. Of her brother John, nothing after his rumored flight to St. Louis (see the entry for March 1ST, 1864) is known.

Although Uncle William was a judge, the Radical Republicans prevented him from taking his elected seat in Congress in 1866. The war had cost him most of his property. In 1869 he sold Catalpa Hall to Union sympathizer Elisha Baxter, who became governor and in a turnabout threw out the carpetbagger scourge. In 1871 for $8,000 William's 148 acres in Jackson County became the site of Newport, designated as railhead for the new railroad and therefore destined to eclipse the old county seat and river port of Jacksonport.[2] Uncle William later became superintendent of Indian affairs in Fort Smith and in 1881 died at Cousin Ann's in Memphis, where he was buried. Additional information on Uncle William and Aunt Emma appears in Appendix 3.

---

2. Abstract of Title, Lots 7, 8, & 9, Newport, Ark., 1995.

Mary Adelia Byers Neill, Sarah, Willie, and their children with visitors at the Neills' Batesville home, July 1893.

Mary is shown here on holiday from her duties as a congressman's wife in Washington. *Rear:* Esther Annie "Betty" Neill; Clare Neill*; William Wilson Byers; Kate McFarland of Olathe, Kansas; John Byers Dickinson; Hugh Neill; Robert Neill, Jr. *Front:* Allen Ramsay Dickinson; Anne Ocheltree of Olathe; Ernest Neill; Eleanor Neill; Aurelia Adelia "Rilla" Dickinson (front); Sarah Byers Dickinson; Mary Byers Neill.

*Clare Neill, the editor's grandmother, is shown here at fifteen, Mary's age when she began this journal.

(Left) Robert Neill, c. 1860. Mary's future husband in homespun vest and homemade Confederate uniform.

(Below) Robert and Mary Adelia Byers Neill, c. 1875.

Mary Adelia Byers Neill, c. 1893. Here she was
a congressman's wife, Robert Neill having won
election to the U.S. House of Representatives in
1892.

Esther Byers's children, c. 1910: Sarah, Mary, Ella, and Willie.
Mary had been widowed three years.
Craig, *My Byers-Bonar-Shannon and Allied Families*, iii.

Batesville

Curtis' Soldiers Find Batesville Is Delightful

This article by Margaret Ross originally was published in the *Arkansas Gazette*, April 30, 1962, and later compiled in *Chronicles of Arkansas: The Years of the Civil War*. Quoted by permission of the *Arkansas Democrat-Gazette*.

———

The Federal soldiers in Curtis' army were very favorably impressed with Batesville. Wilson E. Chapel, of the Thirteenth Illinois, wrote in his diary: "The town is situated on White River. Its streets and residences are beautifully laid out and ornamented. I was much surprised to find so pretty a town." L. G. Bennett, of the Thirty-Sixth Illinois, wrote: "The streets were wide and airy, with good sidewalks, and well built up with substantial business blocks of brick, and scattered here and there were tasty residences, embowered in trees, and from gardens the perfume of roses, then in full bloom, burdened the air.

"A college building, together with three or four churches with spires pointing heavenward, looked homelike, and to men who for months had been wallowing in camps or wandering over the fag ends of creation, it seemed a paradise.

"The people were well dressed, generally well behaved and intelligent, and for once, had the fates so ordered it, the men composing the 36th Illinois would have been content in the performance of garrison duty at Batesville."

Col. George E. Waring, Jr., of the Fourth Missouri Cavalry thought Batesville was a "lovely rose-grown village," but he added: "It had not acquired the picturesque dilapidation, in manner of fences and gates and defective window panes, that marked the Southern domicile during the war."

Although Chapel said that the people of Batesville were "all Secesh," there were many who came in to take the oath of allegiance. Curtis was convinced that some of them were sincere Unionists, and he especially depended upon Elisha Baxter, Calvin C. Bliss, Reuben Harpham, Isaac Murphy, and Col. James M. Johnston.

The men scoured the country for food, and some of the large homes whose occupants had fled were taken over for offices and officers' quarters. Empty warehouses were seized for storage of ordnance or provisions.

Bennett said: "It was evident that this profanation of Rebel mansions by the 'miserable Yankees' created a ripple of excitement in Rebel circles, but never a word of remonstrance was uttered, only volleys of indignant looks and contemptuous gestures showed that the equanimity of the neighborhood, if not of the now slumbering household gods, was disturbed at the intrusion.

"As we walked through the streets it was evident that all whom we met were not friends. Somehow a feeling of hatred towards the North would manifest itself in a thousand different ways.

"If a flag floated over a sidewalk, some fair dame would sweep out into the street to avoid walking under it. If a comely face at an open window attracted attention, a sudden slamming of window-blinds would ensue; but as none of the masculine portion of the inhabitants joined in these petty demonstrations, the young men of the 36th put on their best looks and smiled blandly upon the fair daughters of Secessia, while those who had wives at home enjoyed heartily these dashes of Rebel pepper as giving pungency to their experiences."

Other Views

After the Battle of Pea Ridge in March 1862, the Army of the Southwest passed through Pocahontas and Batesville en route to Helena, Arkansas. The following is excerpted from Shea, "A Semi-Savage State," 91–93 (quoted by permission).

———

Small-town Arkansas females were rarities (there being so few small towns along the army's route), but when encountered they caused something of a sensation. Typical were remarks made by Federals who briefly occupied Pocahontas. The soldiers commandeered the local printing press and cranked out one or two editions of a paper they called the *Division Register*. In a front-page article the military journalists reported the discovery of "something we have not seen since leaving St. Louis—hand-some young ladies." They went on to say that "if those who decamped are as good-looking as our samples, the country must be a paradise for young men. And after seeing the snuff-dipping, tobacco-chewing specimens along our march, they are truly refreshing." Apparently there was a yawning gap between urban and rural life in mid-nineteenth-century Arkansas, even when "urban" usually meant miniature metropolises of only a few hundred souls. . . .

The Army of the Southwest eventually emerged from the highlands and reached Batesville. Located on rolling hills above the White River, the little Independence County community was a sight for sore eyes. Batesville was "the most beautiful town I have seen in the West," enthused an Illinois soldier. . . . A staff officer concluded that "Batesville is one of the prettiest places I have ever seen. It is a perfect grove." An Ohio artilleryman described the town as "the prettiest villa I have seen either in Missouri or Arkansas. The citizens seem to exhibit a good deal of taste in cultivating flowers and laying off their yards to suit the tastes of the fanciful." Not to be outdone, an Illinois cavalryman informed the readers of his hometown newspaper that "a more lovely place cannot be found anywhere." Equally enthusiastic comments can be found in dozens of surviving letters and diaries. (The town seems to have made a better impression than the townspeople. After lavishly praising Batesville in a letter to his wife, an Iowa officer noted, "Were this country settled by intelligent and northern people I would move to Batesville at the close of the war *sure.*" Another Iowan remarked to his fiancée that while Batesville was indeed an attractive little town, it would only become "a place of considerable importance if a few enterprising *Yankees* would settle here.")

Batesville appealed to the Federal soldiers for two reasons. It was, of course, the first real town most of them had seen in quite some time. A weary infantryman . . . noted in his diary that he and his comrades spent most of a day wandering about the streets and "stareing at the houses not having seen civilization for nearly eight months." Probably more important, and certainly more often mentioned, was the fact that Batesville seemed so familiar, so much like what they expected a town to be. An Iowa officer observed significantly that the place "had much the appearance of a northern town." A young and homesick Illinois soldier wrote to his parents that Batesville "seemes like my good old home Trumanburg." Another Illinois soldier, who was born and raised in New Hampshire, informed his wife that the appearance of the town "would lean one to believe that he was walking the streets of a New England village but for the ebony hue and shining ivory of the infernal Darkle which is everywhere visible." A cavalryman writing to the editor of his local newspaper gave Batesville his ultimate accolade. "It is," he said, "the handsomest town I have seen since I left Illinois."

The nearby settlement of Jacksonport was described in quite different terms. . . .

Catalpa Hall (engraving).
Courtesy of the *Arkansas Democrat–Gazette.*

Catalpa Hall

Near Miller's Creek, Ruddell Township, two miles north of Batesville, William Byers began construction of Catalpa Hall around 1840 and continued with interruptions until 1851. The estate farmed cotton and distilled apple and peach brandy, and the family became prosperous. Of "Frontier Monticello" architecture, Catalpa Hall was built facing uphill, so that it was much larger than it appeared upon approach. Down the slope behind it was a tree-shaded lane lined with neat log cabins: the quarters that housed as many as fifty adult slaves plus children.

Historic Home near Batesville

Catalpa Hall, Built Nearly 100 Years Ago by the Late Judge William Byers, is Excellent Example of Early Plantation Architecture.

This article by Eurilda Smith was originally published in the *Arkansas Gazette* on November 13, 1938, and is reproduced in part below by permission of the *Arkansas Democrat-Gazette*. It provides a thorough overview of the history of the building as well as the prominent people who called it home.

———

No dwelling in north Arkansas has more claim to distinction than the large white house just off the public highway two miles north of Batesville. Tradition has woven a halo about this fine old place, which is interesting not only for its age—now nearing the century mark—but also for its association with two outstanding pioneers of the state, Judge William Byers, who built it, and Gov. Elisha Baxter, a later owner, a man who made history in his time.

William Byers came to Arkansas from Ohio in 1838. Opening a law office in Batesville, he established his family on this tract of land within easy driving distance from town. For the site of a permanent home he selected the crest of a gentle slope overlooking pretty little Miller's Creek and began construction about 1840, much of the building material being made on the place. The house was occupied about 1846, though still uncompleted, and when his young wife died soon after, nothing more was done to the place. The first Mrs. Byers was Ann Manning, a descendant of the New England family of Manning. Her death left three children motherless.

Not until after Mr. Byers' second marriage in 1850 was the house completed according to the original plans. It was called Catalpa Hall from the grove of beautiful trees around it.

The building is a noble example of Colonial architecture, simple in line, perfectly proportioned, and so stoutly constructed that foundations, beams and timbers are still in good condition after nearly 100 years. The house is low and broad, the windows small-paned, with green shutters. A wide entrance hall, long enough for "three sets of cotillions to form at once," has a broad stairway leading to the upper floor. On the left are two spacious rooms with great yawning fireplaces, "the parlor and back parlor." On the right are two similar rooms, also with fireplaces. During the Byers' occupancy the rear of these was always "mother's room," and the adjoining side room, shown in the picture (frontispiece to this appendix), was known as the "children's room."

An ell contains the dining room, pantries, kitchen and other workrooms. Across a wide, open porch is a big storeroom designed to hold supplies for a large household. Near this is the large covered cistern for rain water, without which no well-regulated family could exist in those days, no matter how good and plentiful the well water might be. The original outhouses, other buildings disappeared long ago, but the "big house" still is a roomy, comfortable dwelling.

The builder of Catalpa Hall apparently took an active part in state affairs from his arrival, for in February, 1838, the *Arkansas Gazette* mentioned the appointment of "John Drew and William Byers as Directors of the Bank of Arkansas for the Batesville District." From that time he was a leading spirit in everything relating to the progress and development of the state. He became one of the large landholders of the county. He bred fine stock and fast horses, owning some noted racing ponies. As the father of a growing family he was especially interested in education. As president, director, or member of the Board of Trustees, he served untiringly to establish the early schools, notably the Batesville Institute which burned in 1856, the later Soulesbury Institute or College, and still later Arkansas College, now honored as the oldest chartered college in the state. Mr. Byers was a high-ranking Mason and he took a leading part in the work of that order. Governor [William] Fishback [1893–95] once remarked, "At one time William Byers represented the brains, the wealth and the political power of Arkansas."

He served for many years as judge in the Second and in the Seventh Judicial Districts. In 1865 he was elected to Congress and went to Washington, but he and his colleagues were refused admission. Arkansas had no representation in Congress from 1861 to 1868.

In 1850 Mr. Byers married as his second wife the lovely Mrs. Emily Burton Wilson, the daughter of Dr. P. P. Burton of Batesville and Little Rock, a young widow with two small children, George and Nannie Wilson[, who] were reared at Catalpa Hall, with Aurelia, Ann, and Preston Byers, and the five half-brothers and sisters who were born there as the years went by.

Mrs. Emily Byers, "Miss Emmy," energetic and capable, managed her domain with great competency. Her Negroes were well trained as servants, her cooks were famous, the men were skilled workmen, each in his trade. It may be said here that the "Byers Negroes" and their descendants upheld their reputation for industry and thrift long after "freedom come." And to the day of her death, in 1900, they came to "Miss Emmy" for advice and help.

"Miss Emmy" was blest with "green fingers"; her gardens produced marvels of beautiful flowers, strange fruits, or new vegetables. This was true throughout her life, and wherever her home happened to be, it was always surrounded by flowers. It is not strange, therefore that the gardens and grounds of Catalpa Hall made it one of the show places of the district.

Catalpa Hall was early known for lavish hospitality. Every visiting celebrity was entertained there, and a list of guests would be a roster of "Who's Who" in pioneer Arkansas. It would include such names as Albert Pike, Judge [Elbert H.] English, Governor Fishback, Judge U. M. Rose and Mrs. Rose, among many others. Bishop Lay of the Episcopal Church stayed there when he baptized the four youngest children, John, Clayton, Wren, and Nellie.

Three daughters were educated in Memphis. Newspapers of the period are eloquent in describing the dances, dinners, Christmas celebrations, and weddings that brought together the elite of town and country when the young women were at home.

Two home weddings took place here—one in May, 1855, when Aurelia, the oldest daughter, was married to H. C. Smith, a merchant of Batesville, and the other in 1865, when Ann was married to Hugh Stuart [*sic,* Stewart] of Memphis.

Nannie Wilson, the youngest daughter, grew up to be the typical Southern belle of song and story, and it was expected that her wedding would be celebrated with great splendor and her trousseau the finest money could buy. That was not to be.[1] War brought to an end at Catalpa Hall, as elsewhere, the gay life of the old South. While the home escaped the more serious ravages of war, it frequently was visited by marauders in search of food stuff and livestock. The household lived in constant dread of such raids. One night in January, 1863,

---

1. The wedding occurred not in January but on October 5, 1863; see the marriage-license record in the following section.

the family had gathered in the living room after supper, reading, knitting, the young people playing cards. They were alarmed by a great clatter of horses galloping up the road. Bob, the frightened yardboy, ran into the house, crying: "Soldiers, Miss Emmy! Soldiers coming!" It was a tense moment. But the chief concern was for the safety of two guests, Confederate soldier boys, convalescing from typhoid fever. No chance of escape! What to do? But trust "Miss Emmy" to rise to an emergency. Promptly she had the Confederate lads tucked into bed in the children's room and covered with a feather-mattress!

But not for long did the youths have to endure their stifling hideout. The invaders proved to be a band of scouts commanded by the dashing Capt. Carroll H. Wood of Gen. Joe Shelby's staff. He had turned aside to persuade his sweetheart, Miss Nannie, into an immediate marriage. Federal troops en route to Batesville were only 24 hours behind him, and no one knew what might happen or when they would meet again.

Preparations were hastily made. Two scouts were sent into town for the cousins, Mary and Sarah Byers, who came riding behind them, pillion-wise. Another scout brought the Rev. Mr. Kennedy, the Presbyterian minister.[2] Pickets were stationed some distance down the road. When all was ready, Nancy, wearing a simple calico house-dress, with a little "breakfast shawl" thrown round her shoulders, stood up to be married to her soldier-lover. After the ceremony. Captain Wood and his men rode away to join Gen. Robert Shaver.

Of the few guests present at this secret, guarded wedding several became widely known, though along very different lines. Mary Byers, as Mrs. Robert Neill, is remembered by all Southern Methodists for her devotion to the Woman's Missionary Society and Board of Missions, and also for great work in the organization of the state W.C.T.U. Her sister, Sarah Byers, as Mrs. E. M. Dickinson, was equally well known in Episcopal church circles. By contrast, two of the witnesses, soldiers in Captain Wood's band, were Frank and Jesse James, notorious bandits of later years.

After the war Captain Wood and his bride made their home in Batesville. When he became adjutant general on Governor [Augustus H.] Garland's staff in 1874, he moved his family to Little Rock for the period of his service then returned to Batesville.

When Elisha Baxter bought Catalpa Hall in 1869, Judge Byers moved into the Baxter town house. Some of the fine furniture from the hall was sold, some given away. Antique hunters have found relics in Negro cabins. A mahogany

---

2. According to the county marriage-license records and to Mary, a witness, the parson was the Rev. George W. Kennard, a Baptist.

arm chair served as the bishop's chair beside the altar of the old St. Paul's Episcopal Church. Other pieces were given to the Masonic lodge. A remnant of the fine library went to Arkansas College. Among the hall treasures was a life-sized painting of Judge and Mrs. Byers, holding the hand of little Tom, their first child, who died when quite young. Forty years later this painting was burned when fire destroyed the Oklahoma home of his daughter, Nellie, Mrs. Milton McMurtry.[3]

Many pieces of silverware in daily use at the Hall were brought from Virginia. Of other pieces an interesting legend states that they were made in New Orleans especially for Judge Byers, from Mexican silver dollars brought back from the Mexican War. Much of the silver still is being used by great-grandchildren. By a twist of fate two of the 12 famous silver goblets were stolen from the home of his son, Clayton Byers, in Mexico City. They possibly have been melted and recoined into Mexican silver dollars.

No descendant of Judge Byers now lives in Batesville. Those of his daughter Ann, Mrs. Hugh Stuart [*sic*], are well-known in Memphis. Of the others, news of the latest generation places one in Annapolis, Md., and another at Stanford University, California.

From 1869 to 1893 the plantation was known as the "Baxter Place." Every schoolboy knows the history of Elisha Baxter, hero of the "Brooks-Baxter War" of 1873. A native of North Carolina, he came to Batesville in 1852. He struggled through many hardships to reach at last the highest honors in the state. He was a judge of the Supreme Court. He was elected to the United States Senate in 1864 but was not admitted as a member of that body. As an outstanding Republican he had great influence with the party, and the "Baxter Place" became a gathering point for those seeking counsel. Many problems of the Reconstruction era were solved before its great fireplace. It is said that certain archives of state were guarded here during the trouble of 1873–74. It was Governor Baxter's courageous telegram to President Grant ("Either I am governor, or I am not") that decided the serious situation in his favor. . . .

---

3. This painting, now lost, may have been another portrait by Henry Carey Byrd (1804/5–1884). The illustrations to Appendix 3 include two extant works by the artist. After emigrating from England to New Orleans and becoming established at El Dorado and Pine Bluff, Byrd became an itinerant portraitist throughout Arkansas and was in residence at Catalpa Hall about 1843, when he painted Lucy Byers and her children, and again around 1852, when he painted John Byers during a visit to his son, Uncle William. The only known likeness of William Byers is the photograph reproduced herein.

Catalpa Hall, by Neill Phillips, watercolor, c. 1960. "In spring after the daffodils had bloomed, a few pigs were turned loose on the lawns to root up and spread the bulbs for next year's bloom."

The Letter That Never Arrived

A Story of the Day When Romance Flourished in Arkansas. Century-Old House near Batesville Played Host to Blue Coats and Gray, Guerrillas, and a Governor during Dramatic Era.

This article by Lucille Young and Virginia McAdams was originally published in the *Arkansas Democrat* on January 7, 1951, and is reproduced here by permission of the *Arkansas Democrat-Gazette.*

———

One damp evening in February, General Jo Shelby, commanding his Missouri troops, sat in his tent and penned a bread-and-butter letter to a gracious lady at Batesville. She was "Miss Emma," wife of Judge William Byers of Catalpa Hall:

Headquarters Shelby's Brigade
Camp John Moore, Feb. 6, 1864

Mrs. Byers, Batesville, Ark.

Dear Madam: After considerable sailing on the waves and tides of a military life, I am at last settled temporarily on the Washita River, where we shall remain, perhaps, until the thunder of impatient drums and the rattle of musketry breaks the dull lethargy of a camp life. The feelings will naturally contrast our position now and last winter, and sigh for the pleasant associations and fond recollections of the past. I should like very much to visit your quiet home and talk over the pleasures of other days, but the gratification is denied me, and I can only think on the joys that are gone with the wealth of their first embrace.

I have seen your daughter[4] frequently in the last week. She is quite well and boarding in Camden with her husband [Carroll H. Wood]. There is no news of any character around our quiet headquarters, and we are as effectually cut off from the world as if an angel had drawn a wide and deep gulf round the state. All your acquaintances of my brigade desire to be particularly remembered to you. I would write longer but McCoy is just about starting and is impatient at delay.

Hoping that the dark waves of anarchy and desolation, now sweeping over Arkansas with too much rapidity, may spare your bright oasis, I remain, your true friend,

Jo O. Shelby

By an odd quirk of fate, which happens only in swashbuckling novels, Mrs. Byers never received this letter. The courier was Lt. A. C. McCoy, who with a party of men had been ordered to Batesville to pick up deserters. Lieutenant McCoy and one companion were captured by Federal scouts about 40 miles down the river from the Federal headquarters post at Pine Bluff. Shelby's letter fell into the hands of [Col.] Powell Clayton who sent it to General Steele at Little Rock along with his report of the capture.

Their disappointment at finding merely a flowery personal note instead of important military documents can well be imagined.

Perhaps it is just as well, otherwise this letter may not have survived, and we should not have discovered it in the War of the Rebellion Official Records (Vol. XXXIV, Part 2, Page 321).

---

4. Nannie Manning Wilson Wood.

———

The quiet home referred to by Shelby in his letter is a well-known landmark in Independence County. The house stands in a grove of old cedars on a gently rolling hillside just beyond the railroad overpass on Highway 11 north of Batesville. To the present generation it is known as Glennwood, so called for John Glenn, who purchased the property in 1890.

The Glenns, a well-known and very popular family of Batesville, used it as their country home where they entertained with house parties and costume balls. One daughter, Miss Effie Glenn, married Mrs. [*sic*] E. C. Blandford, professor at Arkansas College.

In recent years the Blandford family renovated the old house and lived there for a time, entertaining in traditional style within the broad drawing-rooms so suitably arranged for social gatherings. Residents of Batesville still like to recall these affairs. Many are descendants of those who enjoyed the same warm hospitality in a bygone era.

Judge William Byers built the house in 1846, which fact will remain indisputable as long as the hall stands, as these numerals are fixed in raised lettering upon the molded gutters below the cornice of the west wing.[5] The design of architecture suggests modified Greek revival.

In Civil War days the glazed cupola was often used as a lookout tower. From this vantage point the observer commanded a good view of the surrounding countryside, and quickly detected the approach of Yankee cavalry or lurking marauders, who were numerous in the latter years of the war.

Now beginning its second century, Catalpa Hall's present condition bears witness to its sound construction. Into it were put the good old woods, long seasoned, which have been missing from the market for many a year. Much of the original plastering is still intact. One mark of antiquity can be noted in the plastered ceilings of the two porticos.

Seen from without, the house has a graceful, well-balanced appearance, characteristic of much Southern architecture. Inside, the unusually large rooms appear smaller because of their perfect proportions. The entrance hall, which is broken by an arch, is so large that it served as a ballroom where many a couple whirled through schottiches, polkas, reels and waltzes.

At the end of the hall is a stairway leading up to the "lookout" in the cupola. Halfway up, the stairs turn sharply forming a graceful railed balcony on which, perhaps, were enacted many pretty scenes.

———

5. Although the building itself no longer stands, portions of these gutters bearing the dates have survived.

As in most ante-bellum houses, the extremely broad doorways leading from the hall could accommodate the widest hoop-skirt in the county.

At the time Catalpa Hall contained 17 rooms, including the wine cellar and the offices in the rear. There are 10 rooms in the house proper; the four front parlors which open from the hall, another room directly behind the balcony, four large rooms in the west wing—and the cupola.

In springtime can be seen traces of the once lovely gardens; when lilacs and myrtle, iris and jonquil and old-fashioned roses bloom again. Ivy creeps over much of the lawn and clings to the old cedars; but the catalpas are gone—those handsome trees once the pride of the master of the hall.

——

Many times during the bloody Red River Campaign Jo Shelby and his men must have thought wistfully of the "bright oasis" where, perhaps, for the last time they enjoyed the warm hospitality and carefree living so soon to vanish in a war-torn Southland.

In mid-January, 1863, after intense fighting around Springfield and Hartville, Mo., the Confederates under Marmaduke and Shelby began their march southward into Arkansas. Much suffering was encountered on this journey. Many of the wounded accompanied the troops who marched on frost-bitten feet through snow and ice over impossible roads until they reached the haven of Batesville. There the kind residents of the town and surrounding country cheered the tired heroes and took the wounded and sick into their homes.

The main body of troops ferried the river and camped for a time on the south side. Capt. George Rathbun was selected to do provost marshal duty in Batesville. Almost immediately a skirmish occurred between Confederates and Colonel Waring who led a bold regiment of Federal cavalry into the town. Shelby recrossed the White River with two strong detachments and chased Waring's men back to Missouri; then Captain Rathbun returned to his barracks and the army settled down to enjoy the lovely spring season in camp near Batesville, cloistered in the foothills of the Ozarks.

The Confederates were not the first regimental guests the people of Batesville had received since the beginning of hostilities. The preceding spring had been an unhappy one for the residents. General Curtis marched his armies from Missouri to pay the town a surprise visit early one May morning.

The townspeople were not prepared to resist so large a force, although Colonel Coleman was encamped south of the river with more than a thousand men determined to give battle. But Curtis' armies were estimated at 20,000 strong and closed in upon the town from all points. An old ballad tells the story this way:

'Twas in the year of '62
That Curtis did come down
With all his army dressed in blue
To take our little town.

They came quite early in the day
Before the folks were out. . . .

Chorus:
Yank, Yankee army
Come this way no more
If you knew what was for your good
You'd stay on Northern shore.

However, Curtis' men were received with mixed feelings by the townspeople, some of whom were not unsympathetic toward the Union cause; while many Batesvillians were heart and soul with the Confederacy, the town was not, strictly speaking, part of the solid South. It was several months before these forces left the vicinity to continue their advance upon the state. Most of the citizens were greatly relieved when they withdrew.

—

Then, in the early days of '63, Batesville hailed the return of the men in gray who thundered through the town on their sleek chargers; new hope and confidence rode with them. Once again Catalpa Hall returned to the limelight.

Miss Nannie Wilson, daughter of Mrs. Byers by her first marriage, was a great favorite of the troops, who paid homage to her grace and charm by naming the camp near Batesville in her honor.

Major John N. Edwards, in his book "Shelby and His Men," gives a fitting, though flowery, description of both the young lady and the countryside. He relates that:

Colonel Shelby recrossed White River early in March with his Iron Brigade, now three thousand strong, and selected a beautiful camp among giant oaks, skirting fresh and sparkling streams. This camp, in honor of one of Batesville's most lovely daughters, was named "Camp Nannie Wilson." Rarely ever in life were blended so much purity, beauty, patriotism and grace in the one, and so much nature, freshness and tranquillity in the other. Balls, promenades, flirting, coqueting and match-making followed in rapid succession.

Capt. Carroll H. Wood of Shelby's staff eventually won the lady's hand. In early October, when Shelby's brigade made another raid into Missouri, Captain [Wood] lingered behind to keep an appointment at Catalpa Hall. Like most wartime weddings, the ceremony was performed without the benefit of maline and orange blossoms in an atmosphere charged with the urgency of troop movements and hurried goodbyes.

But, because all brides are beautiful, it little mattered that the bride wore calico. Miss Nannie and Captain Wood were married in Catalpa Hall on a brisk October evening in the presence of her immediate family and a few friends. Captain Wood was attended by a small military escort, among whom were two gentlemen whose names and faces probably passed unnoticed at the time. They were Frank and Jesse James, who were later to carve their names in the legends and folklore of the border region. According to tradition, one of them served as best man—which one, tradition fails to say.

Evidently the turmoil of war upset the county clerk's office at Batesville, since few marriages seem to have been recorded during the mid-war years. This marriage was recorded three years later in the following manner:

From Independence County Marriage License Records—

Carroll H. Wood
To ( ) Marriage
Nannie M. Wilson

We, Mary A. Byers and Sarah Byers, were at the residence of Judge William Byers in the County of Independence, State of Arkansas, on the 5th day of October one thousand eight hundred and sixty-three, and witnessed the solemn rites of marriage by the Rev. George W. Kennard, a minister of the Gospel, between Carroll H. Wood and Nannie M. Wilson, and we hereby so certify on our corporal oaths, this done in the town of Batesville, Independence County, State of Arkansas, on the first day of December, one thousand eight-hundred and sixty-six.

Mary A. Byers
Sarah Byers

(Notarized by J. Searcy, J. P.
Filed by Robt. Neill)[6]

---

6. Robert Neill was Mary's future husband.

With the close of the year 1863 the gay times were at an end for this section of Arkansas. The fall of Vicksburg, Helena, and Little Rock paralyzed the supply lines from the east. Except for the armaments and supplies smuggled across the river at Memphis by a daring few, the forces of the north Arkansas border regions were reduced to short rations and worn equipment. For the remainder of the war the hordes of Federals under Curtis and Steele overran this section, not always on military missions. In January of '64, Catalpa Hall was raided and Judge Byers' life was threatened by a detachment of [the] 6th Missouri State Militia Cavalry.

Col. R. R. Livingston, commanding the district of Batesville at this time, refers to this matter in [the] Rebellion Records (Vol. XXXIV, Pg. 160). Apparently this Yankee officer was disgusted at the shameful breach of conduct among some of his own officers and men:

> I beg to call your attention to the utter impracticability of converting this portion of Arkansas to loyalty while such conduct on the part of our troops is left unpunished and the sufferers unpaid, No reasoning can convince the poor cottager, who is robbed of nearly all he has by both armies, that the Union is a whit safer tor his creed than secession. . . . Judge Byers, a most estimable citizen of this place, residing three miles from town, was rudely assaulted, his life threatened, and his horses and mules stolen from him by these brigands, for I cannot call men soldiers who, using their power for such base purposes, terrify and rob the country they pass through.

In January of '64, Lt. A. N. Harris, a Federal scout, made an expedition from Batesville into the Black River bottoms for the purpose of gaining possession of a herd of beef cattle said to be grazing in the canebrakes. On his way he passed near Catalpa Hall, and included a rough drawing of it in a sketch which he made showing his line of march. (This was found in Rebellion Records (Vol. XXXIV, Pg. 107).)[7]

Wandering like an unhappy shadow through the war years was Elisha Baxter, the man who one day would be master of Catalpa Hall. No doubt, while riding at the head of his Yankee regiment, Colonel Baxter passed the house

---

7. Instead of the sketch map in the *Gazette* article, reproduced here is the original, higher-quality version. U.S. War Department, *War of the Rebellion*, ser. 1, 34(2):107. Harris led his forty men of the Eleventh Missouri Cavalry eastward; mileages in the third column are point to point. The Masonic Hall is in modern Charlotte.

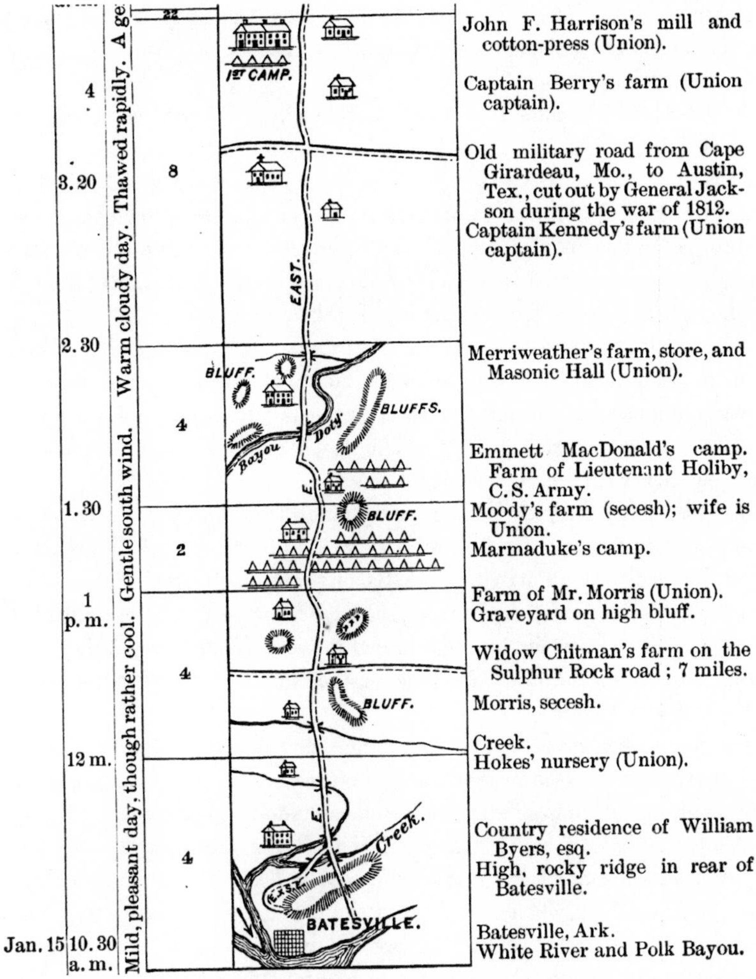
John F. Harrison's mill and cotton-press (Union).
Captain Berry's farm (Union captain).
Old military road from Cape Girardeau, Mo., to Austin, Tex., cut out by General Jackson during the war of 1812.
Captain Kennedy's farm (Union captain).
Merriweather's farm, store, and Masonic Hall (Union).
Emmett MacDonald's camp.
Farm of Lieutenant Holiby, C. S. Army.
Moody's farm (secesh); wife is Union.
Marmaduke's camp.
Farm of Mr. Morris (Union).
Graveyard on high bluff.
Widow Chitman's farm on the Sulphur Rock road; 7 miles.
Morris, secesh.
Creek.
Hokes' nursery (Union).
Country residence of William Byers, esq.
High, rocky ridge in rear of Batesville.
Batesville, Ark.
White River and Polk Bayou.
1ST CAMP.
EAST.
BLUFF.
BLUFFS.
Bayou
Doty
E.
Creek.
BATESVILLE.
Jan. 15
10. 30 a. m.
12 m.
1 p. m.
1. 30
2. 30
3. 20
4
Mild, pleasant day, though rather cool. Gentle south wind. Warm cloudy day. Thawed rapidly. A ge

Route map by Lt. A. N. Harris (USA), 1864.

many times during 1864. His command was the 4th Arkansas Mounted Infantry (Union), which operated in the Batesville district while Livingston was in command of Federal forces there.

Elisha Baxter had come from North Carolina before the war and settled at Batesville, and his young wife had accompanied him on the westward journey. He had been a merchant back East so he opened a store at first, but failed to prosper as he had hoped to in the new land, he soon gave up merchandising and turned to the study of law. By the time war broke out this profession had brought him considerable success. He had passed his bar examination, entered politics, and served two terms in the state legislature.

When talk of secession mounted and war became inevitable, Baxter retired from public life to live quietly with his family at Batesville. And the war brought him nothing but trials and social humiliations, since his political views from the outset were sta[u]nchly pro-Union, while the majority of his friends and neighbors were Southern sympathizers.

The man possessed great courage and honesty, for throughout his career as lawyer, soldier, governor, he held to his principles in the face of all obstacles. After Curtis' arrival in Batesville in '62, Baxter's pro-Union sympathies led him to accept active duty with the Federals, although his temperament was unsuited to military life. When the county returned to Confederate hands early in '63, his admiration for Curtis and the Union caused him to withdraw to Missouri along with these forces.

For Baxter this was an unhappy adventure, since his personal loyalty to his Arkansas neighbors held as strong a grip on his heart as his political beliefs. Eventually this led to misunderstanding and an unfortunate incident.

While in Missouri he had again retired to private life. There Col. Robert Newton and some of Marmaduke's scouts took him into custody and sent him down to Little Rock, where he was jailed and indicted for treason to the Confederacy. Aided by friends, Baxter escaped and found asylum in the old familiar neighborhood of Independence County, where, for a time, he lived in seclusion among other sympathizers with the Union.

The complete fall of Batesville and its subsequent occupation by the Union army gave him another opportunity for active service. As colonel of the 4th Arkansas Mounted Infantry, one finds mention of Elisha Baxter in several reports by Col. R. R. Livingston.

From [the] Rebellion Records (Vol. XXXIV) comes the following:

Batesville, Ark.
March 1, 1864.

Major W. D. Green
Little Rock, Ark.

Major: I have the honor to report that a detachment of this command sent out under command of Col. E. Baxter, Fourth Ark. Mounted Infantry, to recapture the mules taken from a portion of my train by Capt. George W. Rutherford in the 19th Instant, sent hack 14 prisoners captured from him, with the intelligence that they were close on him and with a fair prospect of overtaking him. I have no doubt if my forces overtake him we will recapture a large portion of our lost stock and annihilate his command. He was trying to cross Little Red at the mouth of Devil's Fork at last accounts, but the enemy hereabouts is so erratic I cannot conclude where he will cross.

> I am respectfully, your very obedient servant,
>
> R. R. Livingston
> Colonel First Regt. Nebraska Cav.,Comdg. District.

(According to a report of a later date, Colonel Rutherford did elude Baxter's forces: "Rutherford was not found, he having crossed Little Red River with 140 U.S. mules, captured from my train. . . ."—Report of Livingston.)

Colonel George Rutherford, also a resident of Independence County and a daring officer, was much admired by Jo Shelby, who alluded to him as "the only fighting man in all this country." Giving some idea of the bitterness existing between the opposing factions in this district at that time, Shelby refers to the Federal colonel as "that renegade Baxter."

———

Ironically, this Yankee officer was to become master of the house where Miss Nannie Wilson had once entertained her Confederate beaus. One wonders if phantom booted feet and the clank of spurs ever disturbed his dreams. But perhaps not, for Baxter was a realist, not a dreamer. From the war's end he rose steadily in position and in the respect of the people.

During 1864 he had served in the supreme court of the state, that is, in the Union government then at Little Rock. He had also been chosen to represent Arkansas in the United States Senate but was never allowed to take that seat. Upon his return to Batesville after the war he became circuit judge, serving in this capacity for some time.

It was in 1869 that he purchased the Catalpa House from Judge Byers, and Baxter was living here when elected governor in 1872. From this home he went to Little Rock to assume those duties and play a stirring role in Reconstruction, times which culminated in that exciting interlude remembered by Arkansans as the Brooks-Baxter War. It was an involved affair but brought to an end the carpetbag rule in Arkansas.

The master of Catalpa Hall became the hero of the day. His staunch determination to stand for the people's rights against the evils of the radical party won him the respect and friendship of the Democrats and even the Confederate veterans.

Thus, appreciating his services in their behalf, they offered him the nomination for the next term on the Democratic ticket. This honor he declined, however, preferring to return to his home at Batesville. The Baxter family, which soon included several grandchildren, passed many pleasant years at the old house. About 1890 Baxter sold the property to John Glenn, and, with his family, moved into town, where he resided until his death.

—

Nowadays, Catalpa Hall overlooks a meadows, beyond which is a modern drive-in movie where occasionally the Civil War and frontier days are reenacted in Hollywood trappings. The old road—once the main highway which ran directly past the front door of the house and east toward Elgin on Black River—is no more. The new paved highway gently bypasses the west wing of the hall on its way north to the Missouri border. Time and the weather, life and death, war and peace have left their traces upon this centenarian. It stands today an enduring reminder of an unforgotten romantic period in the state's history.

—

Around the time of publication of this article, the Hall was razed and another dwelling built in its place. All that remains is a historical marker off Highway 233, near Forestry Road and just up from Miller's Creek, citing Catalpa Hall as the residence of three governors, beginning with Elisha Baxter.

Catalpa Hall, postcard, c. 1908.
Courtesy Don A. Heuer.

Catalpa Hall, c. 1930.
Courtesy Don A. Heuer.

Catalpa Hall, front porch, c. 1947.
Courtesy Independence County Historical Society.

Catalpa Hall, north elevation, c. 1947.
Courtesy Independence County Historical Society.

John Byers (1786–1871), by Henry Carey Byrd, c. 1852. A
physician and Methodist Episcopal preacher in Ohio before
moving to Batesville after the war, he was the father of John H.
and William Byers.

Judge William Byers

The following is an excerpt from a biography of Judge Byers published in *Good-speed's Biographical and Historical Memoirs of Northeast Arkansas*, 646–47. In the late nineteenth century, Goodspeed produced dozens of compilations of local history and biography, sold on subscription and covering southern and midwestern states. County chapters are laid out with a detailed history covering early settlement, Civil War events, and more-recent events, followed by biographical sketches of prominent citizens of the area. Comprehensive versions of the Northeast Arkansas volume (in many formats) are available at www.archive.org/details/biographicalhist02good.

———

Pennsylvania has given to Independence County many estimable citizens, but she has contributed none more highly respected, or, for conscientious discharge of duty in every relation of life, more worthy of respect and esteem than was the subject of this sketch.

He was born on the 4th of March, 1810, being a son of Dr. John and Sarah (Bonner) [*sic*, Bonar] Byers, also natives of Pennsylvania. Dr. John Byers was of Irish descent, and had seven brothers, all of whom were soldiers in the Revolutionary War. Judge William Byers remained in his native State until about eight years of age, after which he moved with his parents to near Mount Vernon, Ohio. There he grew to manhood, receiving a limited education, so far as the facilities of schooling were concerned, and might be called a self-made man in every sense of the word. Early in life he commenced the study of law under Mr. Deluo, a very famous lawyer, and was admitted to the bar, at Mount Vernon, Ohio, where he practiced a short time.

He was married the first time at Fredericksburg, Ohio, and came with his family to Batesville, Ark., in about 1838, where he practiced his profession. He soon became very prominent, and was sent to the legislature, where he served one term. He was next elected circuit judge, and served on the bench for a number of years. After this he was elected to Congress, but, owing to some fraudulent circumstances, never took his seat. He never sought office, but was pushed and urged by his friends to accept, and was ever after a public man. He always filled every office with honor and to the satisfaction of his constituents.

Although commencing life with limited means, he became very wealthy, until the late war, when he lost all his property; but it was characteristic of the man that he took everything with the utmost calmness and composure. His

Lucy Adelia Manning Byers (1810–46), by Henry Carey Byrd, c. 1843. She was William Byers's first wife. Lucy is depicted here with her children, William Preston Byers (Cousin Preston), Ann Grow Byers (Cousin Ann), and Aurelia Adelia Byers (Cousin Rilla).

From the Permanent Collection of the Historic Arkansas Museum, Little Rock, and used by permission.

first wife was Miss Lucy Manning, of Ohio, by whom he had three children, only one living, Mrs. Hugh Stewart, of Memphis. He was married the second time, in 1850, to Mrs. Emily (Burton) Wilson, a daughter of Dr. P. P. Burton, a very prominent physician. Six children were born to this union, four now living: John, in Texas; Clayton, a civil engineer, in Old Mexico; Wren; and Nellie, wife of Dr. McMurtle.

Mrs. Byers is a cousin of old Judge Clayton, of Mississippi, who is one of the prominent men of that State. By her marriage to Mr. Wilson, Mrs. Byers became the mother of two children, George, and Nannie, wife of Carroll H. Wood. George Wilson went through the late war.

Mr. Byers was a prominent Mason, and was the father of that secret organization in Batesville. He was for a number of years editor of the *Batesville News.* He died of paralysis at the home of his daughter in Memphis.

Mrs. Byers owns the block where she lives, and is a very wide-awake, energetic lady. She is a member of the Episcopal Church, and is much respected by all who know her. She is of Scotch descent. Her maternal grandmother was born, reared, and educated in Edinburgh, Scotland, and spoke very fluently some seven languages. . . .

The following is an excerpt from the article "Testimony of William Byers of Batesville before the Joint Committee on Reconstruction," published in the *Independence County Chronicle* in 2005.

William Byers was a prominent planter and lawyer who came to Independence County from Ohio in 1837. Born in Pennsylvania, Byers was accompanied here by two brothers—Thomas Newton and John Hancock Byers. Their father, Dr. John Byers, joined them later and lived here until 1871.

William Byers began publishing the *Batesville News* soon after his arrival. It was one of the first newspapers in this part of the state. He was also a real estate investor and represented Independence County in the Arkansas House of Representatives in 1842–43. He was also a respected Mason and served for a time as circuit judge.

After the Civil War, Byers was elected to Congress on the Democratic ticket but was barred from taking his seat by the Radical Republicans then in control of the federal government. He went to Washington anyway and wrote a number of informative letters to friends and constituents which were published in the local papers. This testimony was probably given when he was trying to claim his seat.

Judge Byers was twice married. His first wife, Lucy Adelia Manning, died in 1846. Her grave is marked by a tall monument in Batesville's downtown Pioneer Cemetery. She was the mother of William Preston, a Confederate soldier; Aurelia Adelia, who married prominent merchant Henry C. Smith; and Ann G., who married Hugh Stewart. It is believed that Ann was the daughter with whom Byers spent his last years in Memphis after losing his fortune in Arkansas.

Byers second wife was Emily Burton Wilson, a widow with two children at the time of their marriage. They had four more children.

In 1846, Byers completed the construction of his home, Catalpa Hall, three miles northeast of Batesville. It was considered one of the finest homes in North Arkansas and stood until 1952. William Byers himself died in Memphis in 1881 and is buried there. He has no local descendants.

[From the] Testimony of William Byers of Batesville before the Senate Joint Committee on Reconstruction, Washington, February 2, 1866:

Question: Did you remain in Arkansas during the war?

Answer: Yes, sir, all the time; I was taken down with what some physicians called palsy, other neuralgia, and others rheumatism, about a year before the war commenced, and a great portion of the time I was confined to my house.

Question: Did you take part in the war in any way?

Answer: I was elected judge under the old law. When the convention met and passed the ordinance of secession, they also passed an ordinance requiring every officer in the civil government of the State to take an oath of allegiance to the government of the Confederate States within a certain time, or their offices would be declared vacant. I held courts for about six months after secession, but I never took any oath of allegiance to the Confederate States, and when it would be necessary either to do that or not to hold the courts I tendered my resignation. If that was a participation in the war, holding the courts after the ordinance of secession was passed then I participated in it.

Question: You took no oath to support the Confederacy?

Answer: No, sir; and when General Curtis came into that section of country he adopted a general rule that Union men and all should take the oath of allegiance to the United States government, and I think I was among the first who took it. He told me he wanted me to do it as an example to others. When the amnesty proclamation was issued by President Lincoln, I took the oath of amnesty; and when President Johnson issued the proclamation again, I took the oath again. I did that to encourage the people to take it. . . .

Skirmish at Waugh's Farm

February 19, 1864

This skirmish was the only engagement of any note between Confederate and Federal troops in Independence County. The following may be taken as an official report, for it was originally furnished by the Confederate commanding officer:

> The fight at Waugh's farm in Independence County was one of the minor engagements, but brilliant and decisive. Capt. George W. Rutherford, with a part of his own company of Dobbins' cavalry regiment and Capt. S. J. McGuffin's company of boys called the "Pop-Corn Company," then unattached, Captain McGuffin being second in command, was resting in Knight's Cove (now Stone County), when he received information that a train of 43 foraging wagons with an escort of 147 men from the Eleventh Missouri Cavalry, commanded by Captain Cassell (Castle), was encamped for the night at James Waugh's farm, 11 miles northwest of Batesville, and he determined to attack them with the 83 men he had with him.
>
> Crossing White River above Penter's Bluff, after a night march of some 15 miles, Captain Rutherford reached the Federal camp just after daylight on the 18th of February, 1864, and attacked with such a vigor that he stampeded the escort after a short, sharp fight, killing 13, wounding four, and capturing 17, among the killed being the Federal commander, Captain Cassell. Captain Rutherford captured and carried off 127 mules, with their harness, and 34 horses, with their accoutrements, and burned 43 wagons, losing in the engagement four killed and three wounded.[1]

The corresponding Federal account, by Col. R. R. Livingston:

> There are about 2,000 of the enemy hovering around me, in bands of from 100 to 400 strong each. They are very active and harass my foraging trains constantly. On the 19th instant 35 wagons, escorted by 100 men, were surprised only 12 miles from here and all captured, together with 82 of this command captured, 10 wounded, and 4 killed.

---

1. R. Neill, "Reminiscences of Independence County," 26–27.

Captain Castle, Eleventh Missouri Cavalry, in charge of escort, paid the penalty of his neglect with his life. The whole affair was most disgraceful to our arms, as the enemy was just about our own strength and not as well armed or equipped.

We cannot move, no matter how cautions or secret we endeavor to be, without the inhabitants betraying us. The principal messengers are women, just such bitter enemies as Mrs. Neeby [Neely] and her eldest daughter [Elvira Denton], who have been caught in flagrante delicto.[2]

---

2. U.S. War Department, *War of the Rebellion,* ser. 1, 34:147.

Bibliography

Abstract of Title, Lots 7, 8, & 9, Block 17, Newport, Ark., 1995.

Agnew, Mary Elizabeth (Mrs. John F. Allen). "Speaking of Things: Mary Elizabeth Agnew's Friendship Book." *Independence County Chronicle* 49, no. 2 (2008): 3–33.

"Batesville: Personal Recollections of 1863." In *Confederate Women of Arkansas, 1861–65: Memorial Reminiscences.* Little Rock: United Confederate Veterans, Arkansas Division, 1907.

Boone, James V., and Melissa A. Gibbs. "Calvin Comins Bliss (1823–1891)." In *Encyclopedia of Arkansas History & Culture.* Article last updated June 15, 2009. www.encyclopediaofarkansas.net/encyclopedia/entry-detail. aspx?search=1&entryID=3610.

Britton, Nancy. *The First Hundred Years of the First Methodist Church in Batesville, Arkansas, 1836–1936.* Little Rock: August House, 1986.

———. *Independence Pioneers.* Batesville, Ark.: Independence County Historical Society, 1986.

———. *Independence Pioneers.* Batesville, Ark.: Independence County Historical Society, 1989.

———. *Worthy of Much Praise: A History of St. Paul's Episcopal Church, Batesville, Arkansas, from Its Earliest Beginnings to 1952.* Newport, Ark.: Craig Printing, 1989.

———. "Methodists, Slavery, and Secession in Independence County." *Independence County Chronicle* 52, no. 1 (2011): 4–19.

Britton, Nancy, and Diane Tebbetts. "Nineteenth-Century Homes of Batesville." *Independence County Chronicle* 20, no. 2 (1979): 35.

Byers, William. "Testimony of William Byers of Batesville before the Joint Committee on Reconstruction, Washington, February 2, 1866." *Independence County Chronicle* 46, no. 1 (2005): 55–62.

Civil War Sites Advisory Commission. Battle Summaries by State. U.S. National Park Service. www.nps.gov/hps/abpp/battles/bystate.htm.

Clements, D. A. "Camden Expedition." In *Encyclopedia of Arkansas History &
Culture.* Article last updated November 18, 2011. www.encyclopediaofar-
kansas.net/encyclopedia/entry-detail.aspx?search=1&entryID=1131.

Craig, Marion Stark. *My Byers-Bonar-Shannon and Allied Families, 1695–1976.*
Little Rock: privately published, 1976.

The Daguerreian Society. www.daguerre.org/.

DeBlack, Thomas A. "'A Remarkably Strong Union Sentiment': Unionism in
Arkansas in 1861." In *The Die Is Cast,* edited by Mark K. Christ, 75–100.
Little Rock: Butler Center Books, 2010.

Dowell, Clare Phillips. "The Job Neill Letters." *Independence County Chronicle*
8, no. 1 (1966): 27–37.

Estes, Claud, comp. *List of Field Officers, Regiments, and Battalions in the
Confederate States Army, 18611865.*Macon, Ga.: J. W. Burke, 1912. Google
eBook, books.google.com/books?id=eBUTAAAAYAAJ&pg=PA1&d
q=List+of+Field+Officers,+Regiments,+and+Battalions+in+the+Con
federate+States+Army&hl=en&sa=X&ei=I4OUUOvPK--42QWM
gIG4Aw&ved=0CDAQ6AEwAA.

Fair, Susan. "Spiritualism & the Civil War." *The Gettysburg Experience.* Ac-
cessed October 2010. www.thegettysburgexperience.com/past_issue_head-
lines/2010/october2010/spiritualism.html.

Gerdes, Edward G. "27th Arkansas Infantry." Last updated July 22,
2002. Edward G. Gerdes Civil War Page. www.couchgenweb.com/
civilwar/27infhis.html.

Griffith, Nancy Snell. "Aaron Woodruff Lyon." *Independence County Chronicle*
35, nos.1–2 (1993–94): 52–67.

———. "Slavery in Independence County." *Independence County Chronicle* 41,
nos. 3/4 (2000): 4–70.

Goodspeed Publishing. *Biographical and Historical Memoirs of Northeast Arkansas.* Chicago, 1889. Available online at www.archive.org/details/biographi-
calhisto2good.

Gravesite markers. Pioneer Cemetery, Batesville.

Hirsch, Aaron. "Memoir." c. 1900. American Jewish Archives, Cincinnati.

Hodge, Michael. "Railroads." *Encyclopedia of Arkansas History & Culture.*
Article last updated March 12, 2012. www.encyclopediaofarkansas.net/
encyclopedia/entry-detail.aspx?entryID_1185.

Independence County Deed Records H-497, I-94, J-384, K-494, M-458.

Johnston, James J. "Peace Society in Fulton County." *Fulton County Chronicles*
11, no. 2 (1996): 2664.

———. "Bullets for Johnny Reb: Confederate Nitre and Mining Bureau in Arkansas." In *Civil War Arkansas: Beyond Battles and Leaders,* edited by Anne J. Bailey and Daniel E. Sutherland, 47–84. Fayetteville: University of Arkansas Press, 2000.

Lankford, George. E. "Town-Making in the Southeastern Ozarks." *Independence County Chronicle* 31, no. 1 (1990): 1–19.

———. *Surprised by Death.* Little Rock: Butler Center for Arkansas Studies, 2009.

———. "Presbyterians, Slavery, and Secession in Independence County." *Independence County Chronicle* 52, no. 1 (2011): 20–32.

———, ed. "A Chronicle of Independence County's Civil War: A Compendium of Diaries, Letters, and Reminiscences." 2012. Old Independence Regional Museum and White River Regional Library, Batesville, and Arkansas Humanities Council, Little Rock. Unpublished typescript.

———. "Batesville (Independence County)." In *Encyclopedia of Arkansas History & Culture.* Article last updated February 28, 2012. www.encyclopediaofarkansas.net/encyclopedia/entry-detail.aspx?search=1&entryID=900.

Lyon, Aaron W. "A History of the Batesville Sabbath School." *Independence County Chronicle* 53, no. 2 (2012): 39–41.

Mackey, Robert R. *The Uncivil War.* Norman: University of Oklahoma Press, 2004.

Maxfield, Elvena. "The Elvena Maxfield Journals." Edited by Nancy Britton and Nancy Griffith. *Independence County Chronicle* 44, no. 2 (2003): 2–62; 44, nos. 3/4 (2004): 3–43.

Maxfield, Lucretia Noland. "The Lucretia Noland Maxfield Journal, 1863–1864." Edited by Nancy Griffith and Nancy Britton. *Independence County Chronicle* 35, nos. 3/4 (1994): 2–71.

McGuire, William Lewis. "The W. L. McGuire Journals: Batesville, Arkansas, 1862–1863." Edited by Nancy Britton. *Independence County Chronicle* 34, nos. 3/4 (1993): 2–47.

Mobley, Freeman K. *Making Sense of the Civil War in Batesville-Jacksonport and Northeast Arkansas, 1861–1874.* Batesville, Ark.: privately published, 2005.

Morgan, James Logan, ed. *Centennial History of Newport, Arkansas, 1875–1975.* Newport, Ark.: Jackson County Historical Society, 1975.

Neill, Robert. "Reminiscences of Independence County." *J. Arkansas Historical Association* (1907). Reprinted in *Independence County Chronicle* 4, no. 3 (1963): 2–29.

Phillips, Neill. "My Story." Privately circulated, 1972. Copy in editor's posses-
    sion.

Shea, William L. "A Semi-Savage State: The Image of Arkansas in the Civil
    War." In *Civil War Arkansas: Beyond Battles and Leaders,* edited by Anne
    J. Bailey and Daniel E. Sutherland, 85–100. Fayetteville: University of
    Arkansas Press, 2000.

Sifakis, Stewart. *Who Was Who in the Civil War.* New York: Facts on File, 1988.

Sutherland, Daniel E., ed. *Guerrillas, Unionists, and Violence on the Confederate
    Home Front.* Fayetteville: University of Arkansas Press, 1999.

———. *A Savage Conflict: The Decisive Role of Guerrillas in the Civil War.* Cha-
    pel Hill: University of North Carolina Press, 2009.

U.S. Census Bureau. 1860 Census, Independence County, Arkansas.

U.S. War Department. *The War of the Rebellion: A Compilation of the Official
    Records of the Union and Confederate Armies.* 130 vols. Washington, D.C.:
    Government Printing Office, 1880–1901. Available online at Making of
    America Collection, Cornell University Library, ebooks.library.cornell.
    edu/m/moawar/waro.html.

Watson, Lady Elizabeth. *Fight and Survive! A History of Jackson County, Arkan-
    sas in the Civil War.* Conway, Ark.: River Road, 1974. Rev. ed., Newport,
    Ark.: Jackson County Historical Society, 1996.

Wright, Marcus J., comp. *Arkansas in the War, 1861–1864.* 1909. Batesville, Ark.:
    Independence County Historical Society, 1963.

Index

References to illustrations are in italic type.

CPSIA information can be obtained
at www.ICGtesting.com
Printed in the USA
FFOW05n2057030314